STUMPTOWN™

PORTLAND, OREGON

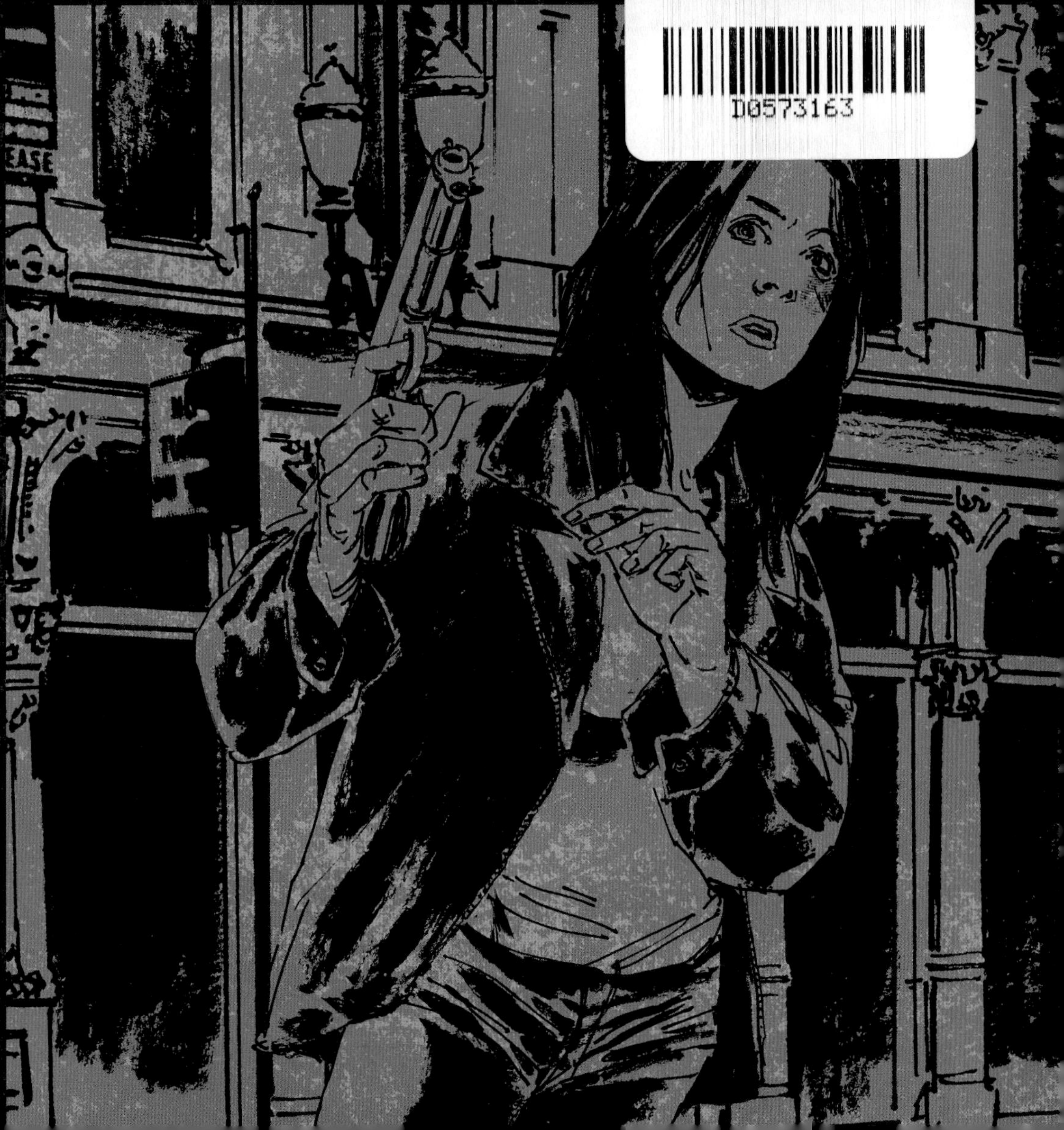

STUMPTOWN™

INVESTIGATIONS • PORTLAND, OREGON

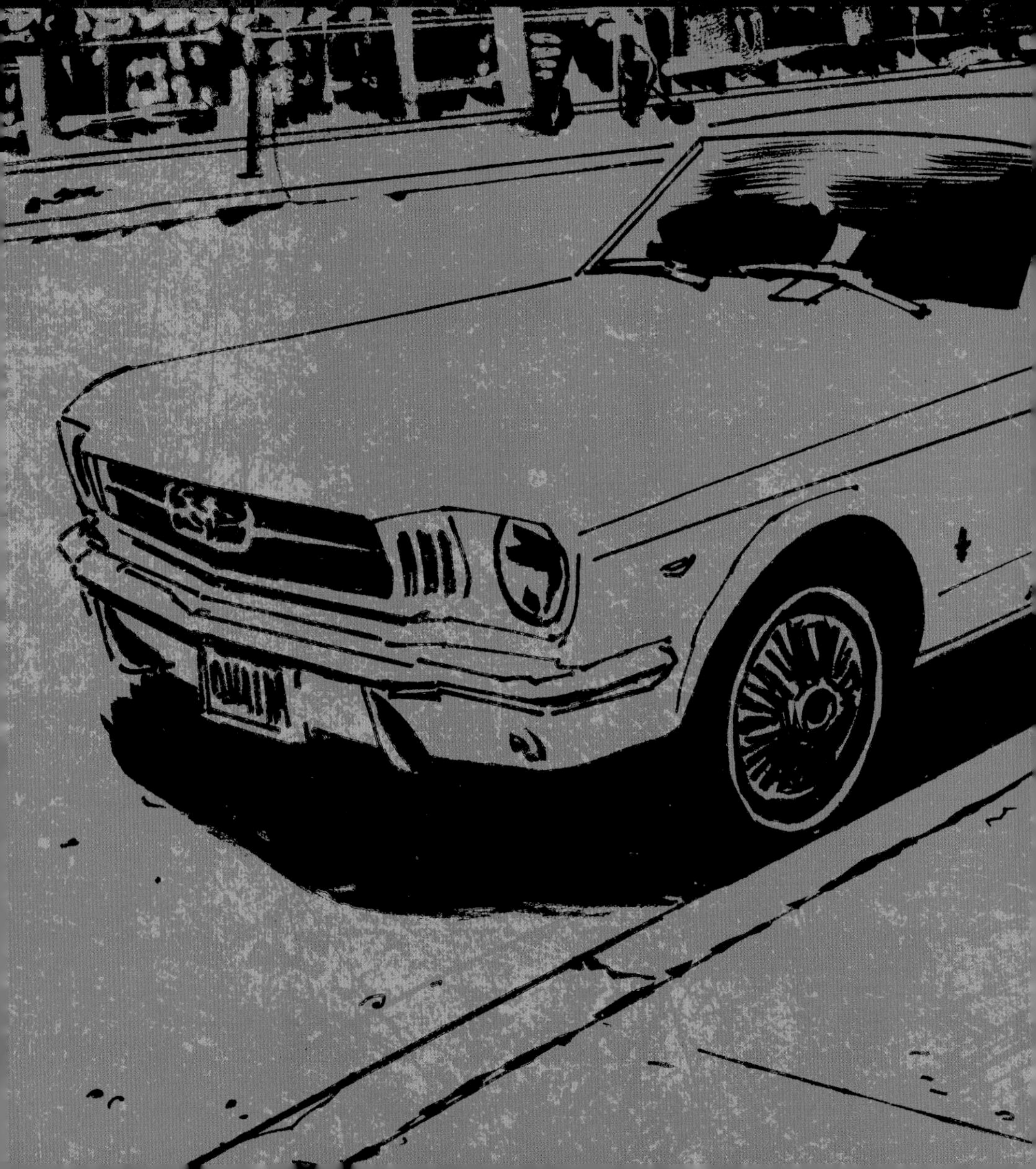

The Case of the Girl Who Took her Shampoo (But Left her Mini)

written by
GREG RUCKA

illustrated by
MATTHEW SOUTHWORTH

colored by
LEE LOUGHRIDGE and RICO RENZI
with **MATTHEW SOUTHWORTH**

Edited by
JAMES LUCAS JONES

Designed by
KEITH WOOD

AN ONI PRESS PRODUCTION

PUBLISHED BY ONI PRESS, INC.

Joe Nozemack, publisher
James Lucas Jones, editor in chief
Brad Rooks, director of operations
David Dissanayake, director of sales
Rachel Reed, publicity manager
Melissa Meszaros MacFadyen, marketing assistant
Troy Look, director of design & production
Hilary Thompson, graphic designer
Kate Z. Stone, junior graphic designer
Angie Dobson, digital prepress technician
Ari Yarwood, managing editor
Charlie Chu, senior editor
Robin Herrera, editor
Alissa Sallah, administrative assistant
Jung Lee, logistics associate

ONI PRESS, INC.
1319 SE Martin Luther King, Jr. Blvd.
Suite 240
Portland, OR 97214

onipress.com
facebook.com/onipress
twitter.com/onipress
onipress.tumblr.com
instagram.com/onipress
onipress.com
gregrucka.com

First Edition: October 2017
978-1-62010-440-8

3 5 7 9 10 8 6 4 2

Library of Congress Control Number: 2017937591

Chapter One

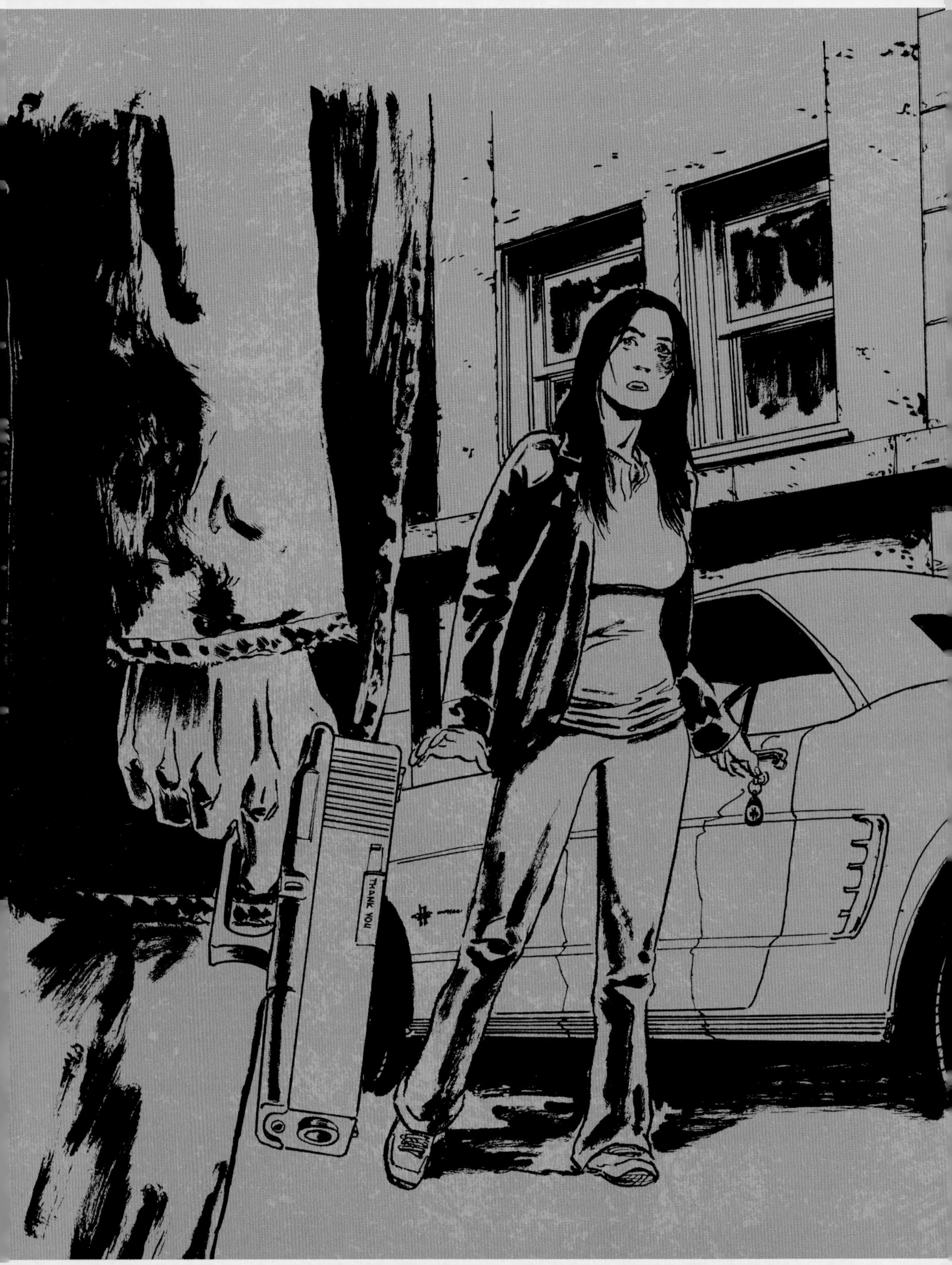
THANK YOU

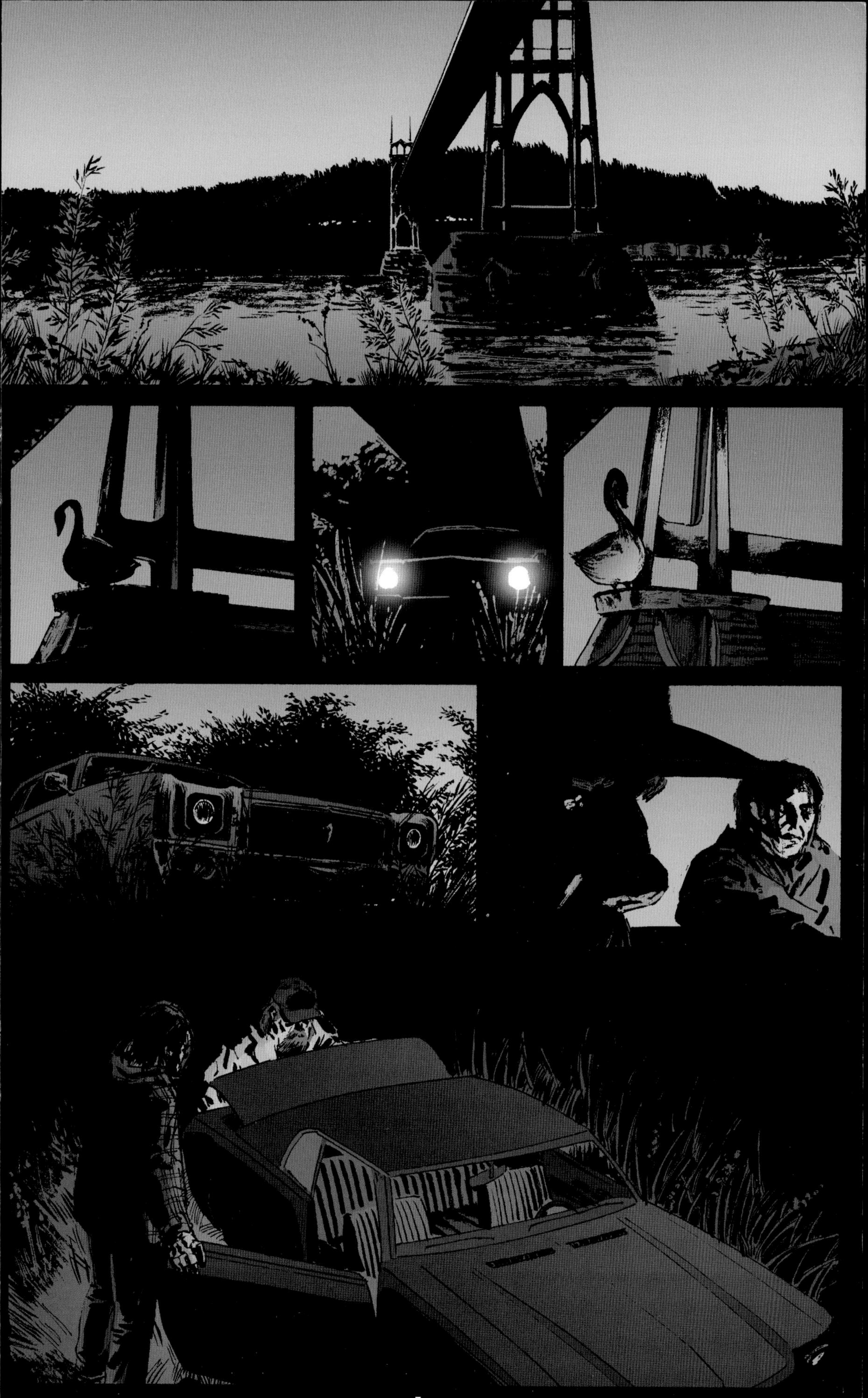

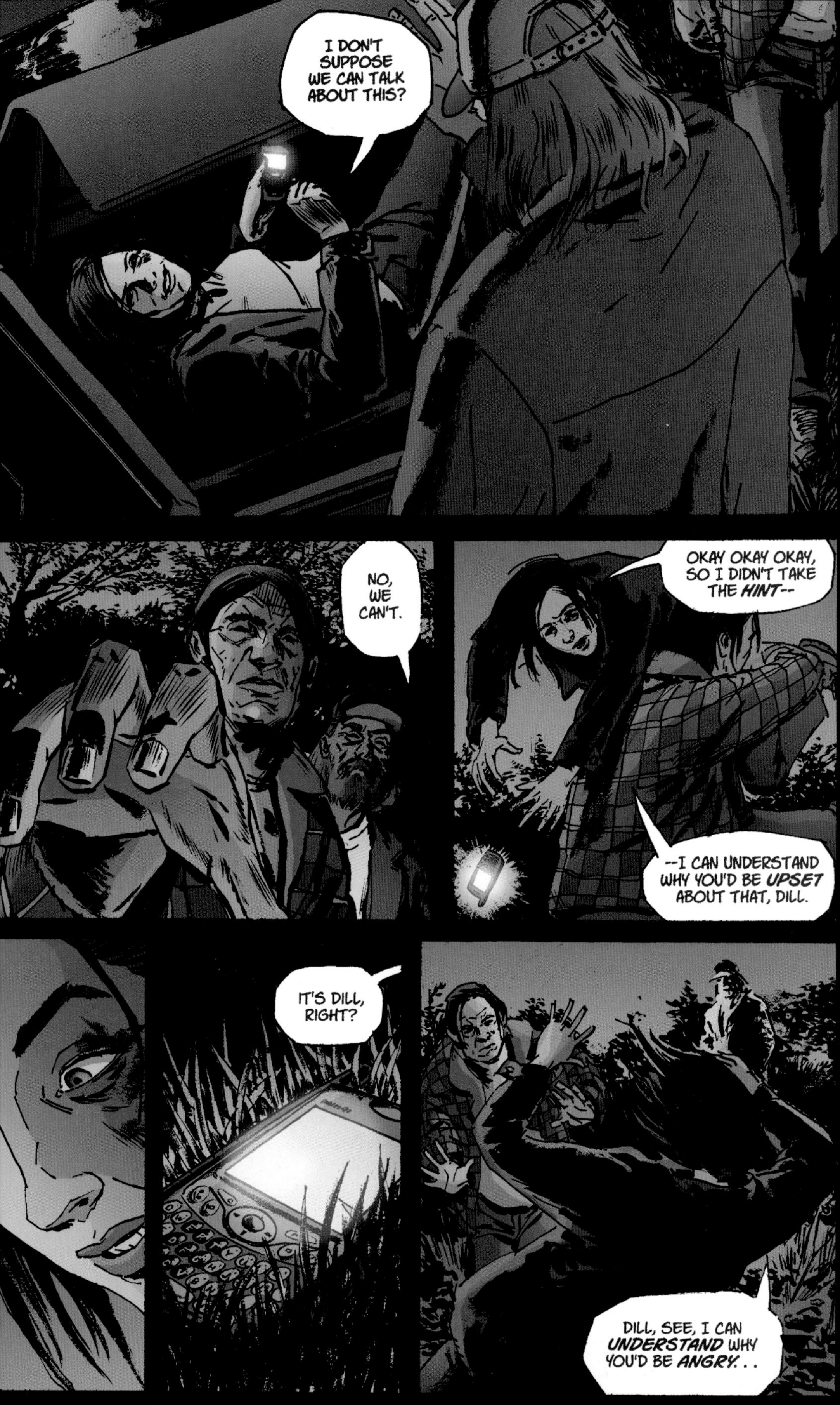
I DON'T SUPPOSE WE CAN TALK ABOUT THIS?
NO, WE CAN'T.
OKAY OKAY OKAY, SO I DIDN'T TAKE THE *HINT*--
--I CAN UNDERSTAND WHY YOU'D BE *UPSET* ABOUT THAT, DILL.
IT'S DILL, RIGHT?
DILL, SEE, I CAN ***UNDERSTAND*** WHY YOU'D BE ***ANGRY*** . . .

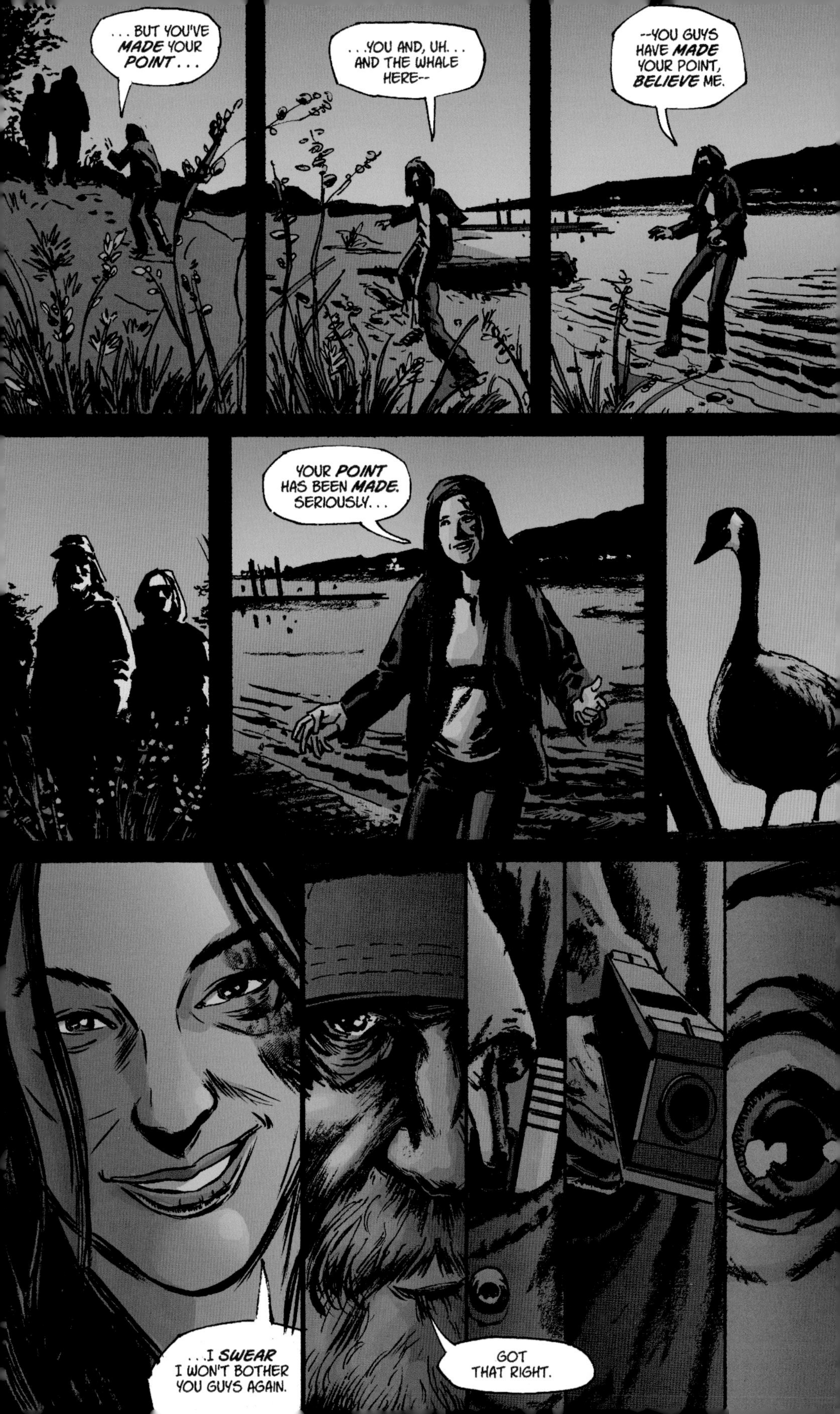
. . . BUT YOU'VE *MADE* YOUR *POINT* . . .
. . .YOU AND, UH. . . AND THE WHALE HERE--
--YOU GUYS HAVE *MADE* YOUR POINT, *BELIEVE* ME.
YOUR *POINT* HAS BEEN *MADE*. SERIOUSLY. . .
. . .I *SWEAR* I WON'T BOTHER YOU GUYS AGAIN.
GOT THAT RIGHT.

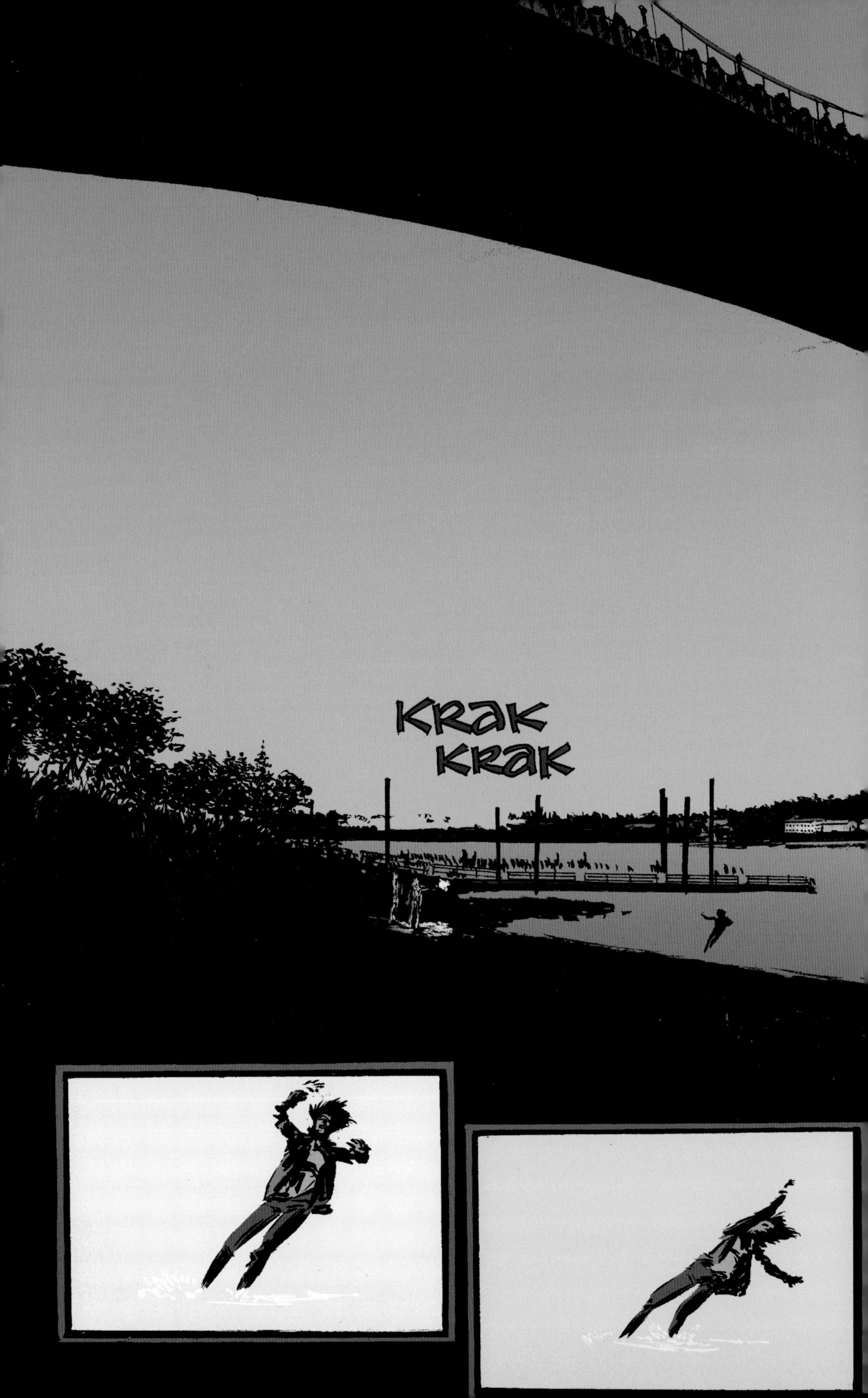
KRAK
KRAK

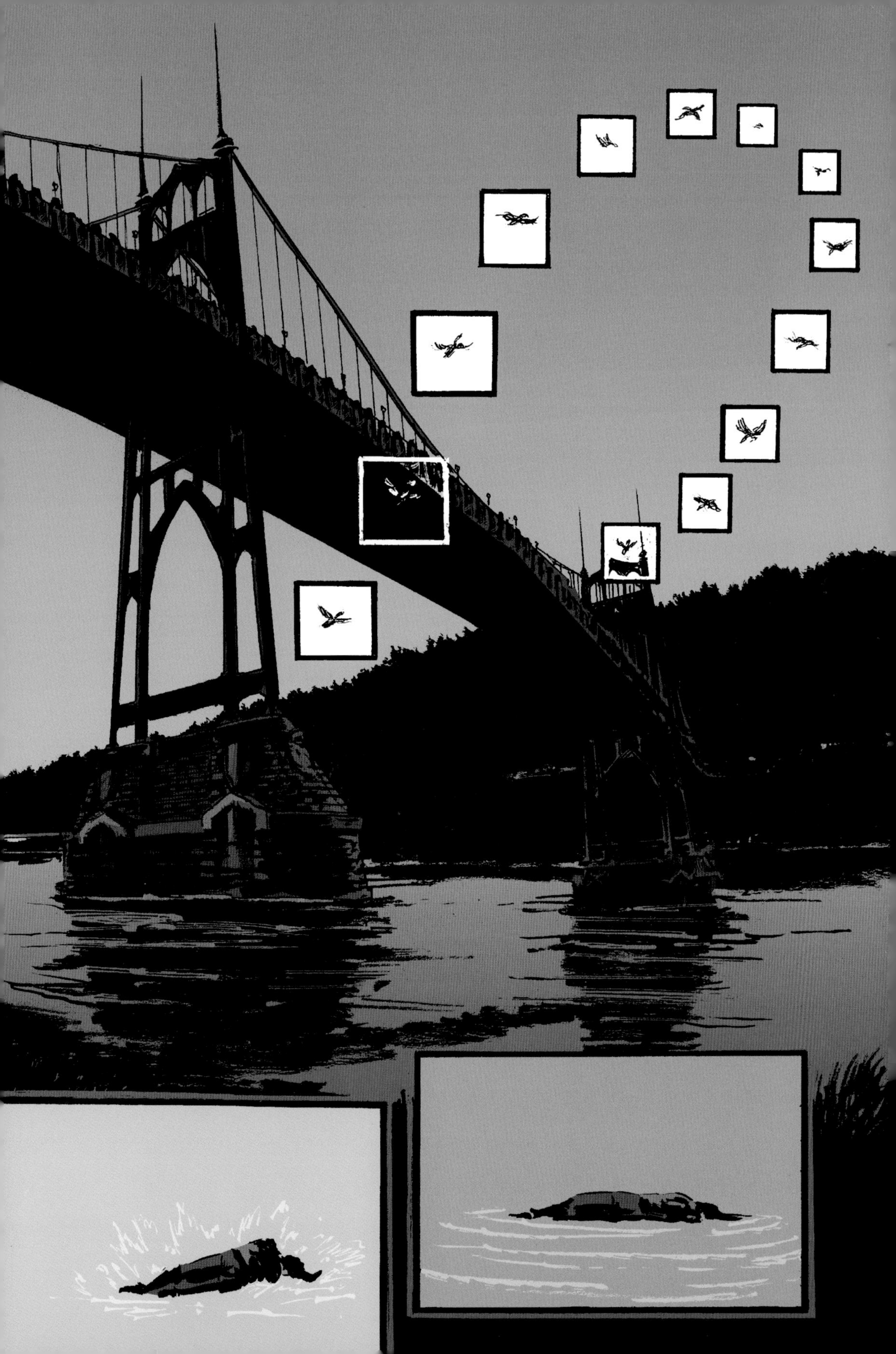

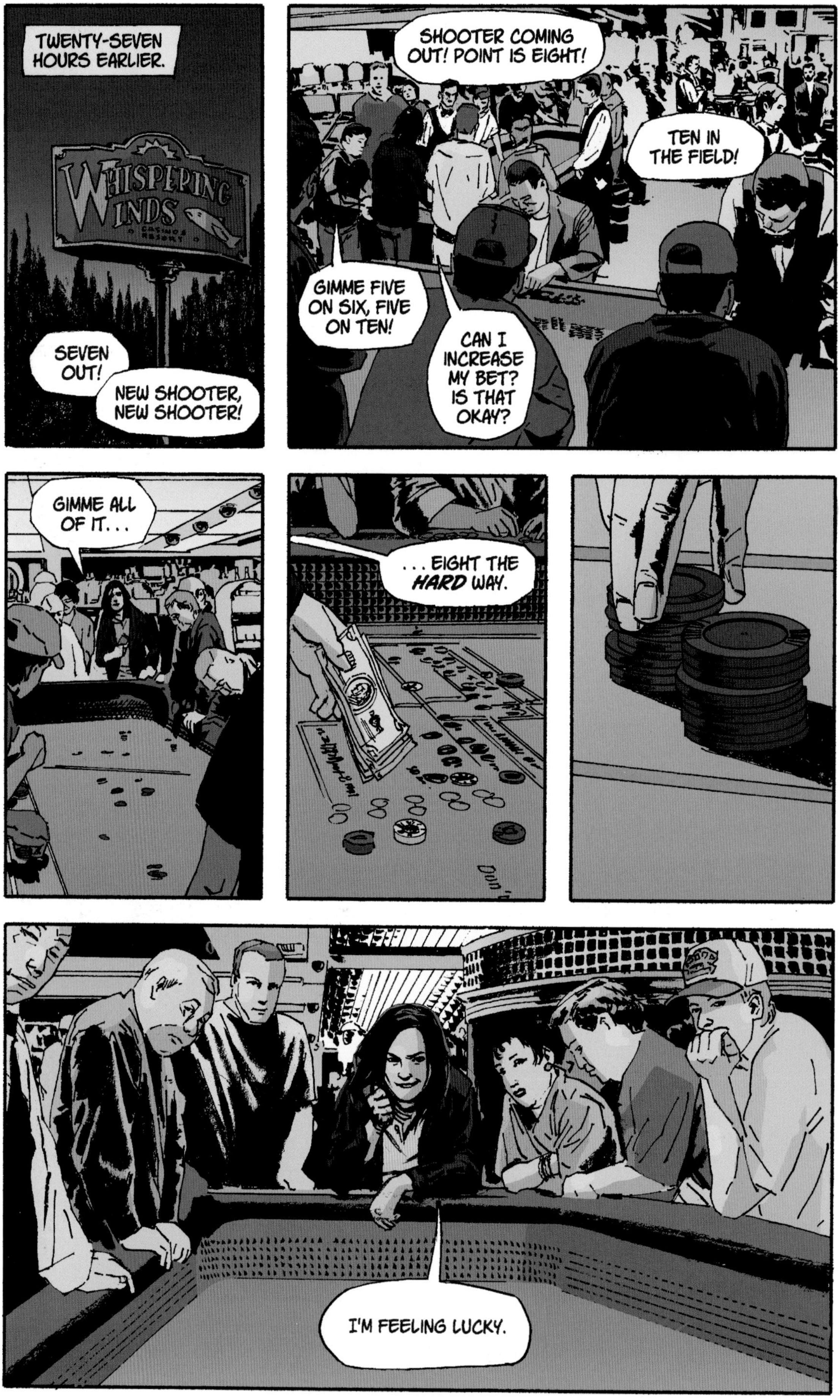
TWENTY-SEVEN HOURS EARLIER.
WHISPERING WINDS
SEVEN OUT!
NEW SHOOTER, NEW SHOOTER!
SHOOTER COMING OUT! POINT IS EIGHT!
TEN IN THE FIELD!
GIMME FIVE ON SIX, FIVE ON TEN!
CAN I INCREASE MY BET? IS THAT OKAY?
GIMME ALL OF IT. . .
. . . EIGHT THE *HARD* WAY.
I'M FEELING LUCKY.

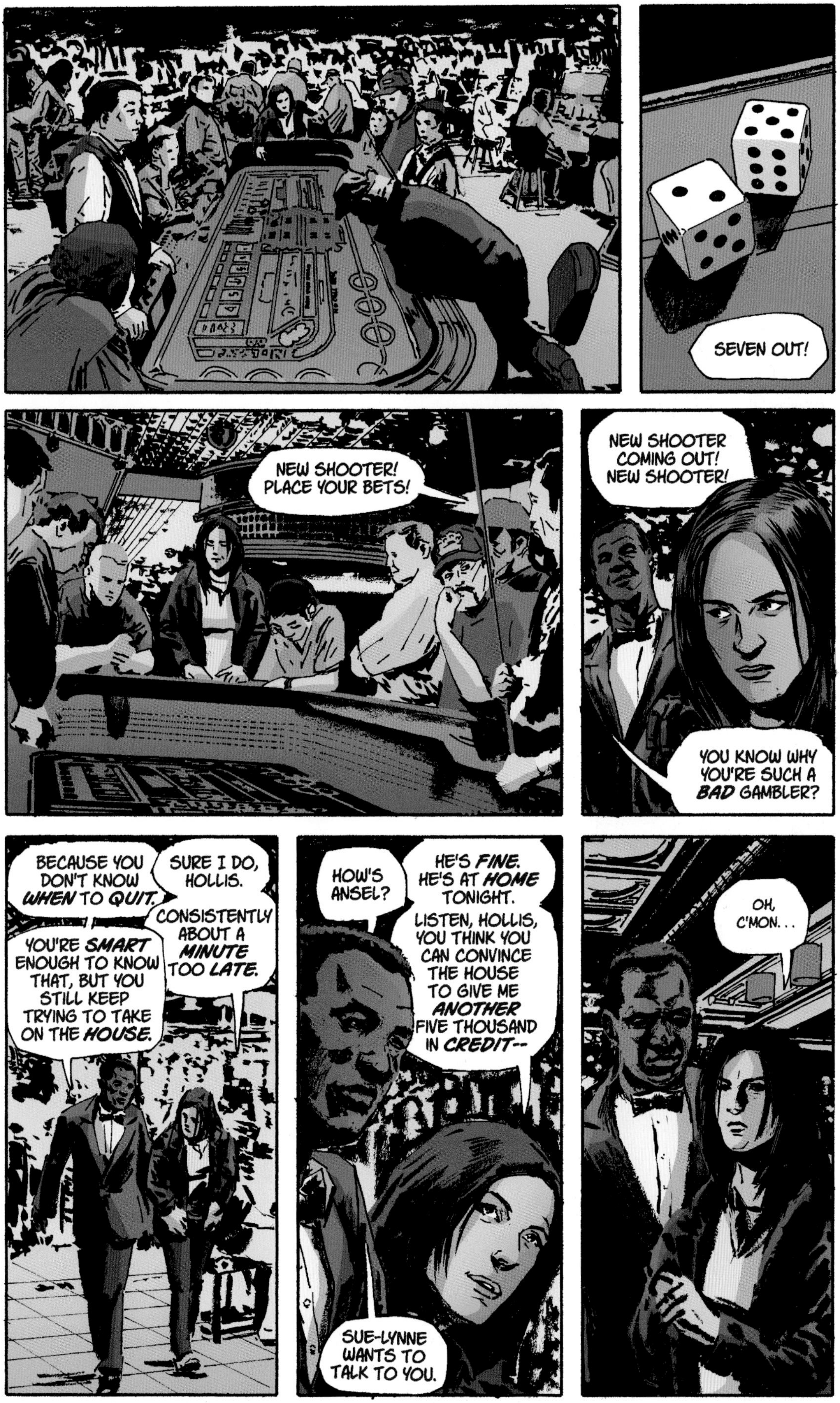
SEVEN OUT!
NEW SHOOTER! PLACE YOUR BETS!
NEW SHOOTER COMING OUT! NEW SHOOTER!
YOU KNOW WHY YOU'RE SUCH A BAD GAMBLER?
SURE I DO, HOLLIS.
BECAUSE YOU DON'T KNOW WHEN TO QUIT.
CONSISTENTLY ABOUT A MINUTE TOO LATE.
YOU'RE SMART ENOUGH TO KNOW THAT, BUT YOU STILL KEEP TRYING TO TAKE ON THE HOUSE.
HOW'S ANSEL?
HE'S FINE. HE'S AT HOME TONIGHT.
LISTEN, HOLLIS, YOU THINK YOU CAN CONVINCE THE HOUSE TO GIVE ME ANOTHER FIVE THOUSAND IN CREDIT--
SUE-LYNNE WANTS TO TALK TO YOU.
OH, C'MON. . .

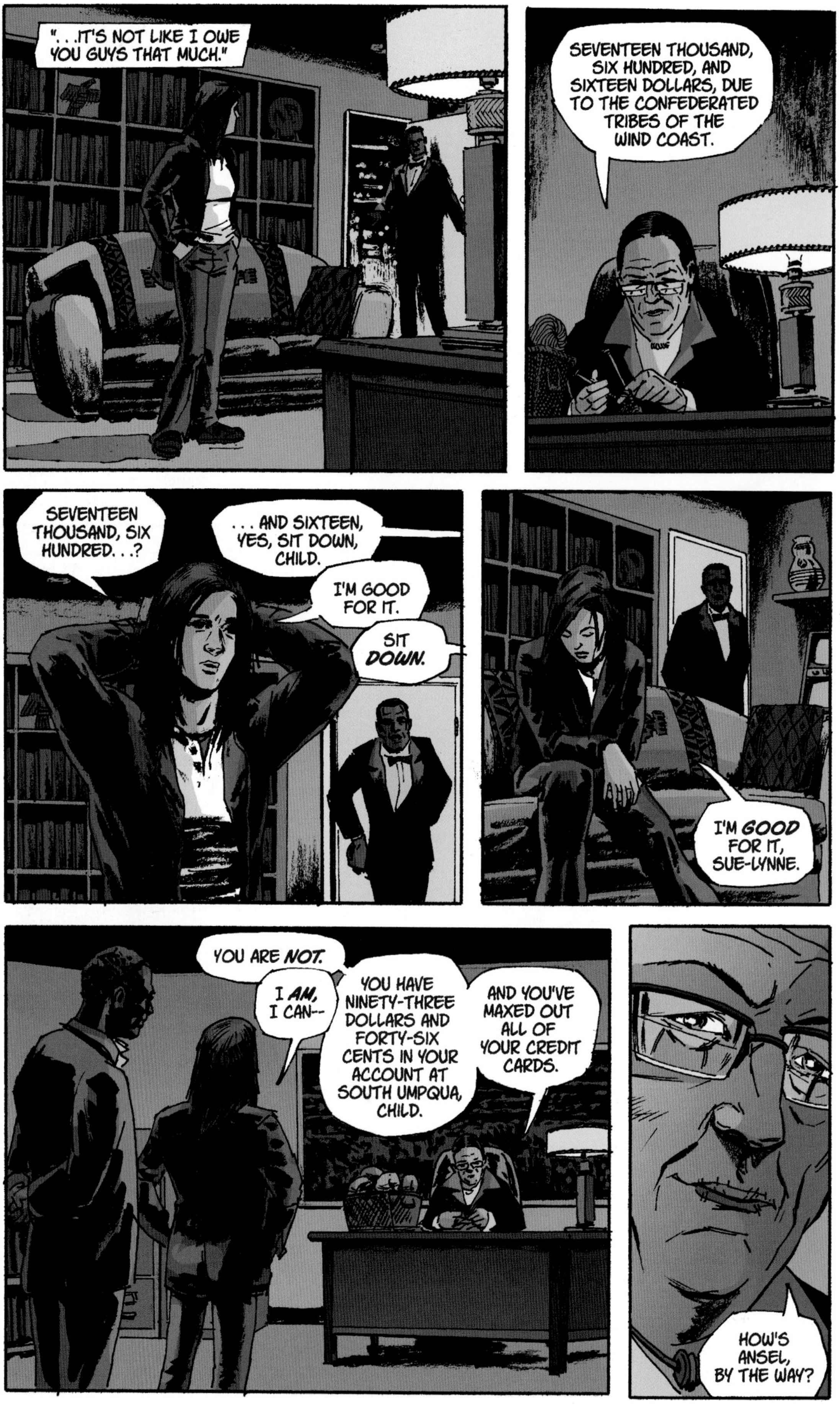
". . .IT'S NOT LIKE I OWE YOU GUYS THAT MUCH."
SEVENTEEN THOUSAND, SIX HUNDRED, AND SIXTEEN DOLLARS, DUE TO THE CONFEDERATED TRIBES OF THE WIND COAST.
SEVENTEEN THOUSAND, SIX HUNDRED. . .?
. . . AND SIXTEEN, YES, SIT DOWN, CHILD.
I'M GOOD FOR IT.
SIT *DOWN*.
I'M *GOOD* FOR IT, SUE-LYNNE.
YOU ARE *NOT*.
I *AM*, I CAN--
YOU HAVE NINETY-THREE DOLLARS AND FORTY-SIX CENTS IN YOUR ACCOUNT AT SOUTH UMPQUA, CHILD.
AND YOU'VE MAXED OUT ALL OF YOUR CREDIT CARDS.
HOW'S ANSEL, BY THE WAY?

HE'S FINE, I'LL TELL HIM YOU ASKED.

YOU DIDN'T BRING ME UP HERE TO TELL ME I'M *BROKE* OR TO ASK ABOUT ANSEL, SUE-LYNNE.

CHARLOTTE'S RUN OFF.

MAYBE WITH A BOY.

YOU'RE GOING TO FIND HER.

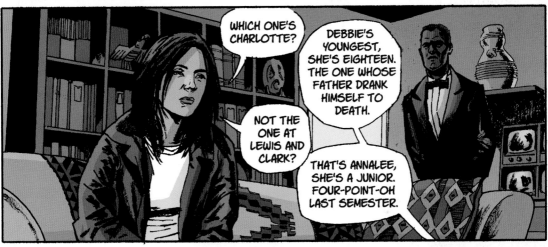

WHICH ONE'S CHARLOTTE?

NOT THE ONE AT LEWIS AND CLARK?

DEBBIE'S YOUNGEST, SHE'S EIGHTEEN. THE ONE WHOSE FATHER DRANK HIMSELF TO DEATH.

THAT'S ANNALEE, SHE'S A JUNIOR. FOUR-POINT-OH LAST SEMESTER.

YOU MUST BE VERY PROUD.

I'M PROUD OF *ALL* OF MY GRAND-CHILDREN.

EVEN THE ONES WHO RUN OFF?

ALL OF MY GRAND-CHILDREN.

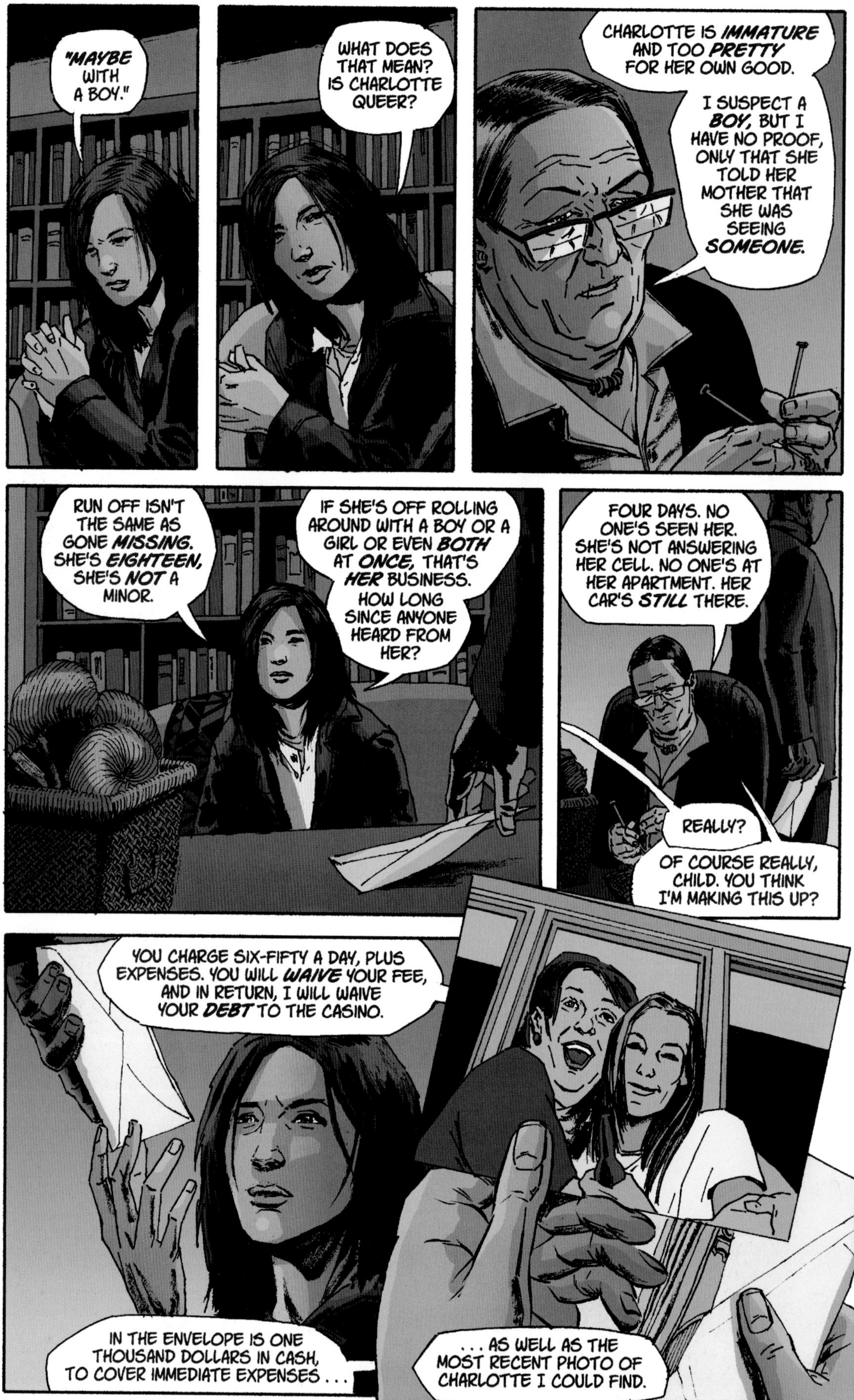
"MAYBE WITH A BOY."
WHAT DOES THAT MEAN? IS CHARLOTTE QUEER?
CHARLOTTE IS *IMMATURE* AND TOO *PRETTY* FOR HER OWN GOOD.
I SUSPECT A *BOY,* BUT I HAVE NO PROOF, ONLY THAT SHE TOLD HER MOTHER THAT SHE WAS SEEING *SOMEONE.*
RUN OFF ISN'T THE SAME AS GONE *MISSING.* SHE'S *EIGHTEEN,* SHE'S *NOT* A MINOR.
IF SHE'S OFF ROLLING AROUND WITH A BOY OR A GIRL OR EVEN *BOTH* AT *ONCE,* THAT'S *HER* BUSINESS.
HOW LONG SINCE ANYONE HEARD FROM HER?
FOUR DAYS. NO ONE'S SEEN HER. SHE'S NOT ANSWERING HER CELL. NO ONE'S AT HER APARTMENT. HER CAR'S *STILL* THERE.
REALLY?
OF COURSE REALLY, CHILD. YOU THINK I'M MAKING THIS UP?
YOU CHARGE SIX-FIFTY A DAY, PLUS EXPENSES. YOU WILL *WAIVE* YOUR FEE, AND IN RETURN, I WILL WAIVE YOUR *DEBT* TO THE CASINO.
IN THE ENVELOPE IS ONE THOUSAND DOLLARS IN CASH, TO COVER IMMEDIATE EXPENSES . . .
. . . AS WELL AS THE MOST RECENT PHOTO OF CHARLOTTE I COULD FIND.

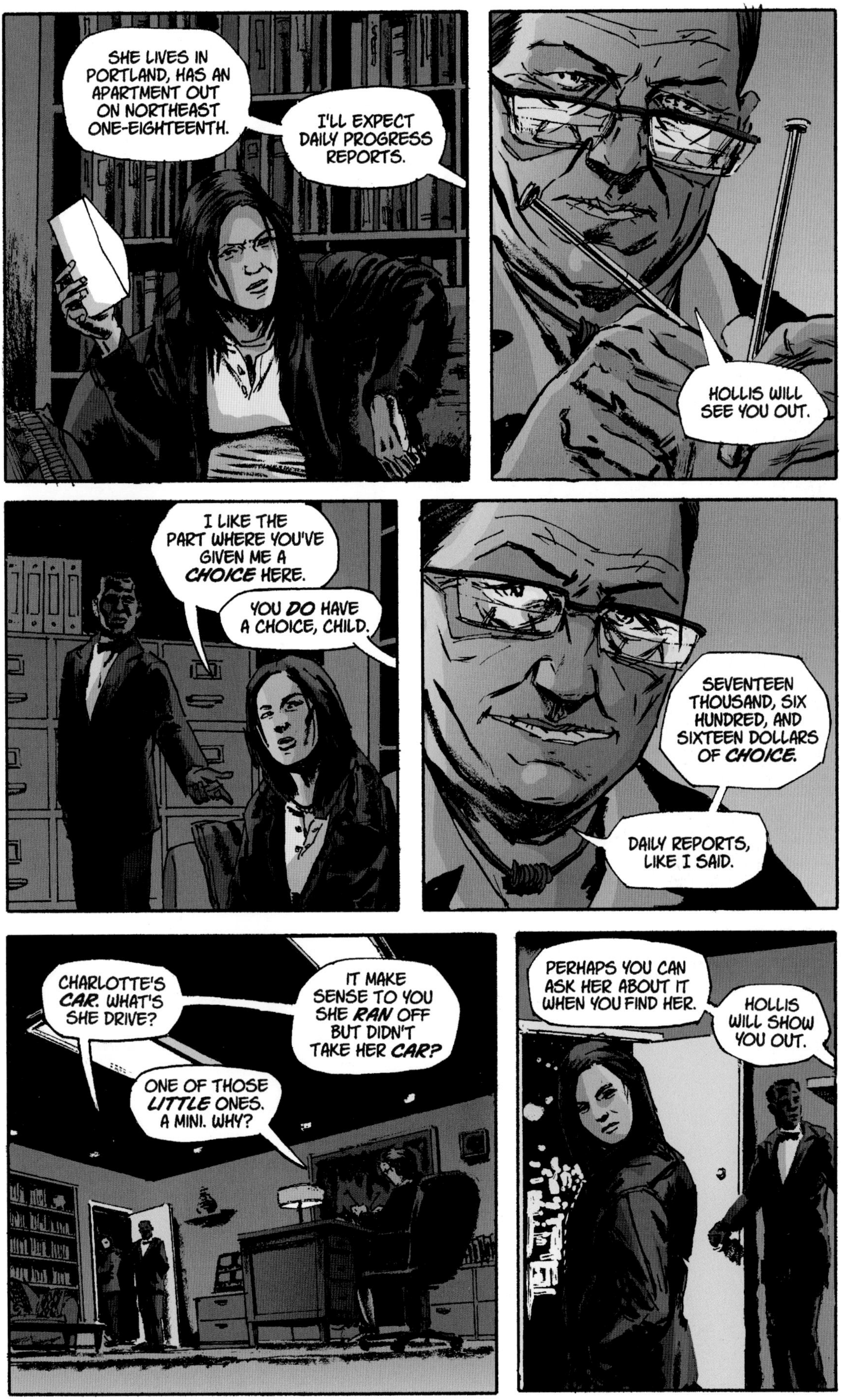
SHE LIVES IN PORTLAND, HAS AN APARTMENT OUT ON NORTHEAST ONE-EIGHTEENTH.
I'LL EXPECT DAILY PROGRESS REPORTS.
HOLLIS WILL SEE YOU OUT.
I LIKE THE PART WHERE YOU'VE GIVEN ME A *CHOICE* HERE.
YOU *DO* HAVE A CHOICE, CHILD.
SEVENTEEN THOUSAND, SIX HUNDRED, AND SIXTEEN DOLLARS OF *CHOICE*.
DAILY REPORTS, LIKE I SAID.
CHARLOTTE'S *CAR*. WHAT'S SHE DRIVE?
ONE OF THOSE *LITTLE* ONES. A MINI. WHY?
IT MAKE SENSE TO YOU SHE *RAN* OFF BUT DIDN'T TAKE HER *CAR?*
PERHAPS YOU CAN ASK HER ABOUT IT WHEN YOU FIND HER.
HOLLIS WILL SHOW YOU OUT.

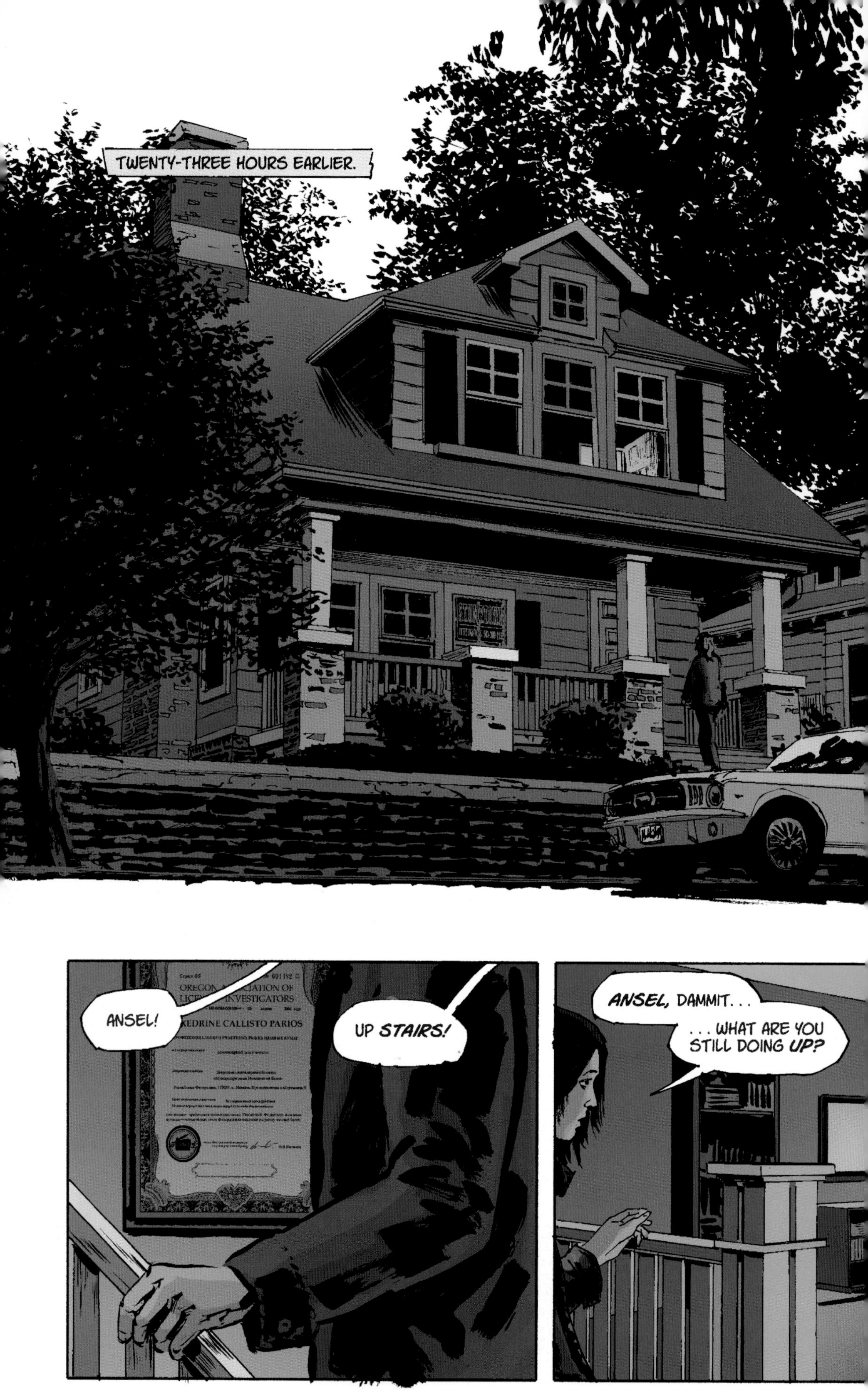
TWENTY-THREE HOURS EARLIER.
ANSEL!
UP STAIRS!
ANSEL, DAMMIT. . .
. . . WHAT ARE YOU STILL DOING UP?

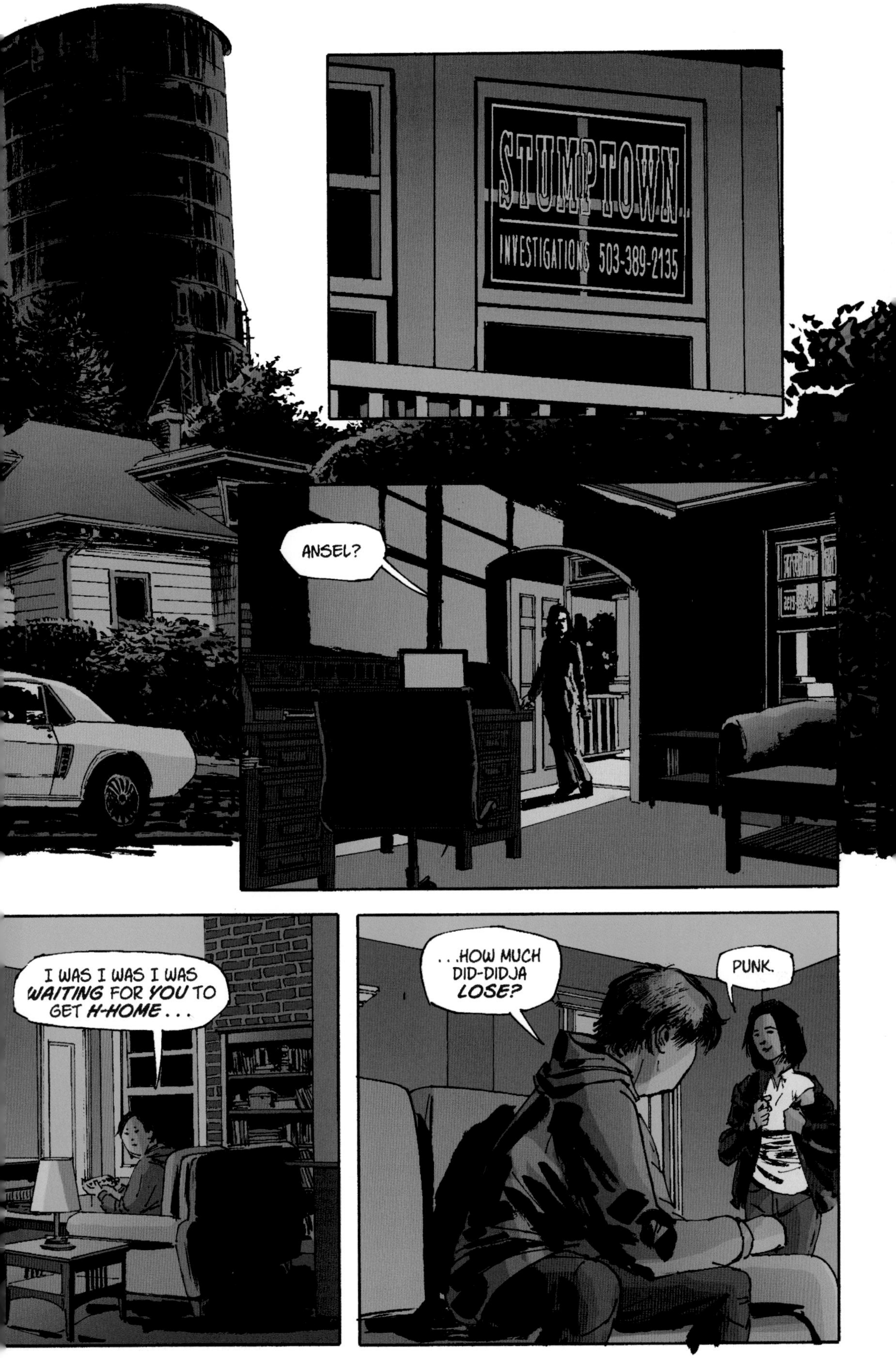
STUMPTOWN
INVESTIGATIONS 503-389-2135
ANSEL?
I WAS I WAS I WAS WAITING FOR YOU TO GET H-HOME . . .
. . .HOW MUCH DID-DIDJA LOSE?
PUNK.

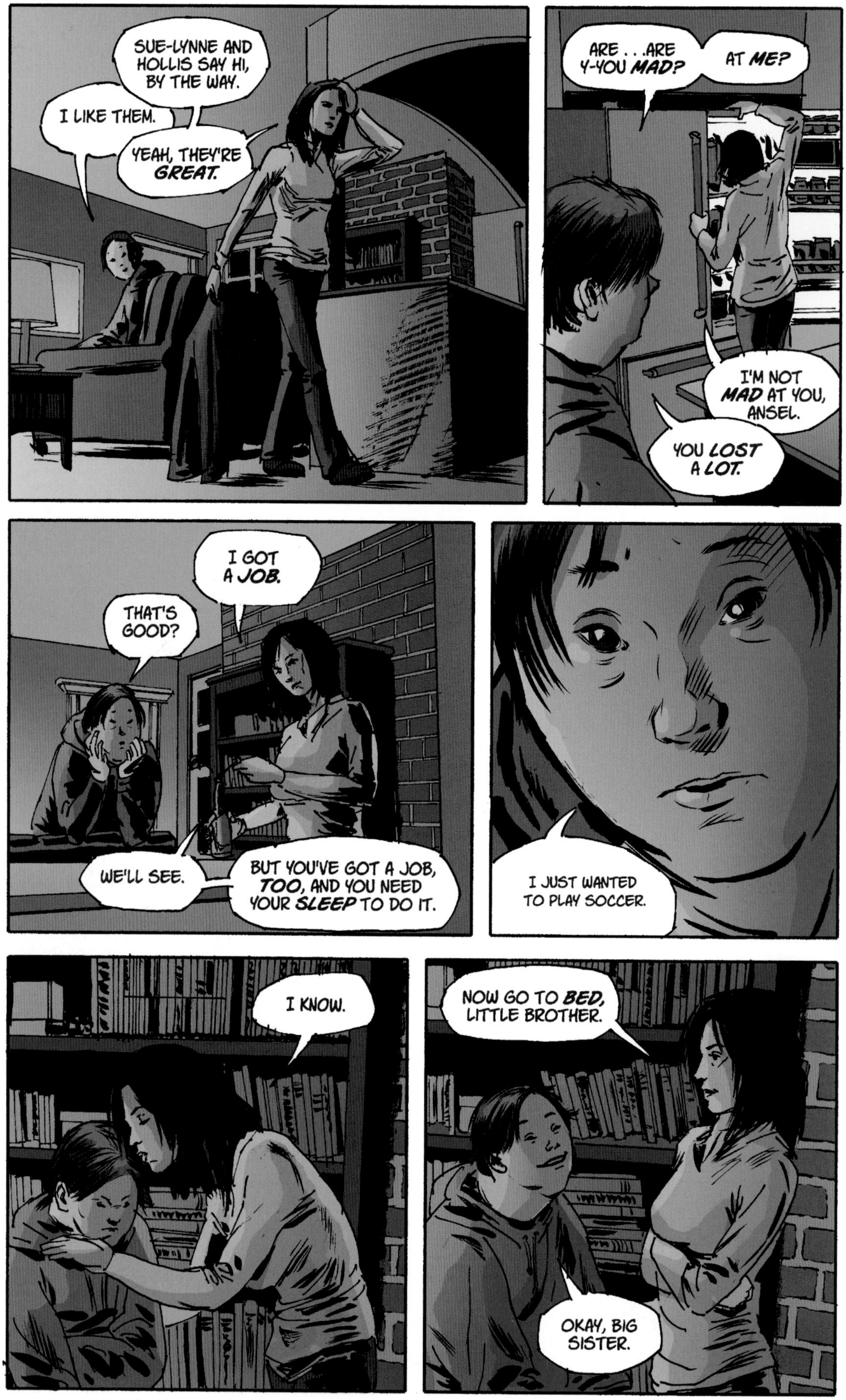

SUE-LYNNE AND HOLLIS SAY HI, BY THE WAY.
I LIKE THEM.
YEAH, THEY'RE GREAT.
ARE . . . ARE Y-YOU MAD?
AT ME?
I'M NOT MAD AT YOU, ANSEL.
YOU LOST A LOT.
I GOT A JOB.
THAT'S GOOD?
WE'LL SEE.
BUT YOU'VE GOT A JOB, TOO, AND YOU NEED YOUR SLEEP TO DO IT.
I JUST WANTED TO PLAY SOCCER.
I KNOW.
NOW GO TO BED, LITTLE BROTHER.
OKAY, BIG SISTER.

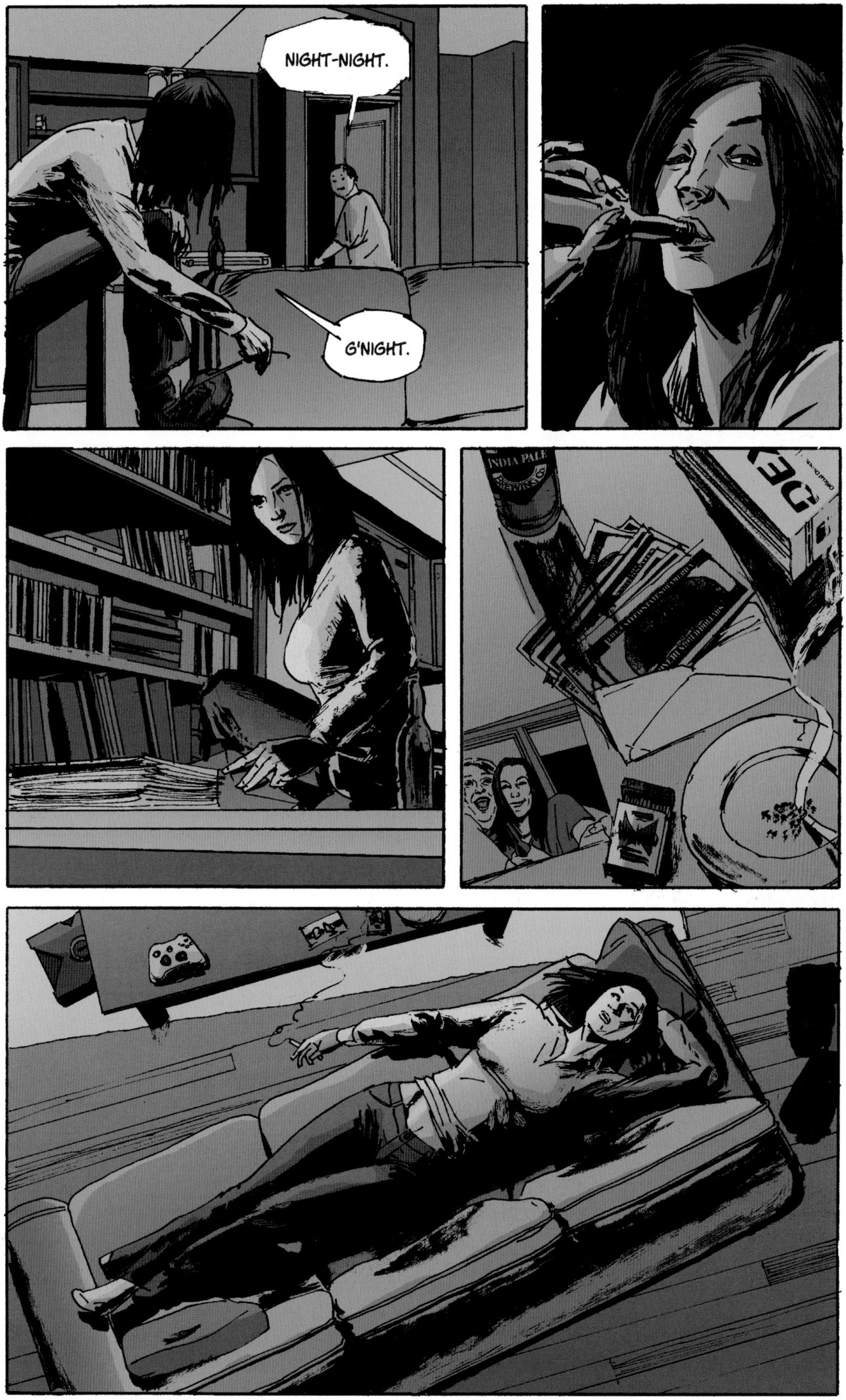
NIGHT-NIGHT.
G'NIGHT.
INDIA PALE

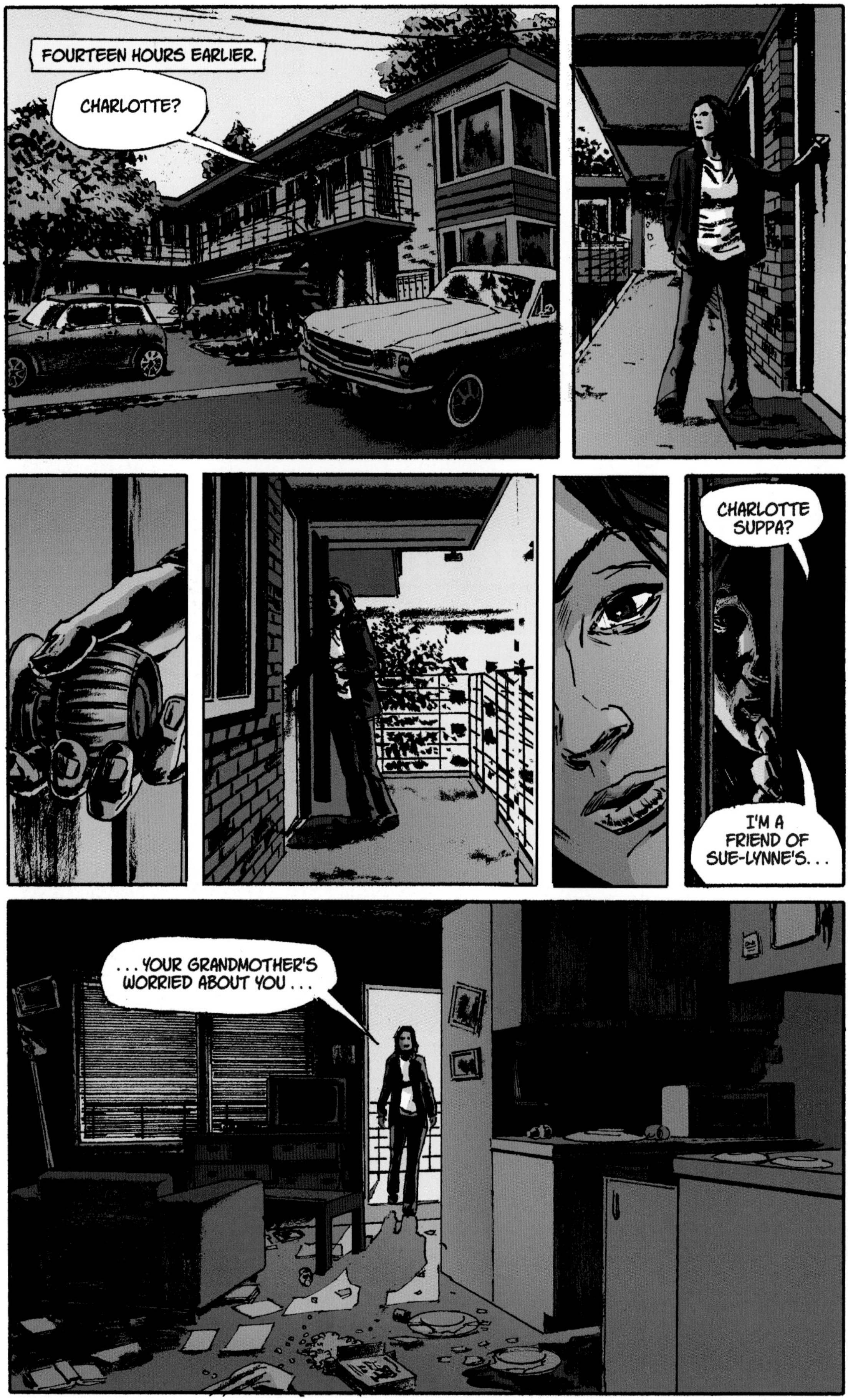
FOURTEEN HOURS EARLIER.
CHARLOTTE?
CHARLOTTE SUPPA?
I'M A FRIEND OF SUE-LYNNE'S. . .
. . . YOUR GRANDMOTHER'S WORRIED ABOUT YOU . . .

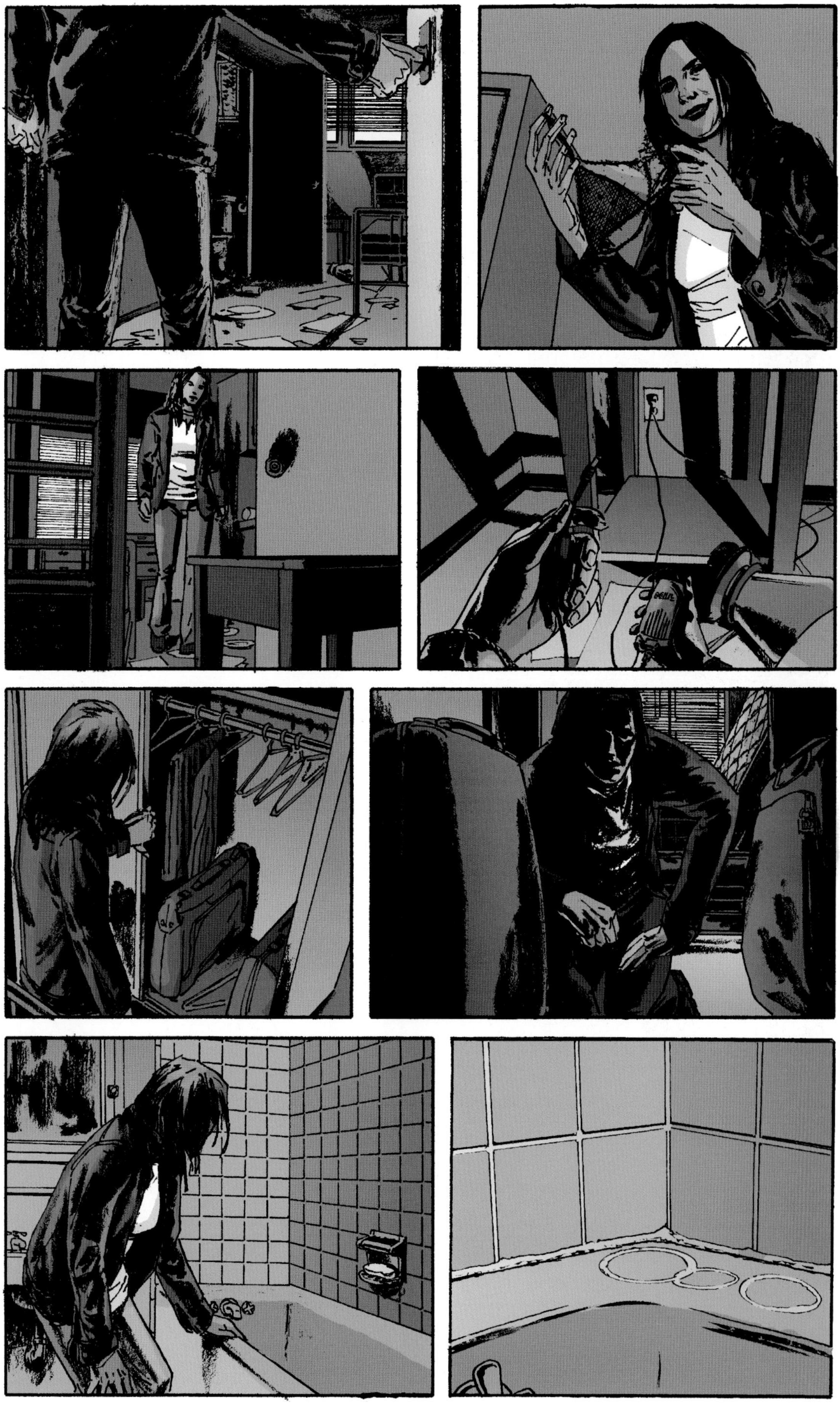

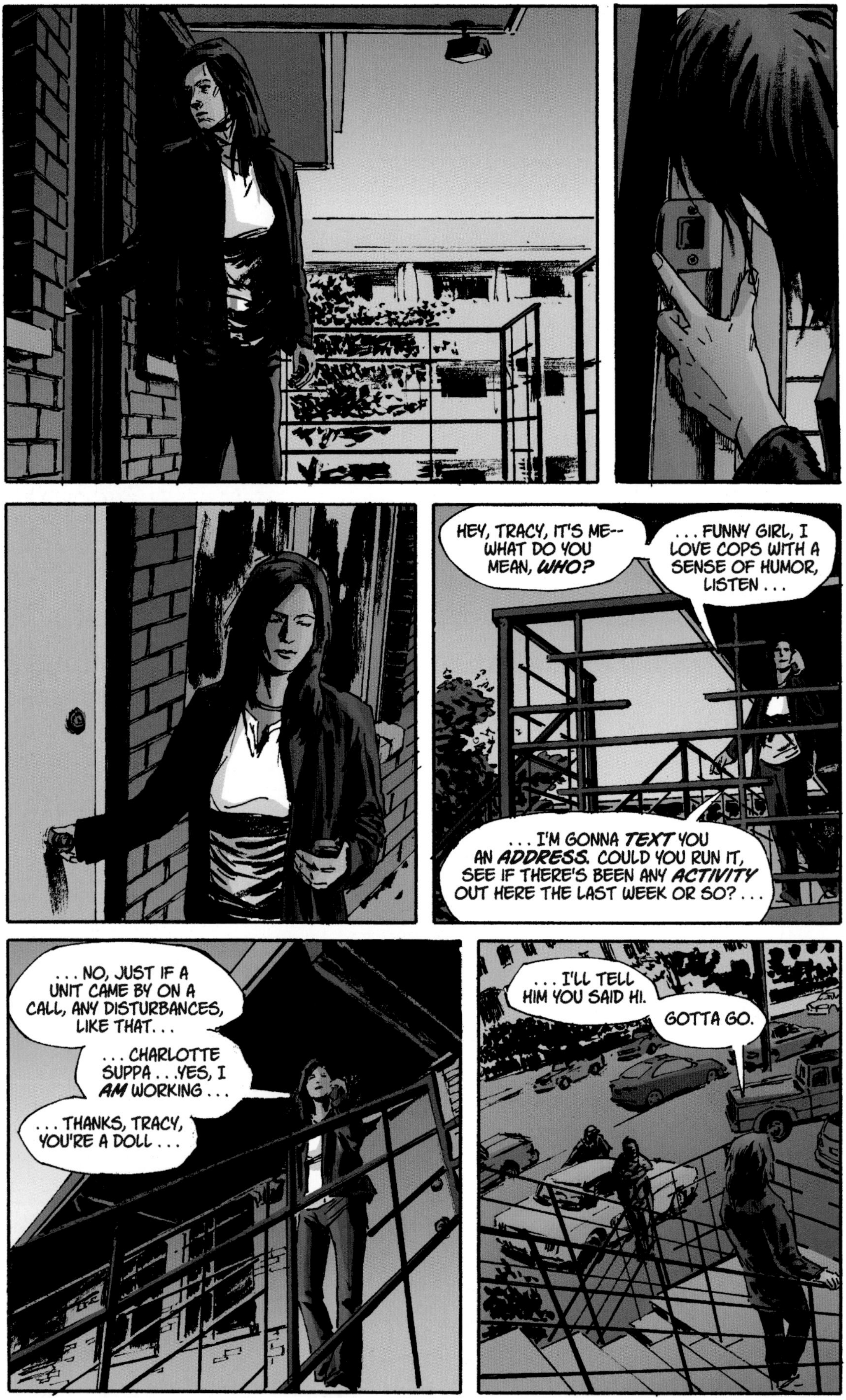
HEY, TRACY, IT'S ME-- WHAT DO YOU MEAN, WHO?
. . . FUNNY GIRL, I LOVE COPS WITH A SENSE OF HUMOR, LISTEN . . .
. . . I'M GONNA TEXT YOU AN ADDRESS. COULD YOU RUN IT, SEE IF THERE'S BEEN ANY ACTIVITY OUT HERE THE LAST WEEK OR SO? . . .
. . . NO, JUST IF A UNIT CAME BY ON A CALL, ANY DISTURBANCES, LIKE THAT . . .
. . . CHARLOTTE SUPPA . . . YES, I AM WORKING . . .
. . . THANKS, TRACY, YOU'RE A DOLL . . .
. . . I'LL TELL HIM YOU SAID HI.
GOTTA GO.

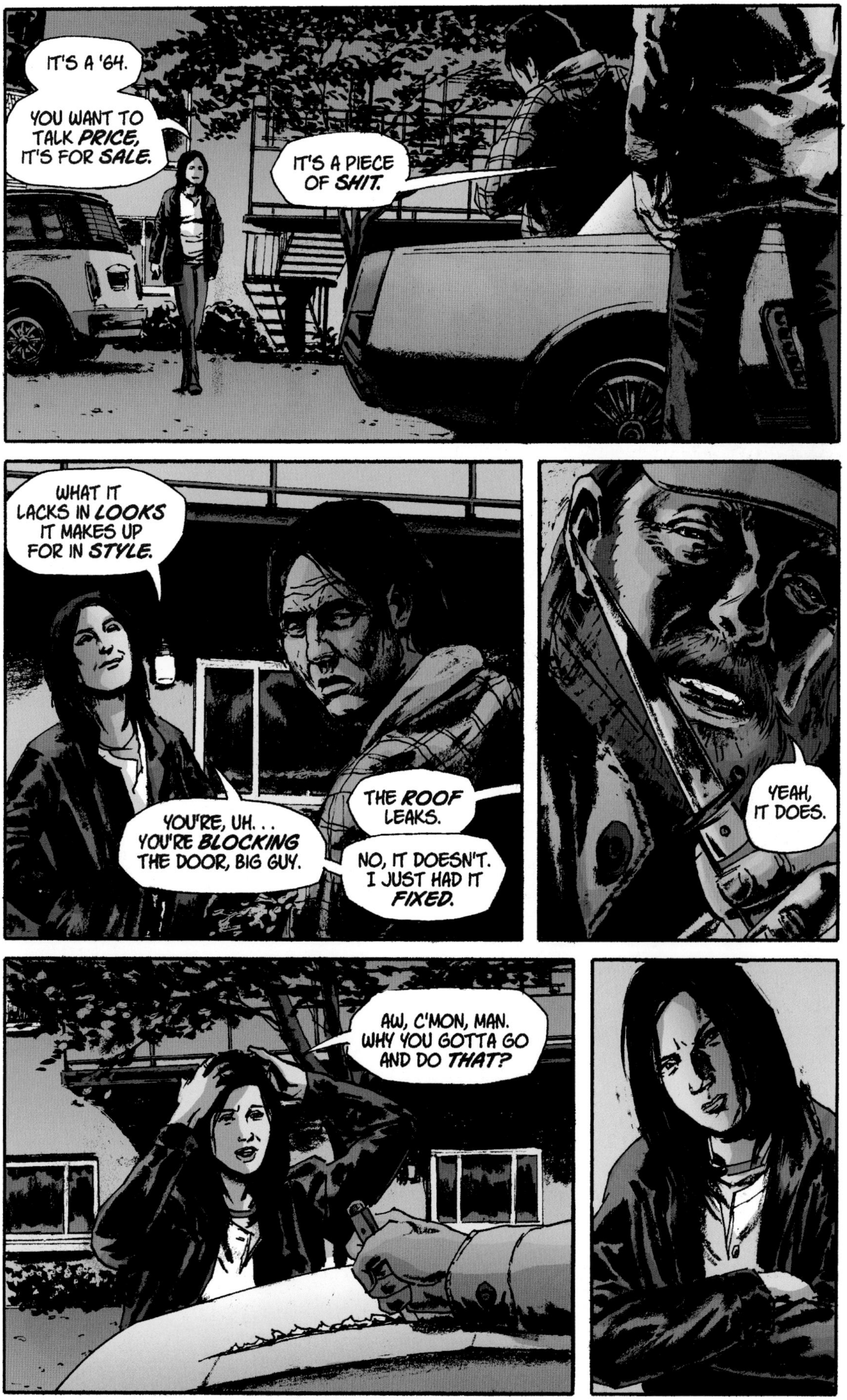

IT'S A '64.
YOU WANT TO TALK PRICE, IT'S FOR SALE.
IT'S A PIECE OF SHIT.
WHAT IT LACKS IN LOOKS IT MAKES UP FOR IN STYLE.
THE ROOF LEAKS.
NO, IT DOESN'T. I JUST HAD IT FIXED.
YOU'RE, UH. . . YOU'RE BLOCKING THE DOOR, BIG GUY.
YEAH, IT DOES.
AW, C'MON, MAN. WHY YOU GOTTA GO AND DO THAT?

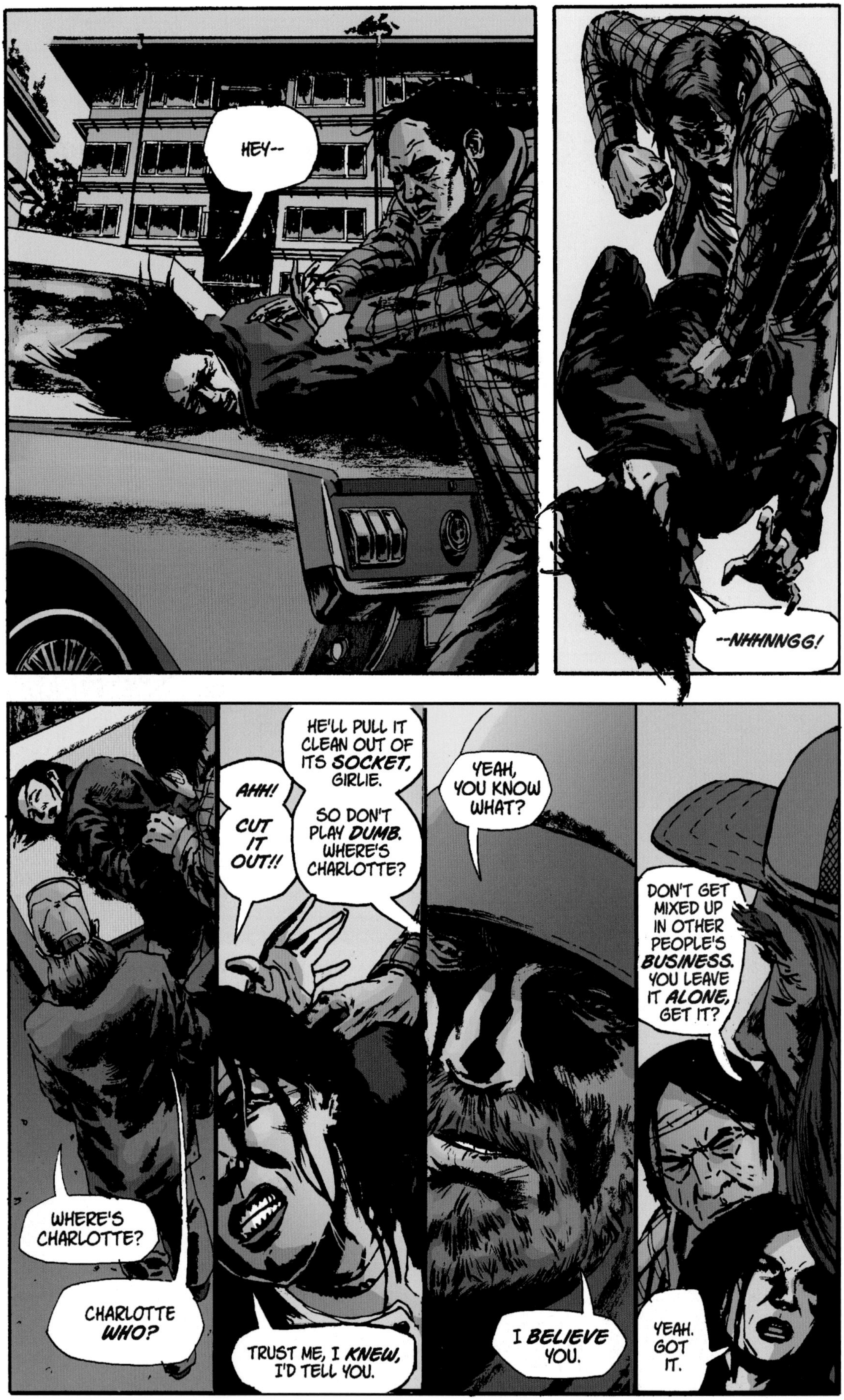
HEY--
--NHHNNGG!
WHERE'S CHARLOTTE?
CHARLOTTE WHO?
AHH! CUT IT OUT!!
HE'LL PULL IT CLEAN OUT OF ITS SOCKET, GIRLIE.
SO DON'T PLAY DUMB. WHERE'S CHARLOTTE?
TRUST ME, I KNEW, I'D TELL YOU.
YEAH, YOU KNOW WHAT?
I BELIEVE YOU.
DON'T GET MIXED UP IN OTHER PEOPLE'S BUSINESS. YOU LEAVE IT ALONE, GET IT?
YEAH. GOT IT.

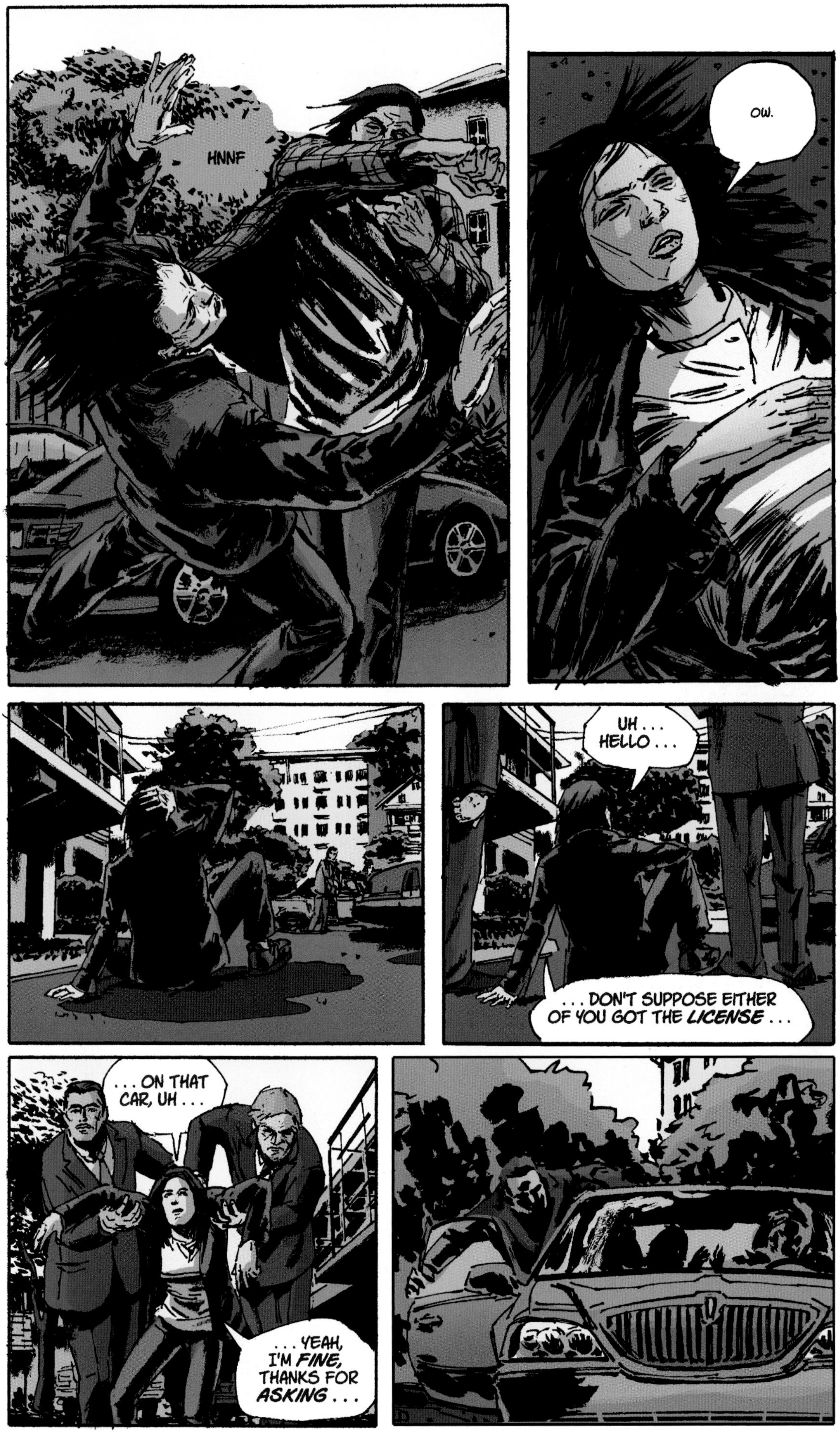
HNNF
OW.
UH . . . HELLO . . .
. . . DON'T SUPPOSE EITHER OF YOU GOT THE *LICENSE* . . .
. . . ON THAT CAR, UH . . .
. . . YEAH, I'M *FINE,* THANKS FOR *ASKING* . . .

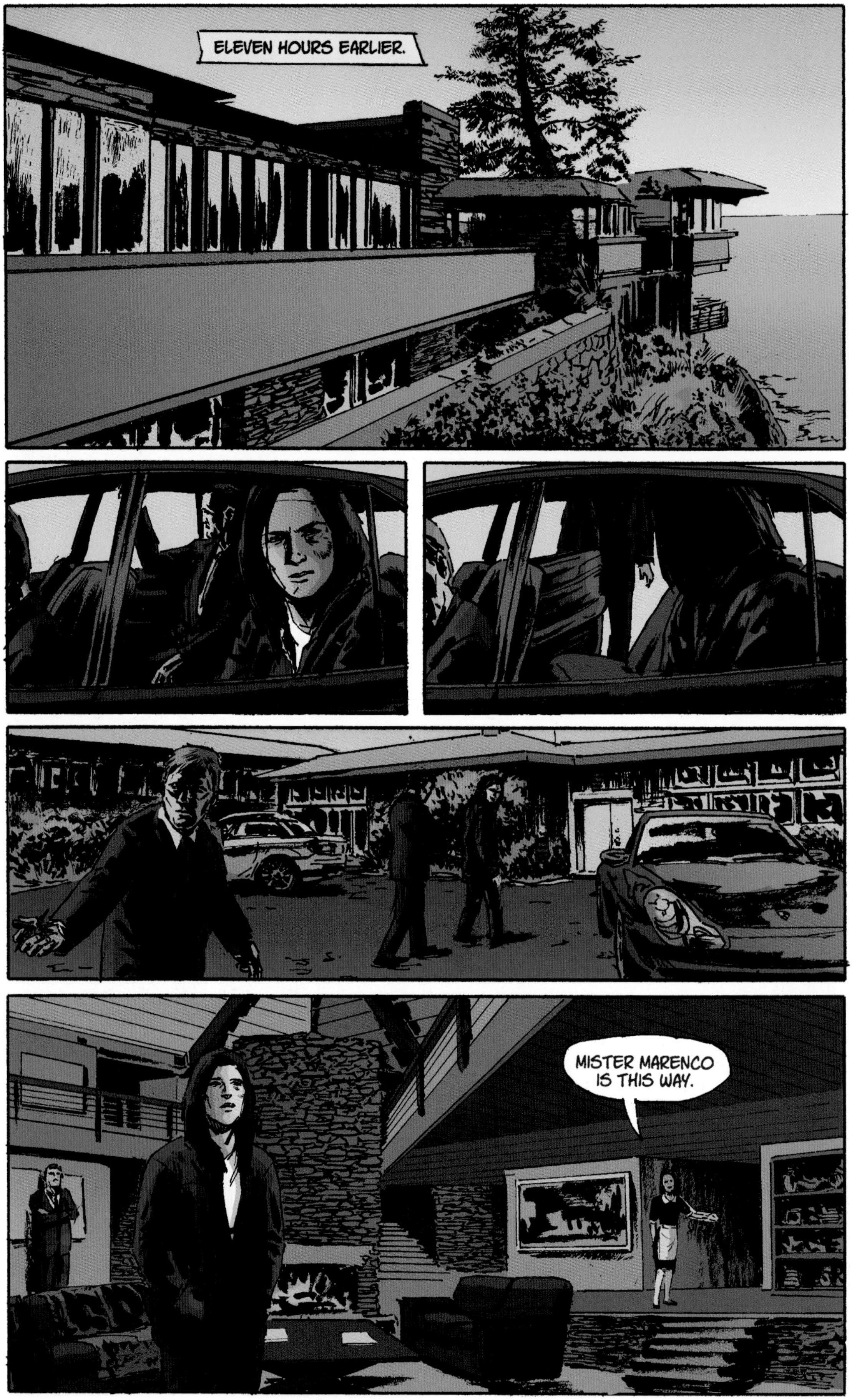
ELEVEN HOURS EARLIER.
MISTER MARENCO IS THIS WAY.

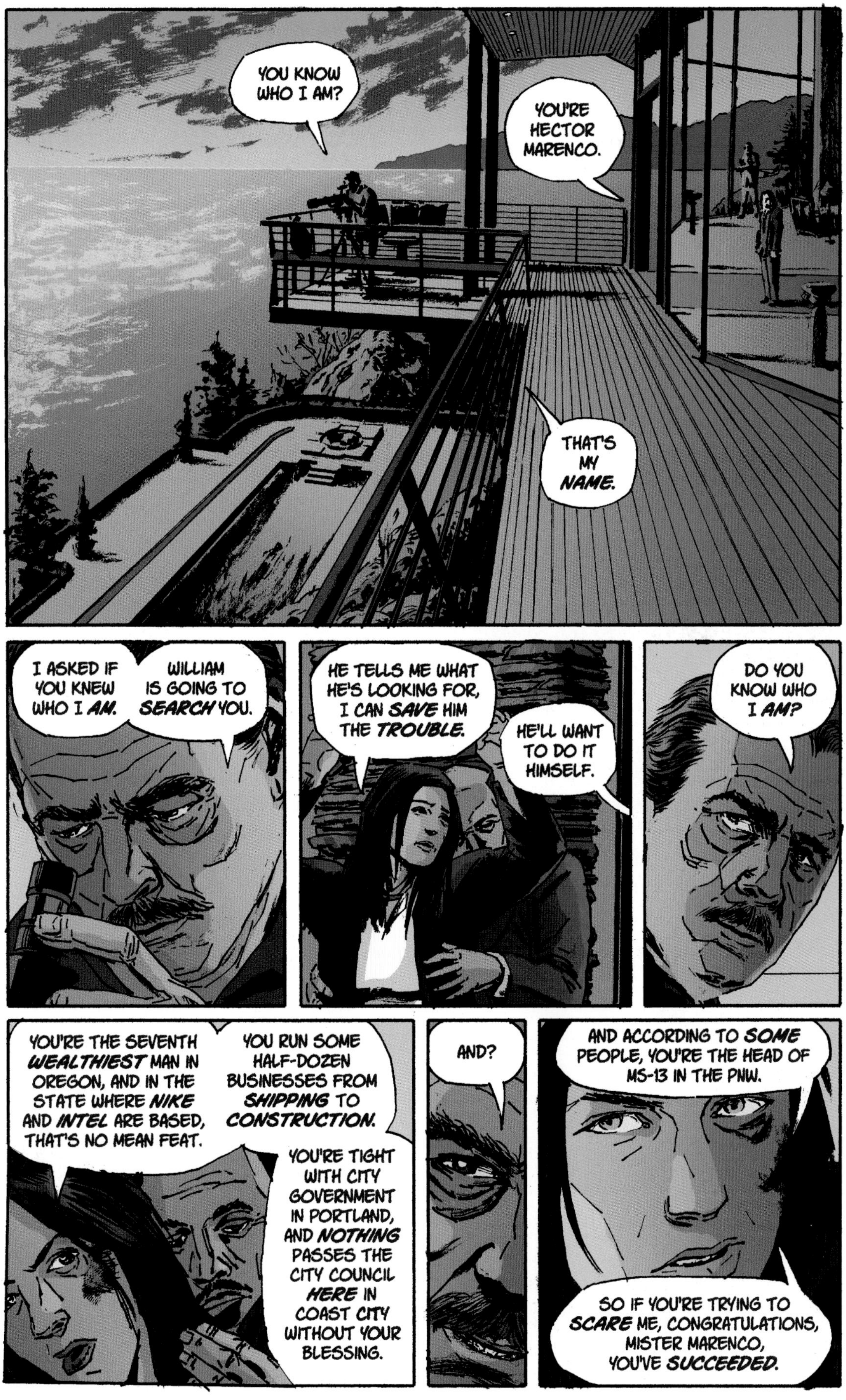
YOU KNOW WHO I AM?
YOU'RE HECTOR MARENCO.
THAT'S MY NAME.
I ASKED IF YOU KNEW WHO I AM.
WILLIAM IS GOING TO SEARCH YOU.
HE TELLS ME WHAT HE'S LOOKING FOR, I CAN SAVE HIM THE TROUBLE.
HE'LL WANT TO DO IT HIMSELF.
DO YOU KNOW WHO I AM?
YOU'RE THE SEVENTH WEALTHIEST MAN IN OREGON, AND IN THE STATE WHERE NIKE AND INTEL ARE BASED, THAT'S NO MEAN FEAT.
YOU RUN SOME HALF-DOZEN BUSINESSES FROM SHIPPING TO CONSTRUCTION.
YOU'RE TIGHT WITH CITY GOVERNMENT IN PORTLAND, AND NOTHING PASSES THE CITY COUNCIL HERE IN COAST CITY WITHOUT YOUR BLESSING.
AND?
AND ACCORDING TO SOME PEOPLE, YOU'RE THE HEAD OF MS-13 IN THE PNW.
SO IF YOU'RE TRYING TO SCARE ME, CONGRATULATIONS, MISTER MARENCO, YOU'VE SUCCEEDED.

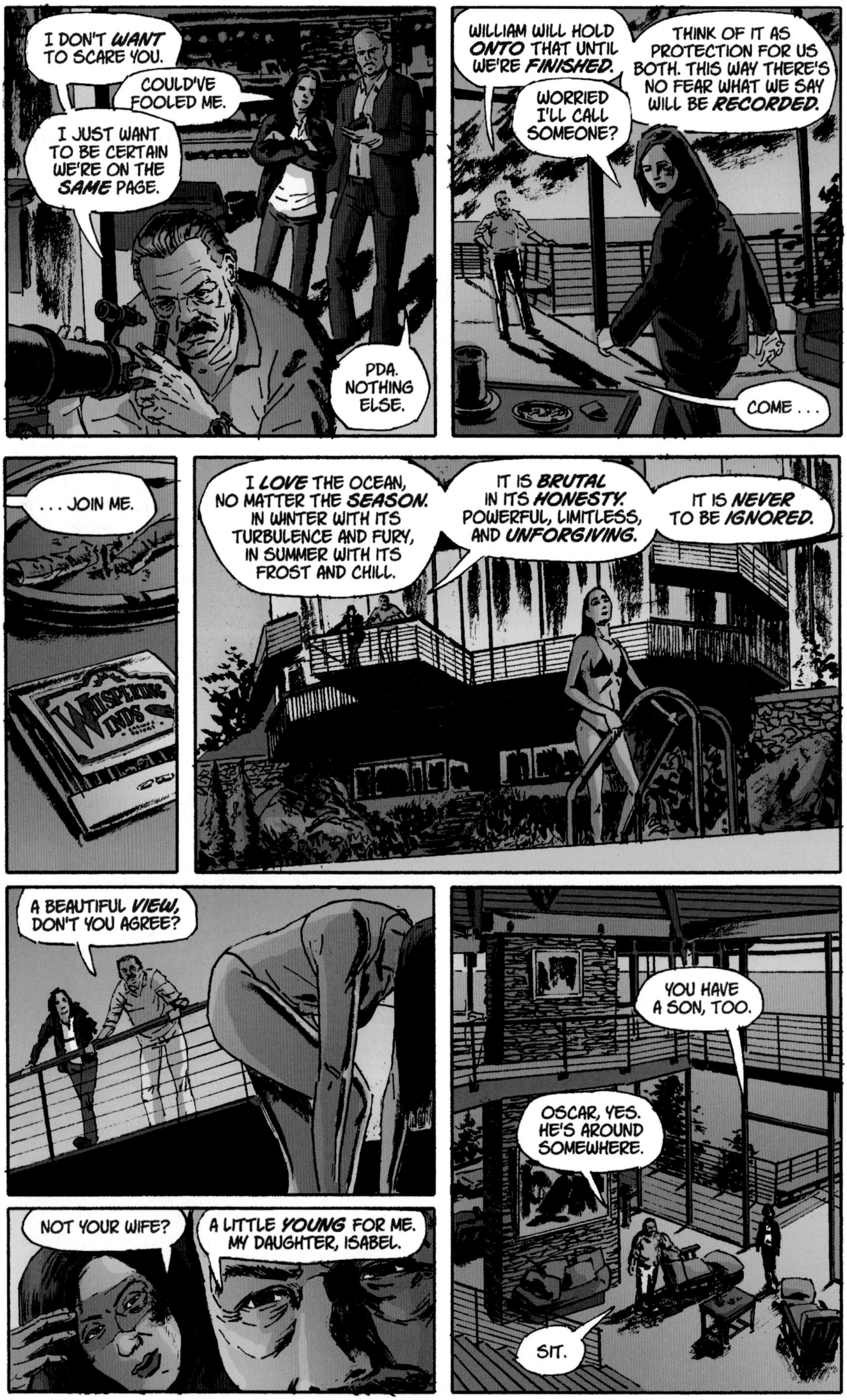
I DON'T WANT TO SCARE YOU.
COULD'VE FOOLED ME.
I JUST WANT TO BE CERTAIN WE'RE ON THE SAME PAGE.
PDA. NOTHING ELSE.
WILLIAM WILL HOLD ONTO THAT UNTIL WE'RE FINISHED.
WORRIED I'LL CALL SOMEONE?
THINK OF IT AS PROTECTION FOR US BOTH. THIS WAY THERE'S NO FEAR WHAT WE SAY WILL BE RECORDED.
COME . . .
. . . JOIN ME.
WHISPERING WINDS
I LOVE THE OCEAN, NO MATTER THE SEASON. IN WINTER WITH ITS TURBULENCE AND FURY, IN SUMMER WITH ITS FROST AND CHILL.
IT IS BRUTAL IN ITS HONESTY. POWERFUL, LIMITLESS, AND UNFORGIVING.
IT IS NEVER TO BE IGNORED.
A BEAUTIFUL VIEW, DON'T YOU AGREE?
NOT YOUR WIFE?
A LITTLE YOUNG FOR ME. MY DAUGHTER, ISABEL.
YOU HAVE A SON, TOO.
OSCAR, YES. HE'S AROUND SOMEWHERE.
SIT.

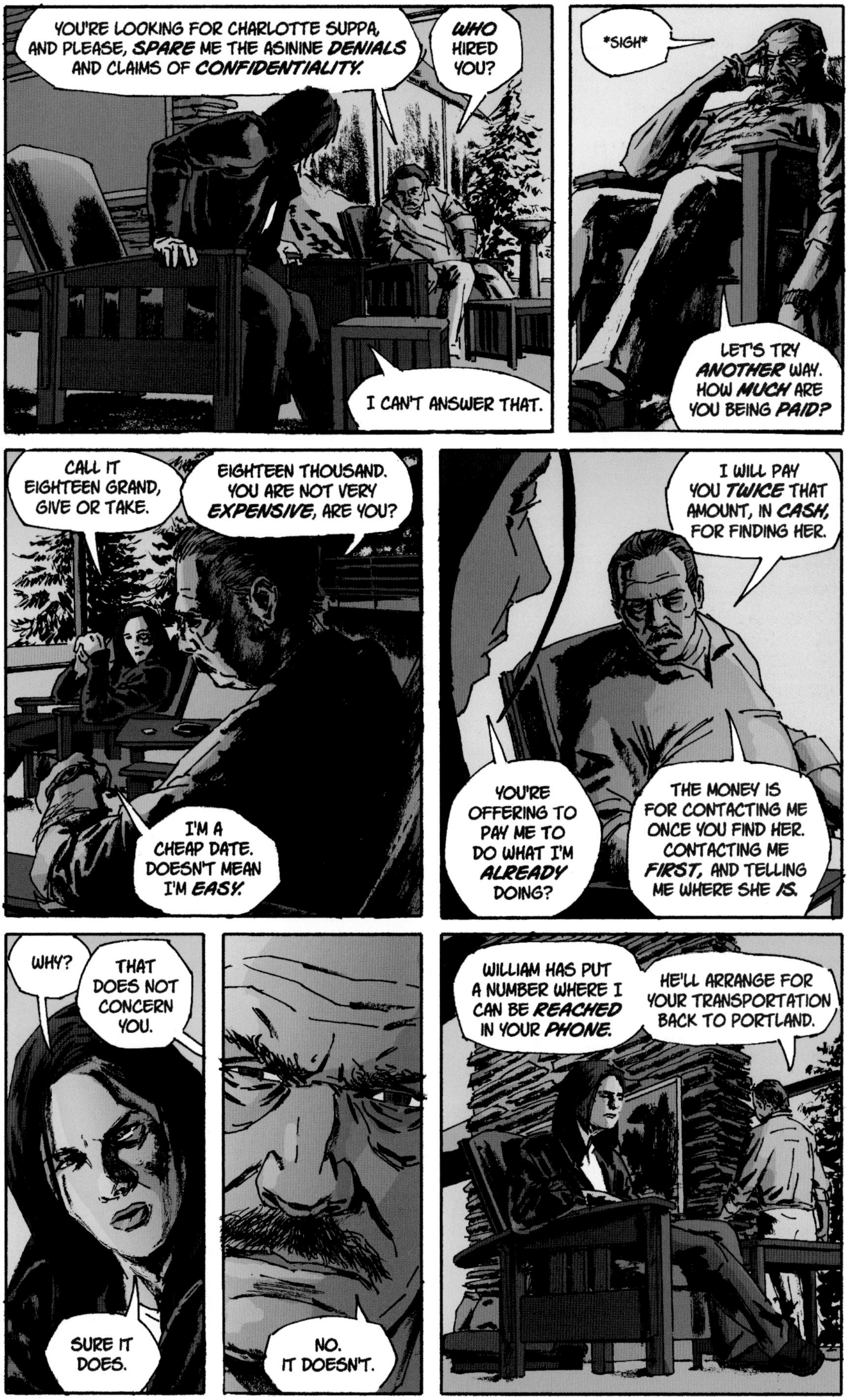
YOU'RE LOOKING FOR CHARLOTTE SUPPA, AND PLEASE, SPARE ME THE ASININE DENIALS AND CLAIMS OF CONFIDENTIALITY.
WHO HIRED YOU?
I CAN'T ANSWER THAT.
SIGH
LET'S TRY ANOTHER WAY. HOW MUCH ARE YOU BEING PAID?
CALL IT EIGHTEEN GRAND, GIVE OR TAKE.
EIGHTEEN THOUSAND. YOU ARE NOT VERY EXPENSIVE, ARE YOU?
I'M A CHEAP DATE. DOESN'T MEAN I'M EASY.
I WILL PAY YOU TWICE THAT AMOUNT, IN CASH, FOR FINDING HER.
YOU'RE OFFERING TO PAY ME TO DO WHAT I'M ALREADY DOING?
THE MONEY IS FOR CONTACTING ME ONCE YOU FIND HER. CONTACTING ME FIRST, AND TELLING ME WHERE SHE IS.
WHY?
THAT DOES NOT CONCERN YOU.
SURE IT DOES.
NO. IT DOESN'T.
WILLIAM HAS PUT A NUMBER WHERE I CAN BE REACHED IN YOUR PHONE.
HE'LL ARRANGE FOR YOUR TRANSPORTATION BACK TO PORTLAND.

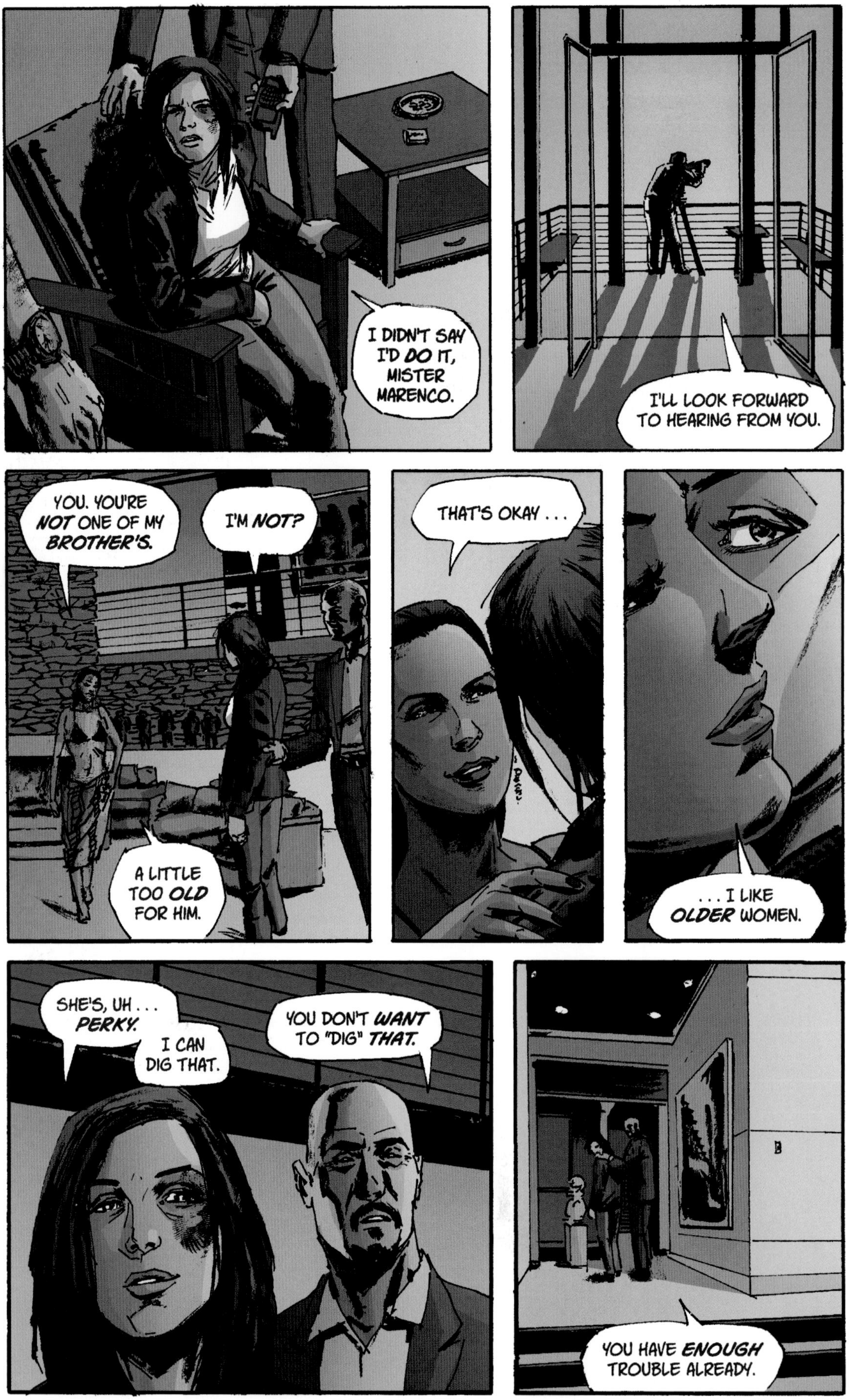
I DIDN'T SAY I'D DO IT, MISTER MARENCO.
I'LL LOOK FORWARD TO HEARING FROM YOU.
YOU. YOU'RE NOT ONE OF MY BROTHER'S.
I'M NOT?
A LITTLE TOO OLD FOR HIM.
THAT'S OKAY . . .
. . . I LIKE OLDER WOMEN.
SHE'S, UH . . . PERKY.
I CAN DIG THAT.
YOU DON'T WANT TO "DIG" THAT.
YOU HAVE ENOUGH TROUBLE ALREADY.

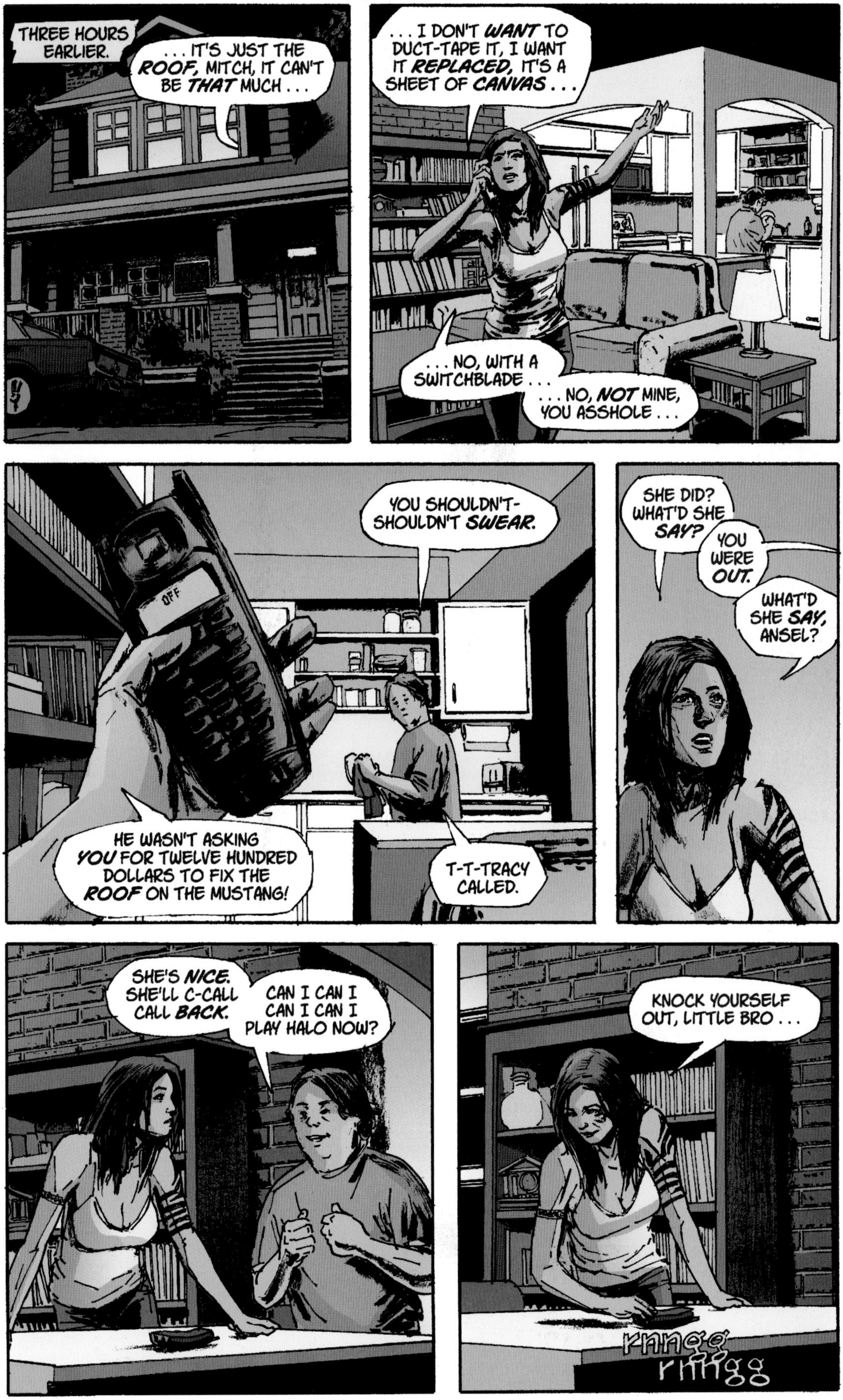
THREE HOURS EARLIER.
. . . IT'S JUST THE ROOF, MITCH, IT CAN'T BE THAT MUCH . . .
. . . I DON'T WANT TO DUCT-TAPE IT, I WANT IT REPLACED, IT'S A SHEET OF CANVAS . . .
. . . NO, WITH A SWITCHBLADE . . .
. . . NO, NOT MINE, YOU ASSHOLE . . .
OFF
YOU SHOULDN'T-SHOULDN'T SWEAR.
HE WASN'T ASKING YOU FOR TWELVE HUNDRED DOLLARS TO FIX THE ROOF ON THE MUSTANG!
T-T-TRACY CALLED.
SHE DID? WHAT'D SHE SAY?
YOU WERE OUT.
WHAT'D SHE SAY, ANSEL?
SHE'S NICE. SHE'LL C-CALL CALL BACK.
CAN I CAN I CAN I CAN I PLAY HALO NOW?
KNOCK YOURSELF OUT, LITTLE BRO . . .
rrinngg rrinngg

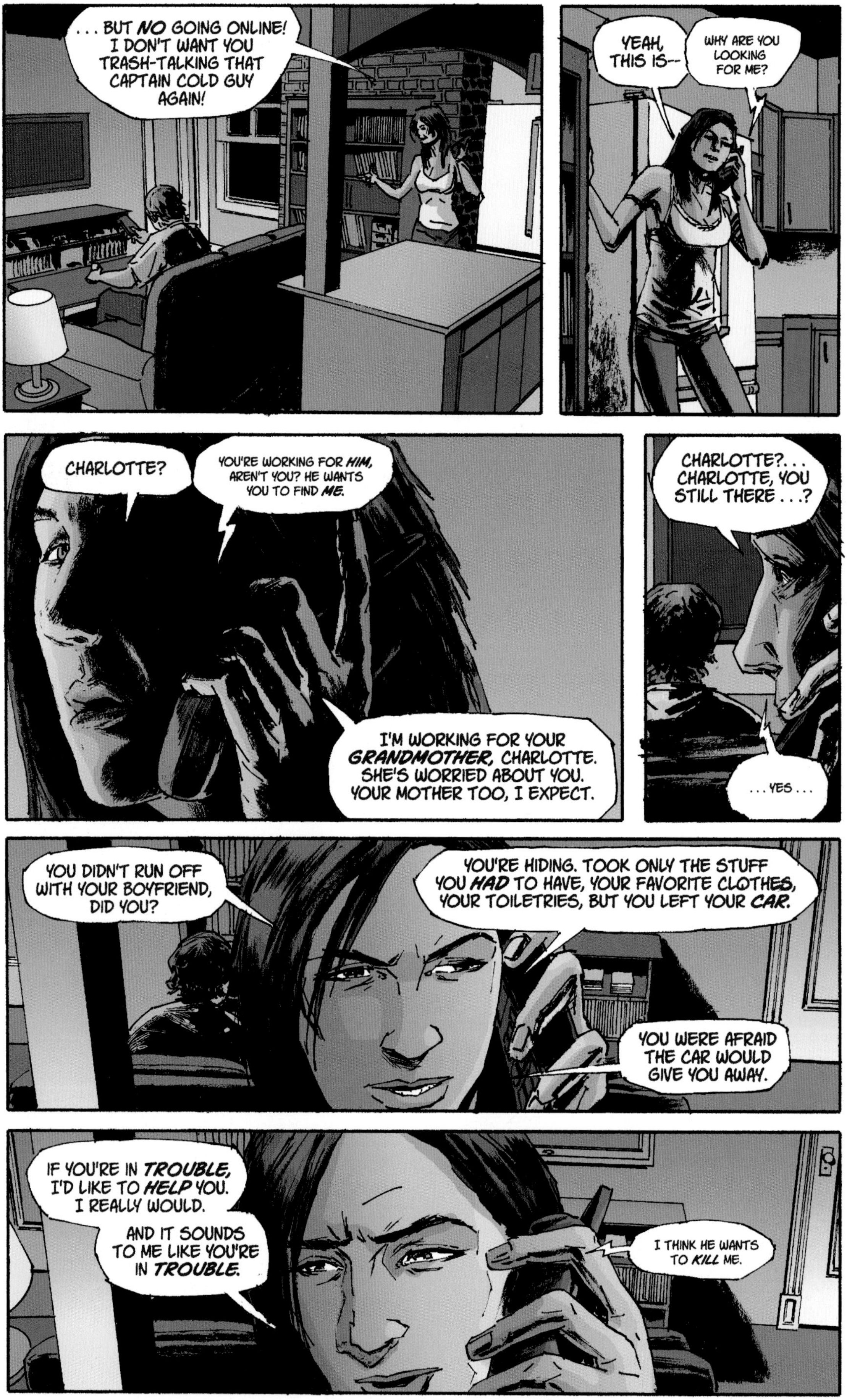

. . . BUT NO GOING ONLINE! I DON'T WANT YOU TRASH-TALKING THAT CAPTAIN COLD GUY AGAIN!
YEAH, THIS IS--
WHY ARE YOU LOOKING FOR ME?
CHARLOTTE?
YOU'RE WORKING FOR HIM, AREN'T YOU? HE WANTS YOU TO FIND ME.
I'M WORKING FOR YOUR GRANDMOTHER, CHARLOTTE. SHE'S WORRIED ABOUT YOU. YOUR MOTHER TOO, I EXPECT.
CHARLOTTE?. . . CHARLOTTE, YOU STILL THERE . . .?
. . . YES . . .
YOU DIDN'T RUN OFF WITH YOUR BOYFRIEND, DID YOU?
YOU'RE HIDING. TOOK ONLY THE STUFF YOU HAD TO HAVE, YOUR FAVORITE CLOTHES, YOUR TOILETRIES, BUT YOU LEFT YOUR CAR.
YOU WERE AFRAID THE CAR WOULD GIVE YOU AWAY.
IF YOU'RE IN TROUBLE, I'D LIKE TO HELP YOU. I REALLY WOULD.
AND IT SOUNDS TO ME LIKE YOU'RE IN TROUBLE.
I THINK HE WANTS TO KILL ME.

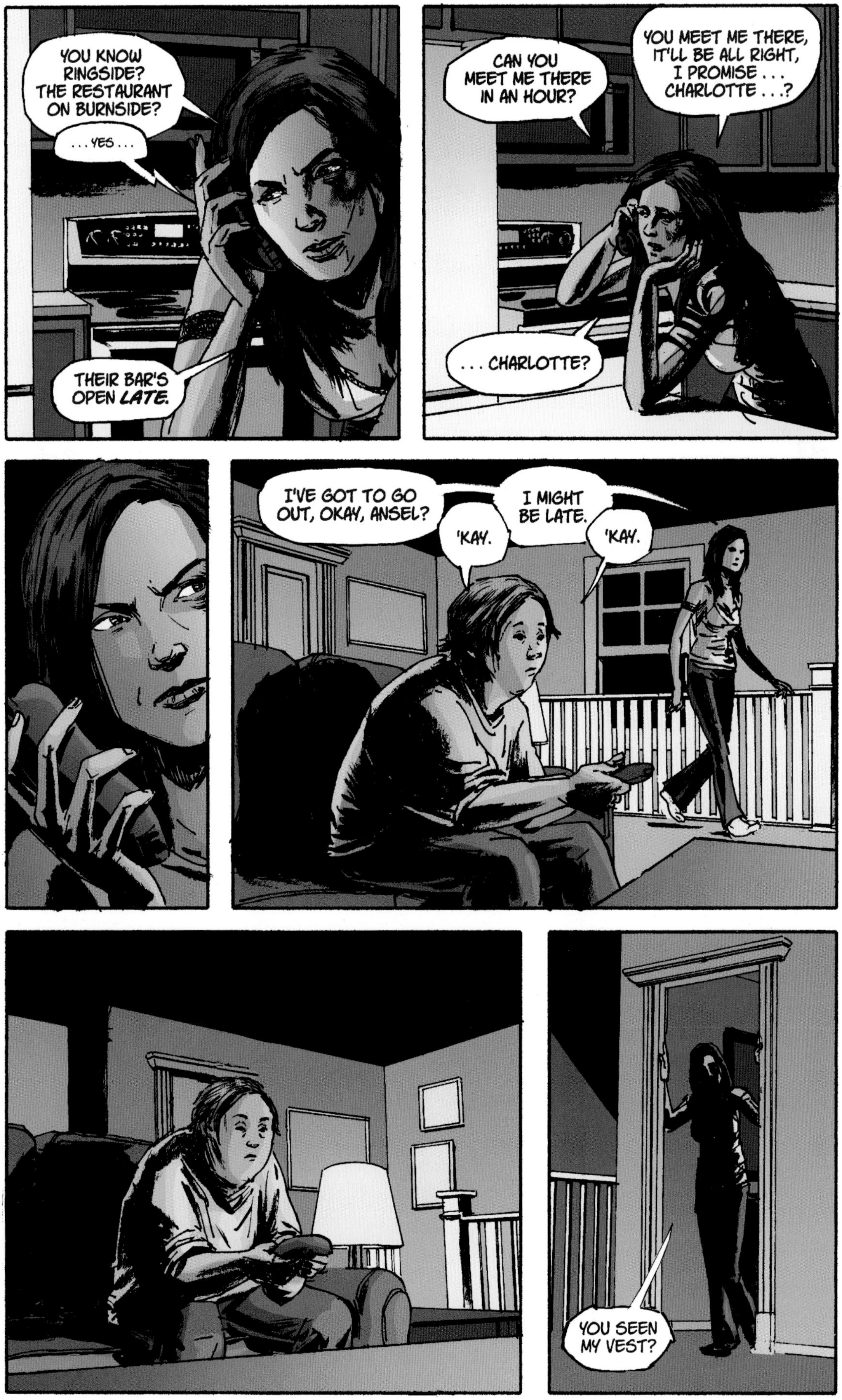
YOU KNOW RINGSIDE? THE RESTAURANT ON BURNSIDE?
. . . YES . . .
THEIR BAR'S OPEN *LATE*.
CAN YOU MEET ME THERE IN AN HOUR?
YOU MEET ME THERE, IT'LL BE ALL RIGHT, I PROMISE . . . CHARLOTTE . . .?
. . . CHARLOTTE?
I'VE GOT TO GO OUT, OKAY, ANSEL?
'KAY.
I MIGHT BE LATE.
'KAY.
YOU SEEN MY VEST?

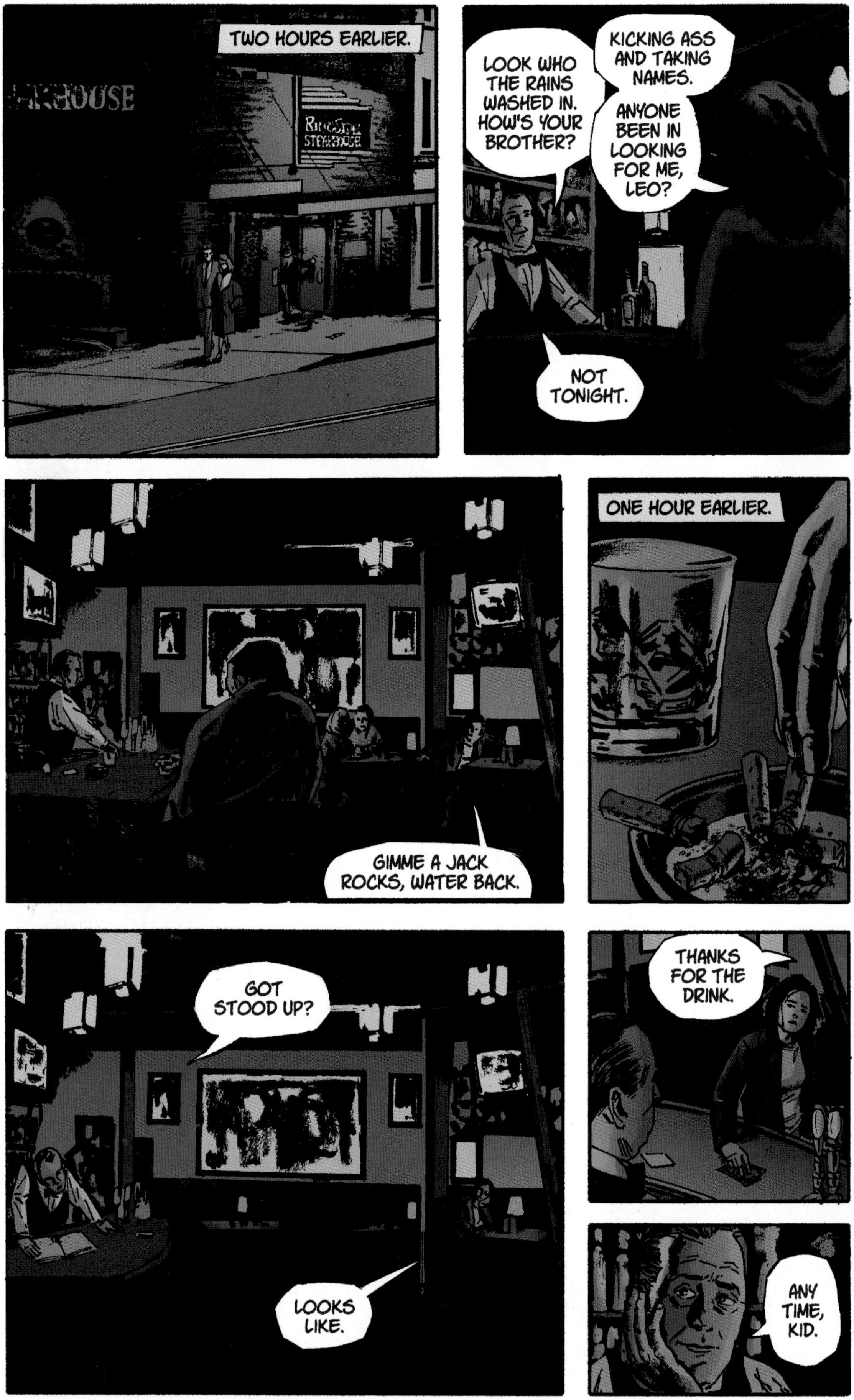
TWO HOURS EARLIER.
RINGSIDE STEAKHOUSE
LOOK WHO THE RAINS WASHED IN. HOW'S YOUR BROTHER?
KICKING ASS AND TAKING NAMES.
ANYONE BEEN IN LOOKING FOR ME, LEO?
NOT TONIGHT.
GIMME A JACK ROCKS, WATER BACK.
ONE HOUR EARLIER.
GOT STOOD UP?
LOOKS LIKE.
THANKS FOR THE DRINK.
ANY TIME, KID.

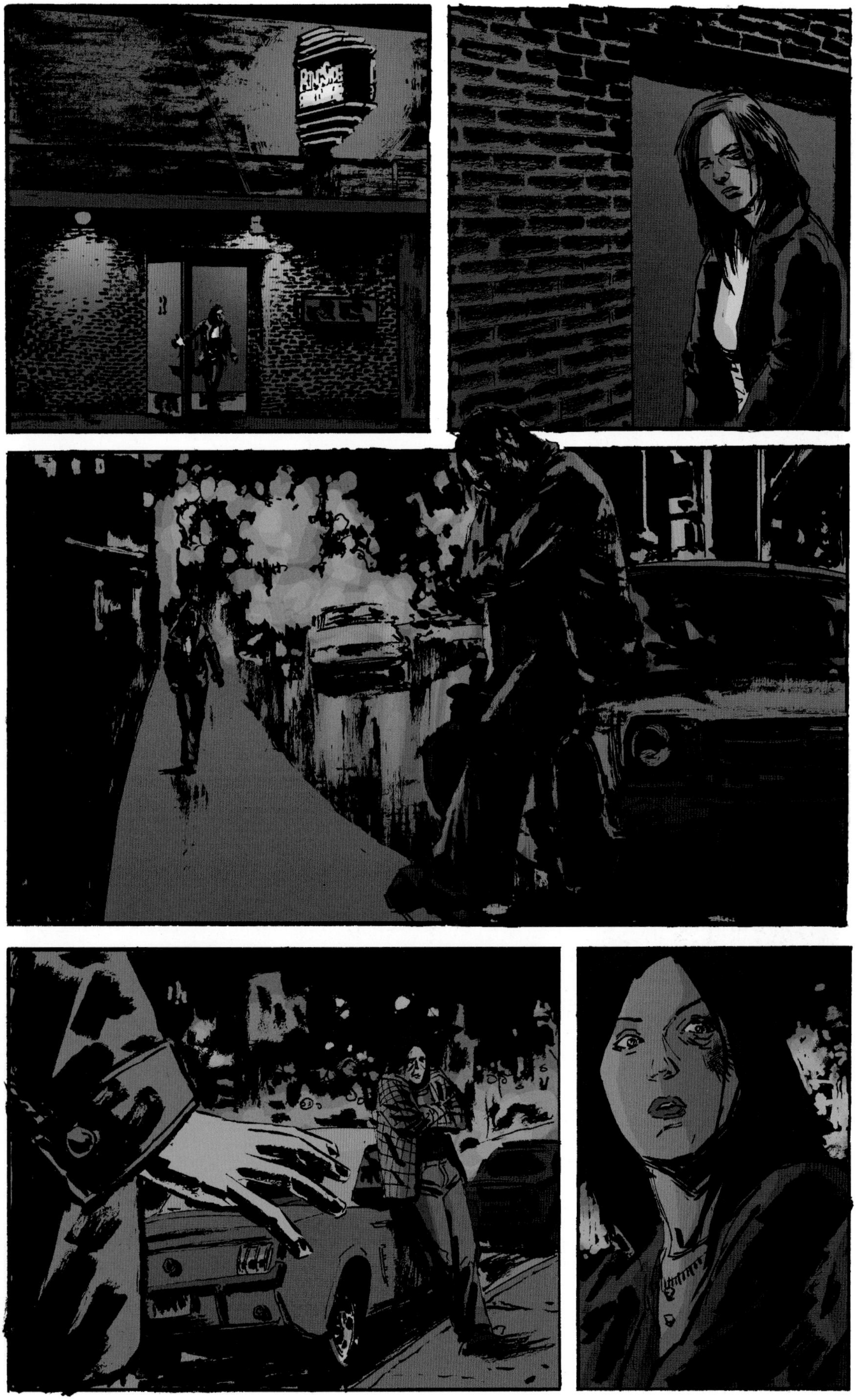

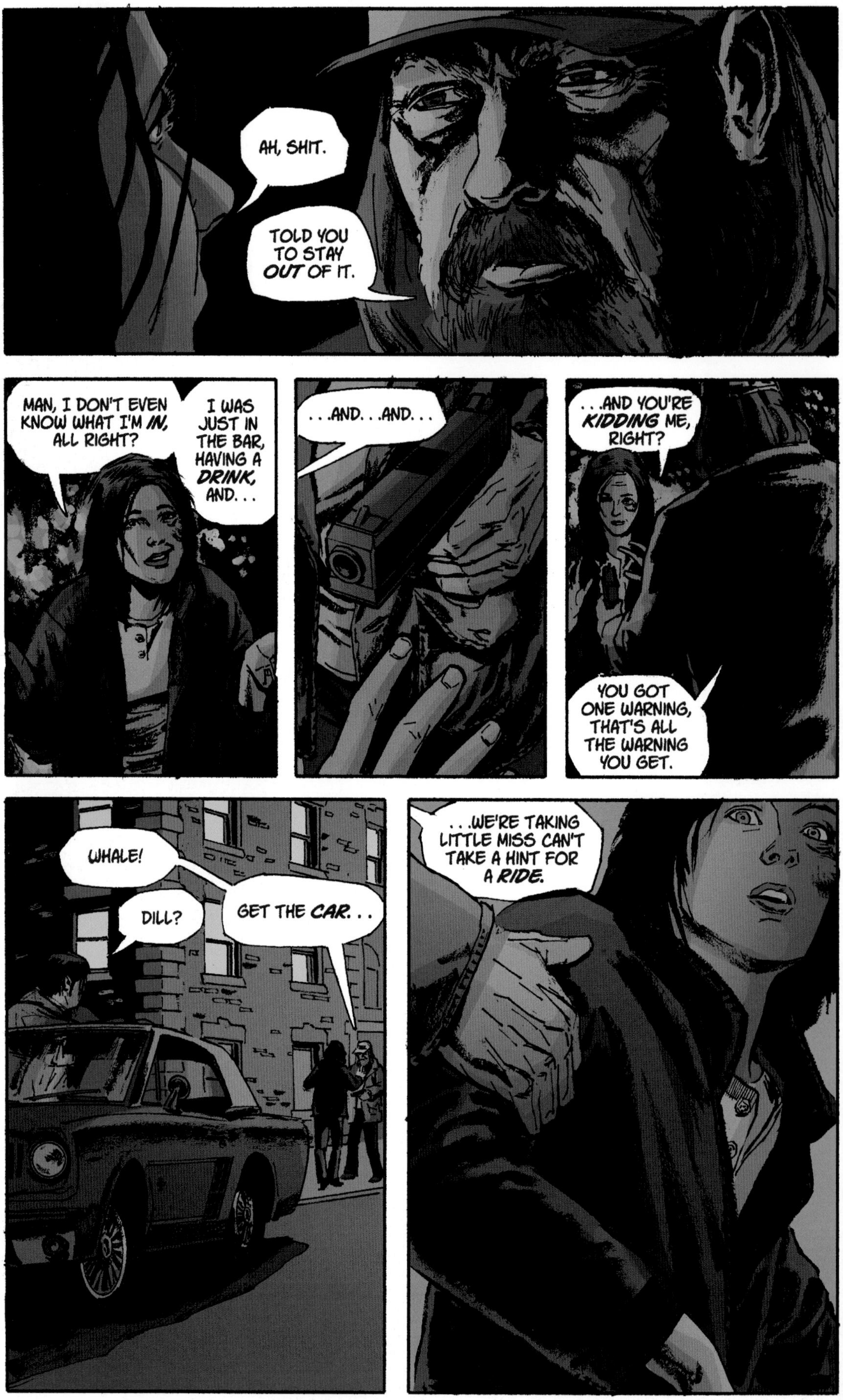
AH, SHIT.
TOLD YOU TO STAY *OUT* OF IT.
MAN, I DON'T EVEN KNOW WHAT I'M *IN*, ALL RIGHT?
I WAS JUST IN THE BAR, HAVING A *DRINK*, AND...
...AND...AND...
...AND YOU'RE *KIDDING* ME, RIGHT?
YOU GOT ONE WARNING, THAT'S ALL THE WARNING YOU GET.
WHALE!
DILL?
GET THE *CAR*...
...WE'RE TAKING LITTLE MISS CAN'T TAKE A HINT FOR A *RIDE*.

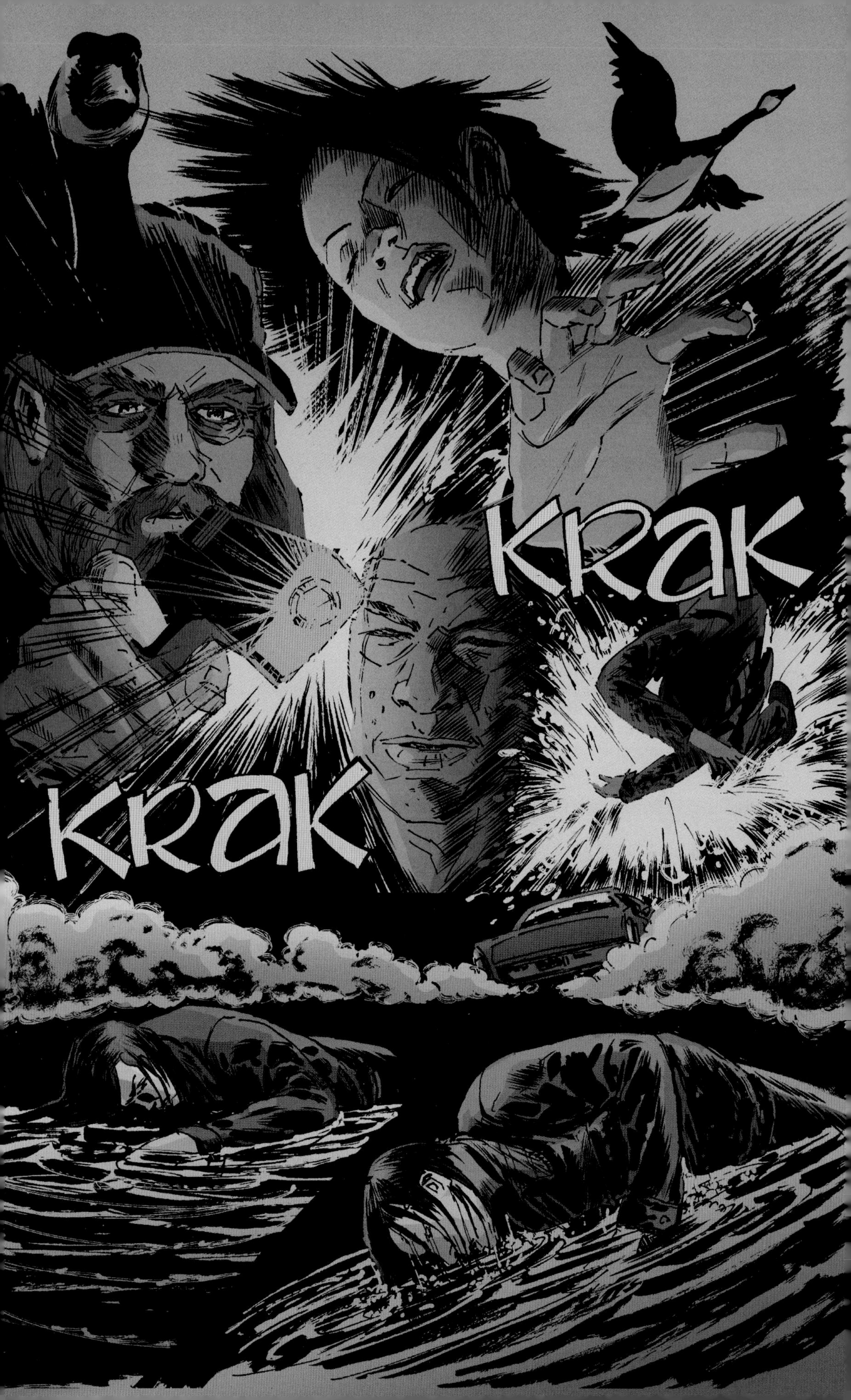
KRAK
KRAK

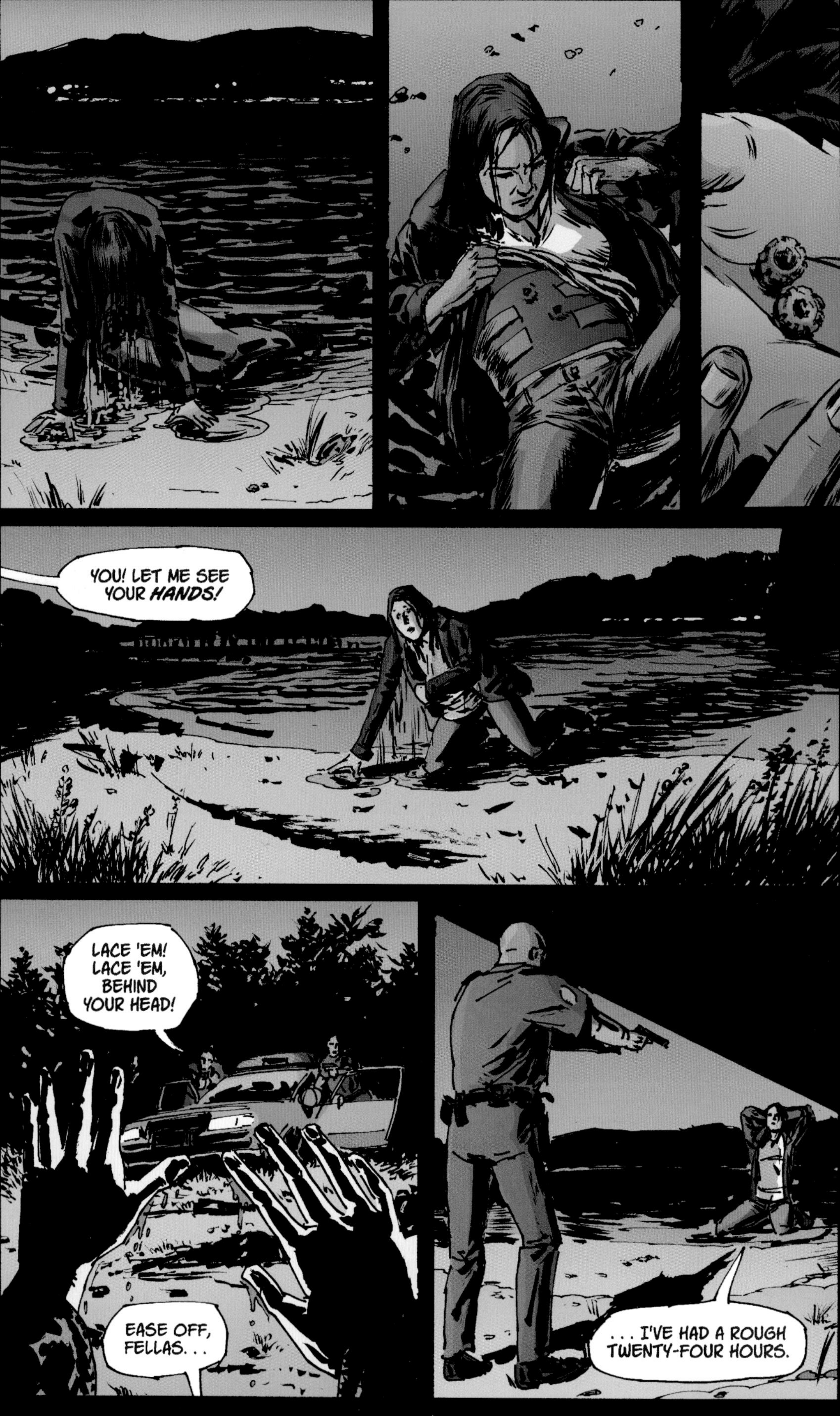
YOU! LET ME SEE YOUR HANDS!
LACE 'EM! LACE 'EM, BEHIND YOUR HEAD!
EASE OFF, FELLAS. . .
. . . I'VE HAD A ROUGH TWENTY-FOUR HOURS.

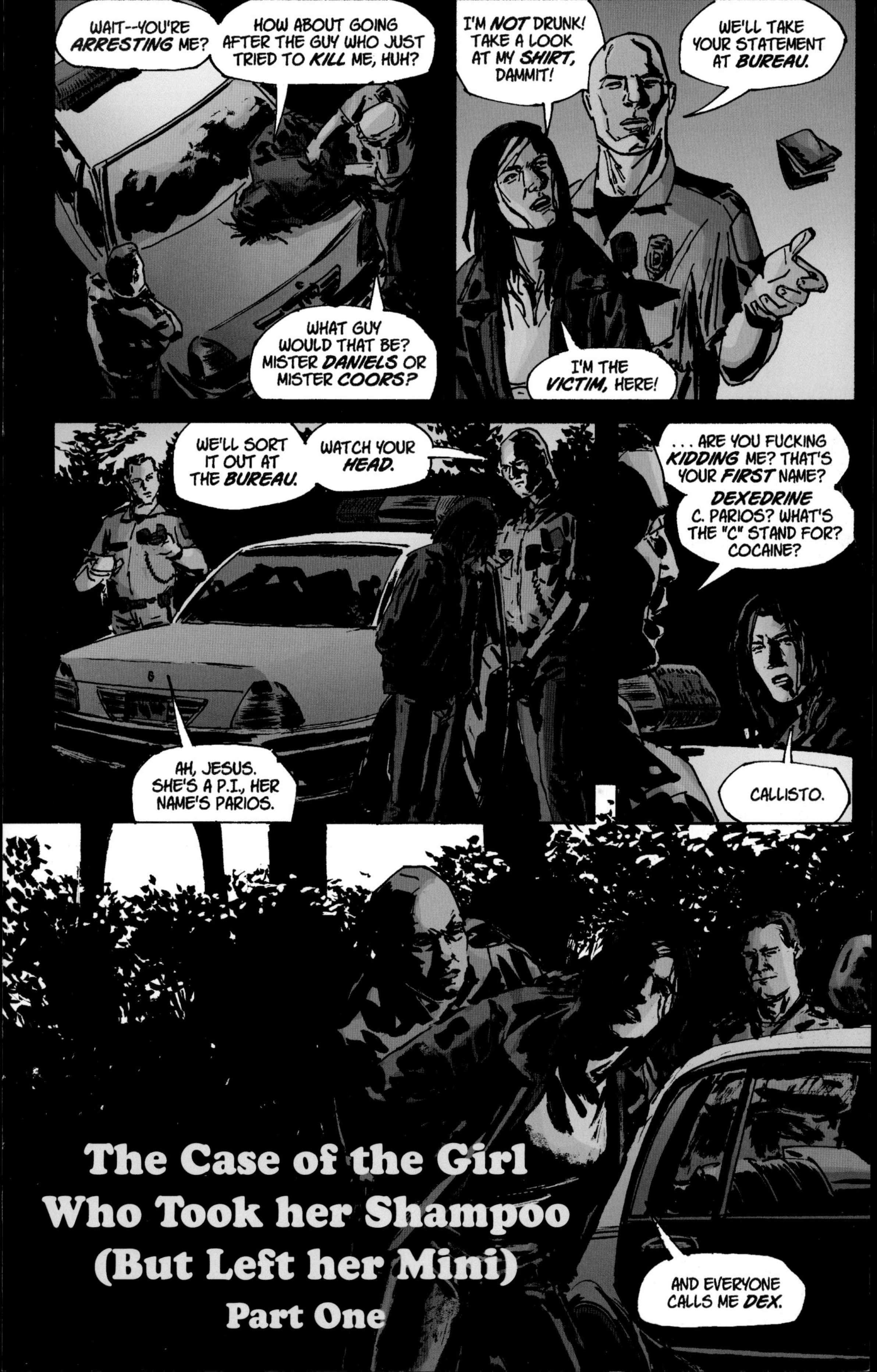
WAIT--YOU'RE ARRESTING ME?
HOW ABOUT GOING AFTER THE GUY WHO JUST TRIED TO KILL ME, HUH?
WHAT GUY WOULD THAT BE? MISTER DANIELS OR MISTER COORS?
I'M NOT DRUNK! TAKE A LOOK AT MY SHIRT, DAMMIT!
WE'LL TAKE YOUR STATEMENT AT BUREAU.
I'M THE VICTIM, HERE!
WE'LL SORT IT OUT AT THE BUREAU.
WATCH YOUR HEAD.
AH, JESUS. SHE'S A P.I., HER NAME'S PARIOS.
. . . ARE YOU FUCKING KIDDING ME? THAT'S YOUR FIRST NAME?
DEXEDRINE C. PARIOS? WHAT'S THE "C" STAND FOR? COCAINE?
CALLISTO.
The Case of the Girl Who Took her Shampoo (But Left her Mini)
Part One
AND EVERYONE CALLS ME DEX.

Chapter Two

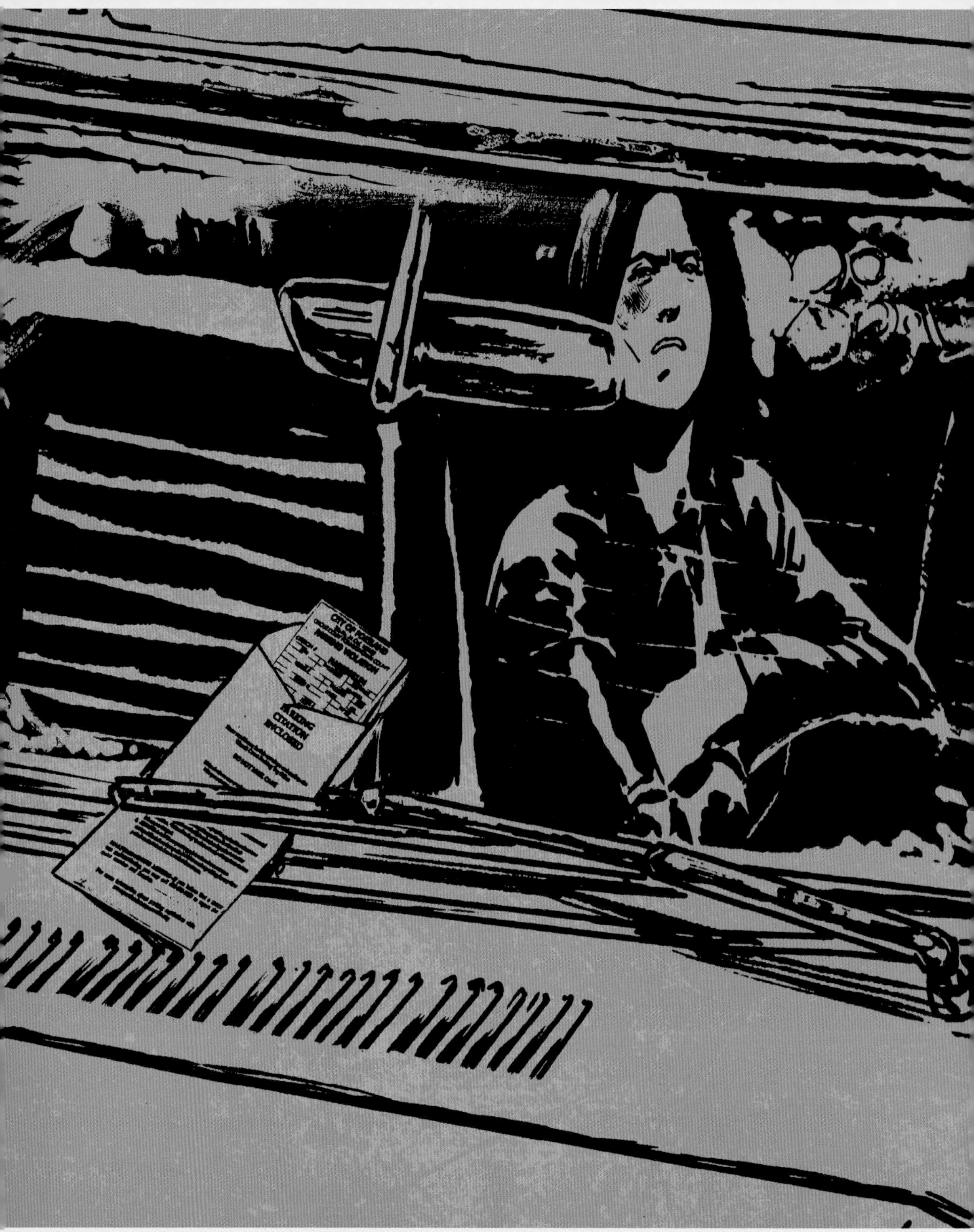
CITY OF PORTLAND
PARKING VIOLATION
CITATION
ENCLOSED

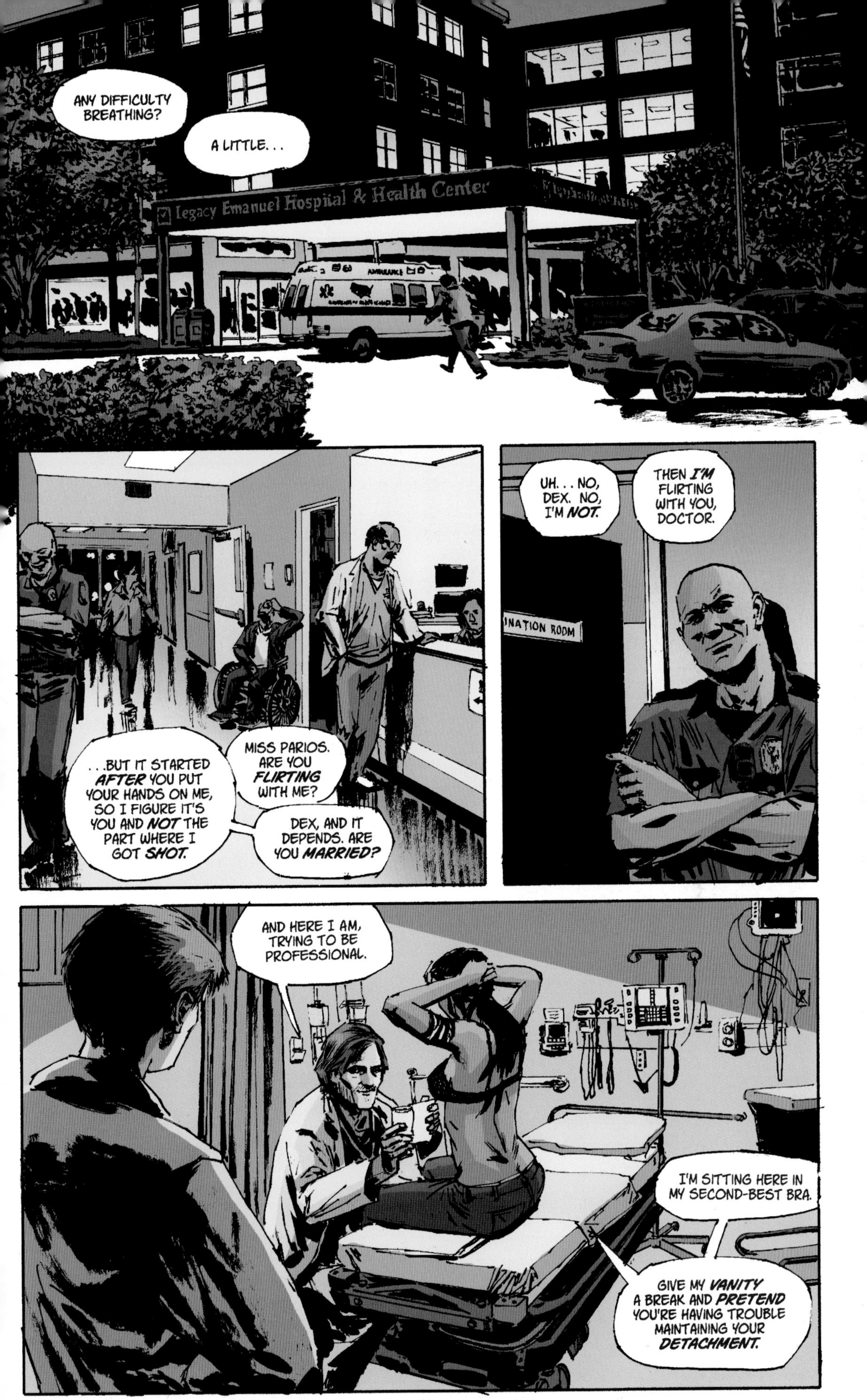
ANY DIFFICULTY BREATHING?
A LITTLE. . .
Legacy Emanuel Hospital & Health Center
. . .BUT IT STARTED *AFTER* YOU PUT YOUR HANDS ON ME, SO I FIGURE IT'S YOU AND *NOT* THE PART WHERE I GOT *SHOT.*
MISS PARIOS. ARE YOU *FLIRTING* WITH ME?
DEX, AND IT DEPENDS. ARE YOU *MARRIED?*
UH. . . NO, DEX. NO, I'M *NOT.*
THEN *I'M* FLIRTING WITH YOU, DOCTOR.
INATION ROOM
AND HERE I AM, TRYING TO BE PROFESSIONAL.
I'M SITTING HERE IN MY SECOND-BEST BRA.
GIVE MY *VANITY* A BREAK AND *PRETEND* YOU'RE HAVING TROUBLE MAINTAINING YOUR *DETACHMENT.*

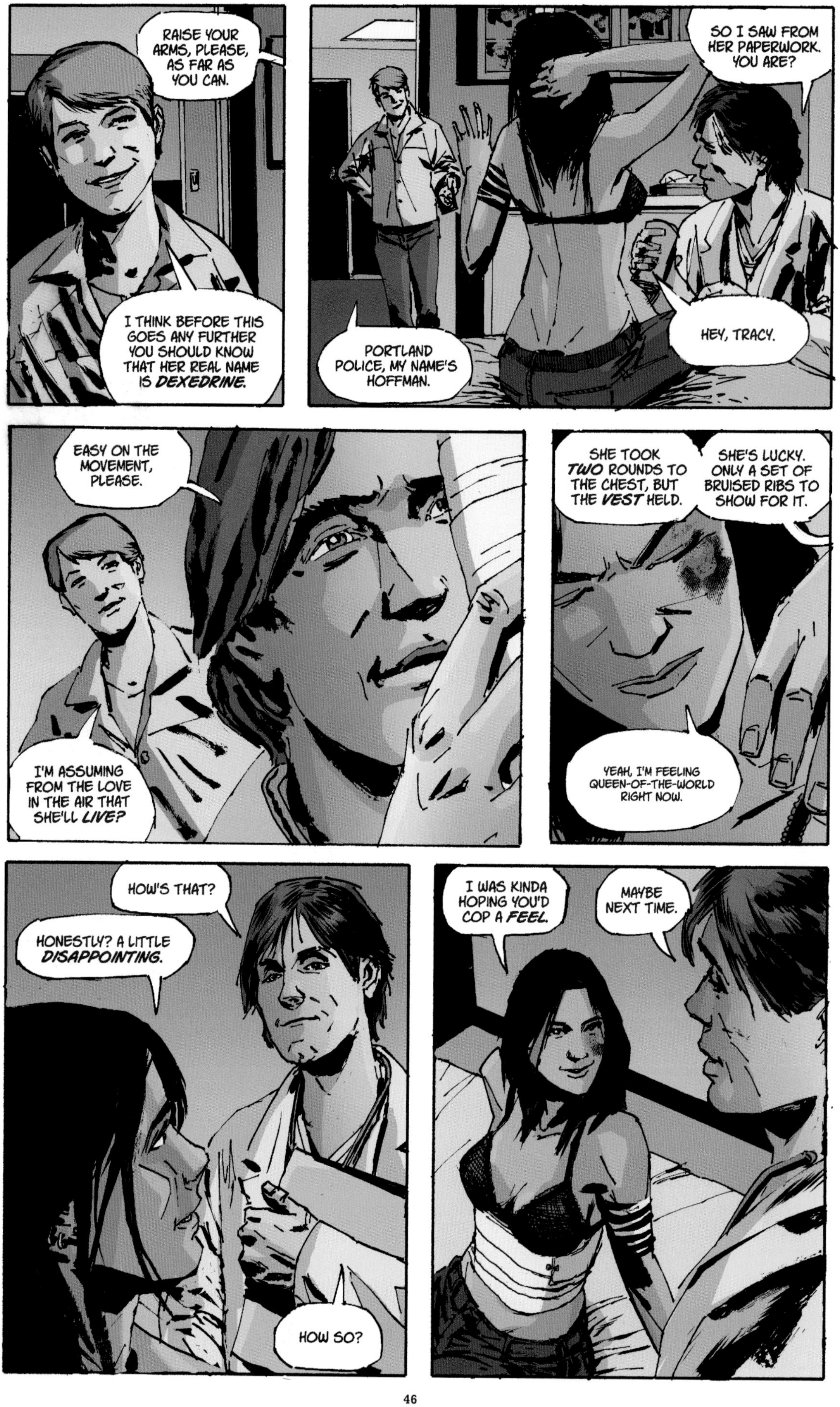
RAISE YOUR ARMS, PLEASE, AS FAR AS YOU CAN.
I THINK BEFORE THIS GOES ANY FURTHER YOU SHOULD KNOW THAT HER REAL NAME IS *DEXEDRINE.*
SO I SAW FROM HER PAPERWORK. YOU ARE?
PORTLAND POLICE, MY NAME'S HOFFMAN.
HEY, TRACY.
EASY ON THE MOVEMENT, PLEASE.
I'M ASSUMING FROM THE LOVE IN THE AIR THAT SHE'LL *LIVE?*
SHE TOOK *TWO* ROUNDS TO THE CHEST, BUT THE *VEST* HELD.
SHE'S LUCKY. ONLY A SET OF BRUISED RIBS TO SHOW FOR IT.
YEAH, I'M FEELING QUEEN-OF-THE-WORLD RIGHT NOW.
HOW'S THAT?
HONESTLY? A LITTLE *DISAPPOINTING.*
HOW SO?
I WAS KINDA HOPING YOU'D COP A *FEEL.*
MAYBE NEXT TIME.

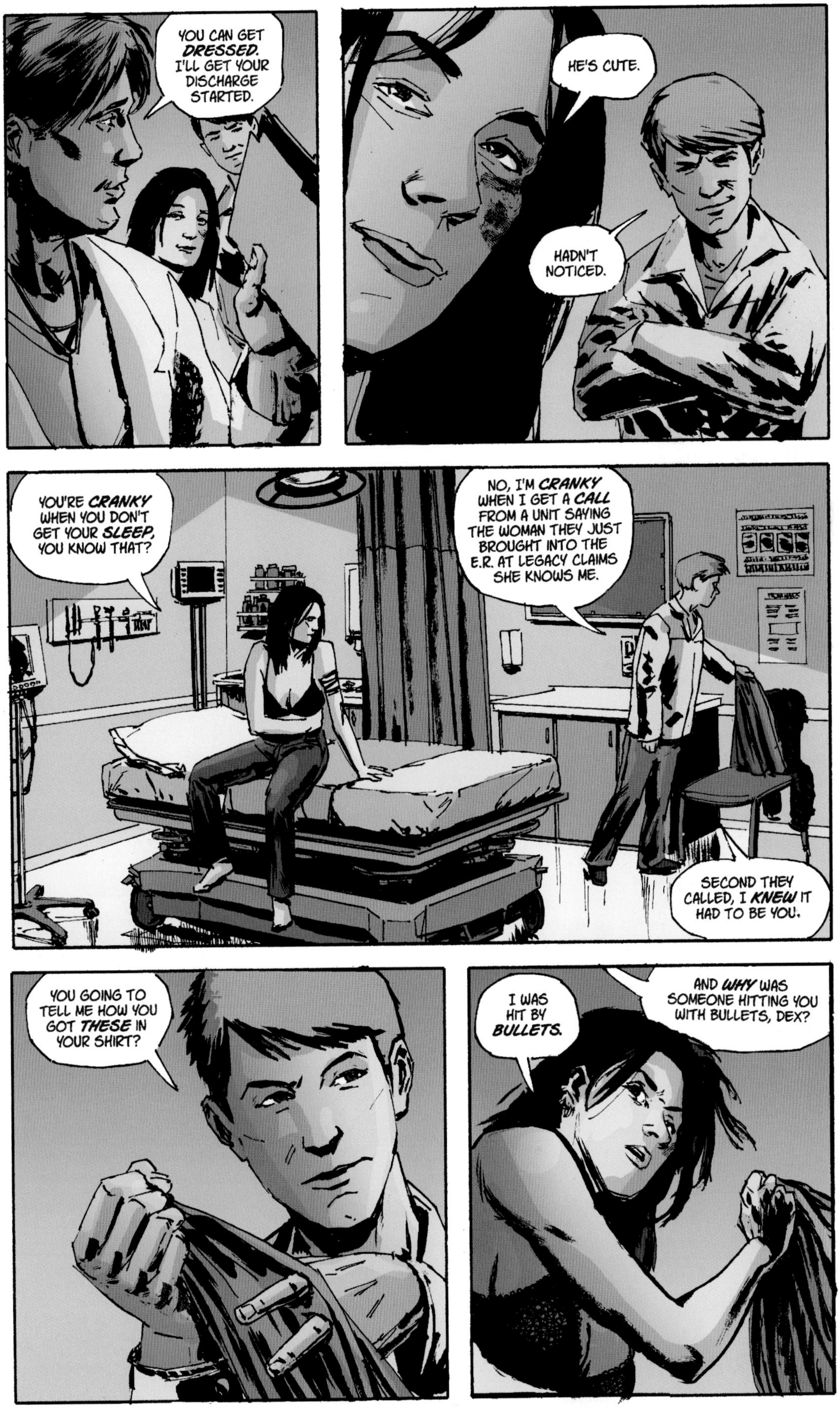
YOU CAN GET DRESSED. I'LL GET YOUR DISCHARGE STARTED.
HE'S CUTE.
HADN'T NOTICED.
YOU'RE CRANKY WHEN YOU DON'T GET YOUR SLEEP, YOU KNOW THAT?
NO, I'M CRANKY WHEN I GET A CALL FROM A UNIT SAYING THE WOMAN THEY JUST BROUGHT INTO THE E.R. AT LEGACY CLAIMS SHE KNOWS ME.
SECOND THEY CALLED, I KNEW IT HAD TO BE YOU.
YOU GOING TO TELL ME HOW YOU GOT THESE IN YOUR SHIRT?
I WAS HIT BY BULLETS.
AND WHY WAS SOMEONE HITTING YOU WITH BULLETS, DEX?

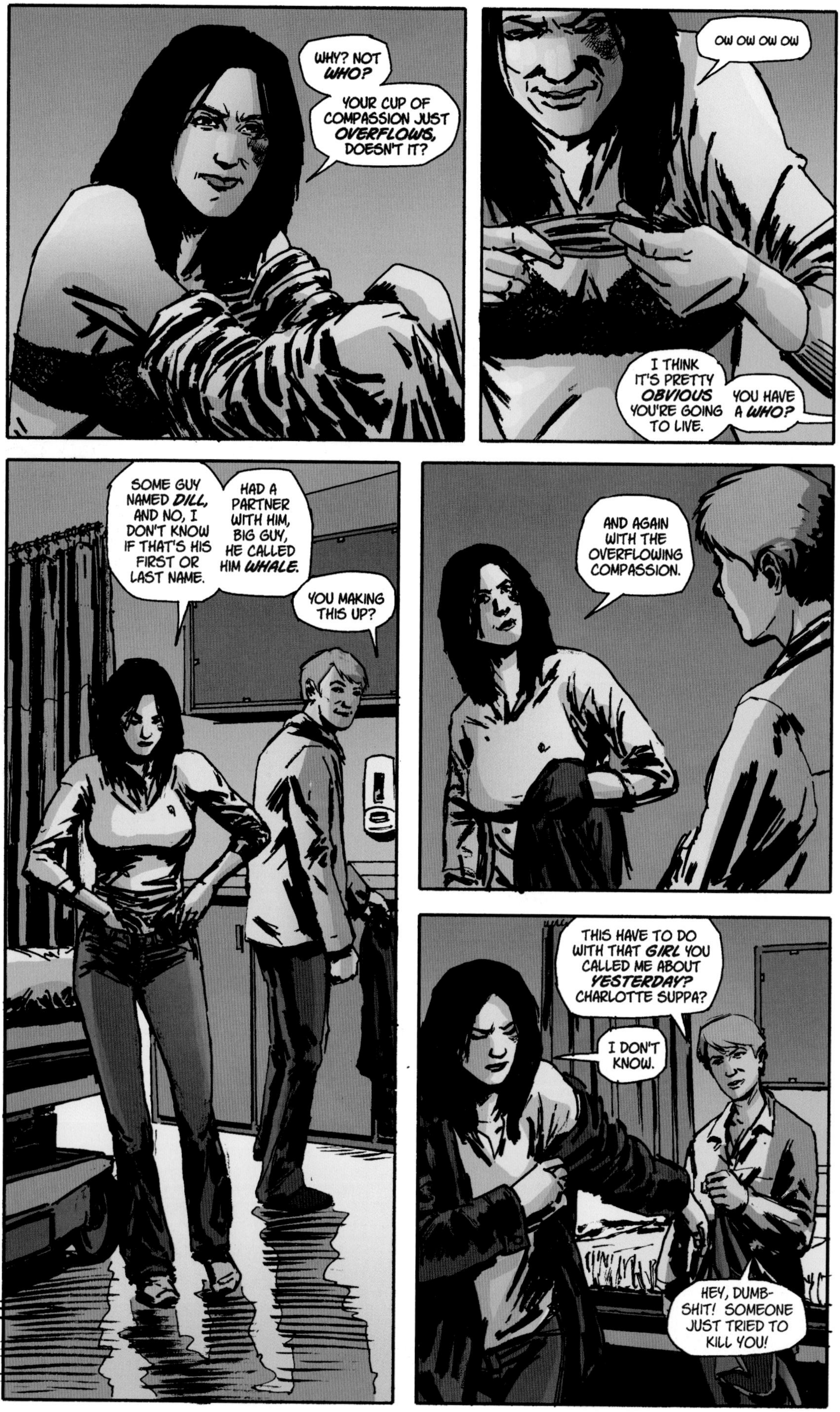
WHY? NOT WHO?
YOUR CUP OF COMPASSION JUST OVERFLOWS, DOESN'T IT?
OW OW OW OW
I THINK IT'S PRETTY OBVIOUS YOU'RE GOING TO LIVE.
YOU HAVE A WHO?
SOME GUY NAMED DILL, AND NO, I DON'T KNOW IF THAT'S HIS FIRST OR LAST NAME.
HAD A PARTNER WITH HIM, BIG GUY, HE CALLED HIM WHALE.
YOU MAKING THIS UP?
AND AGAIN WITH THE OVERFLOWING COMPASSION.
THIS HAVE TO DO WITH THAT GIRL YOU CALLED ME ABOUT YESTERDAY? CHARLOTTE SUPPA?
I DON'T KNOW.
HEY, DUMB-SHIT! SOMEONE JUST TRIED TO KILL YOU!

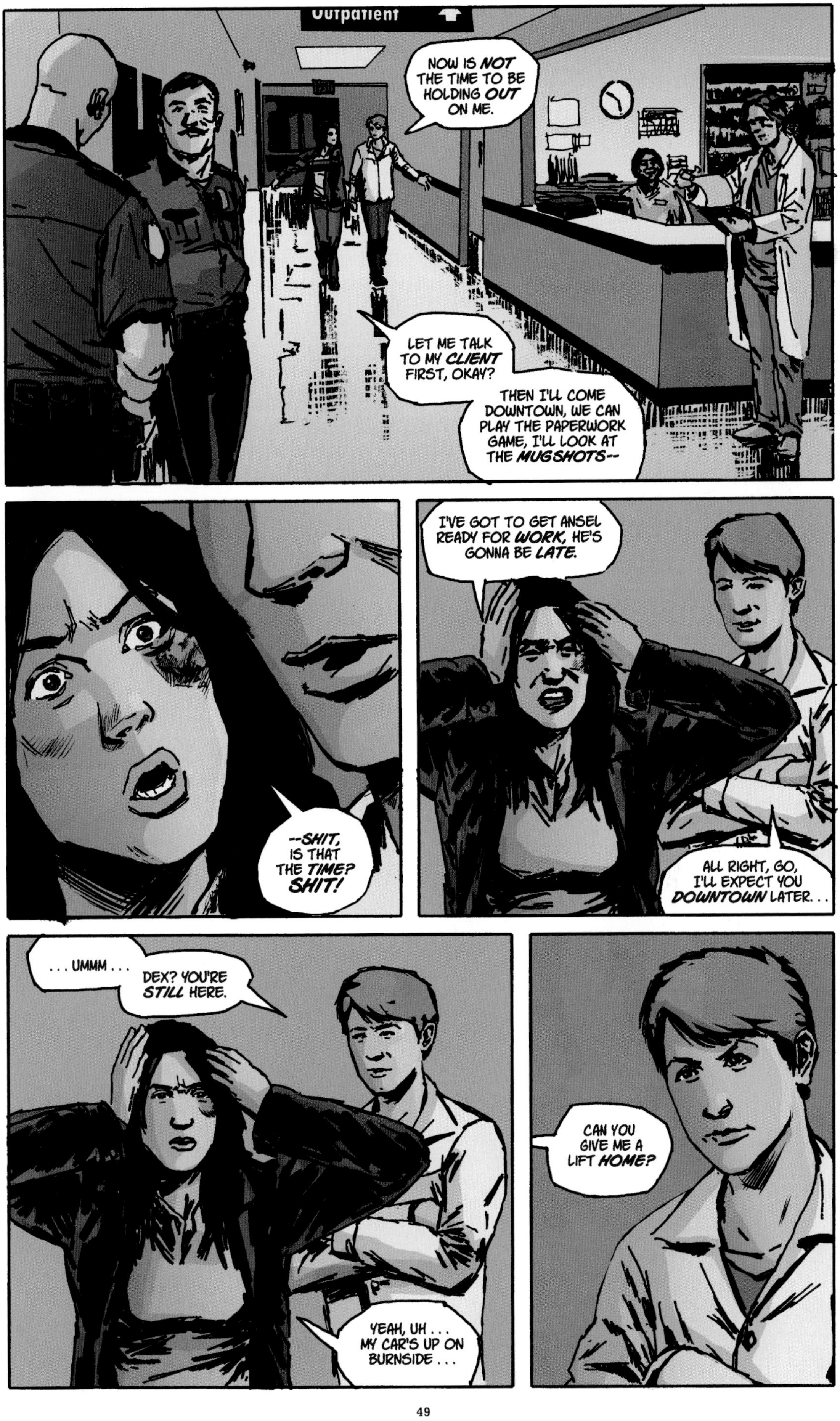
Outpatient
NOW IS NOT THE TIME TO BE HOLDING OUT ON ME.
LET ME TALK TO MY CLIENT FIRST, OKAY?
THEN I'LL COME DOWNTOWN, WE CAN PLAY THE PAPERWORK GAME, I'LL LOOK AT THE MUGSHOTS--
--SHIT, IS THAT THE TIME? SHIT!
I'VE GOT TO GET ANSEL READY FOR WORK, HE'S GONNA BE LATE.
ALL RIGHT, GO, I'LL EXPECT YOU DOWNTOWN LATER . . .
. . . UMMM . . .
DEX? YOU'RE STILL HERE.
YEAH, UH . . . MY CAR'S UP ON BURNSIDE . . .
CAN YOU GIVE ME A LIFT HOME?

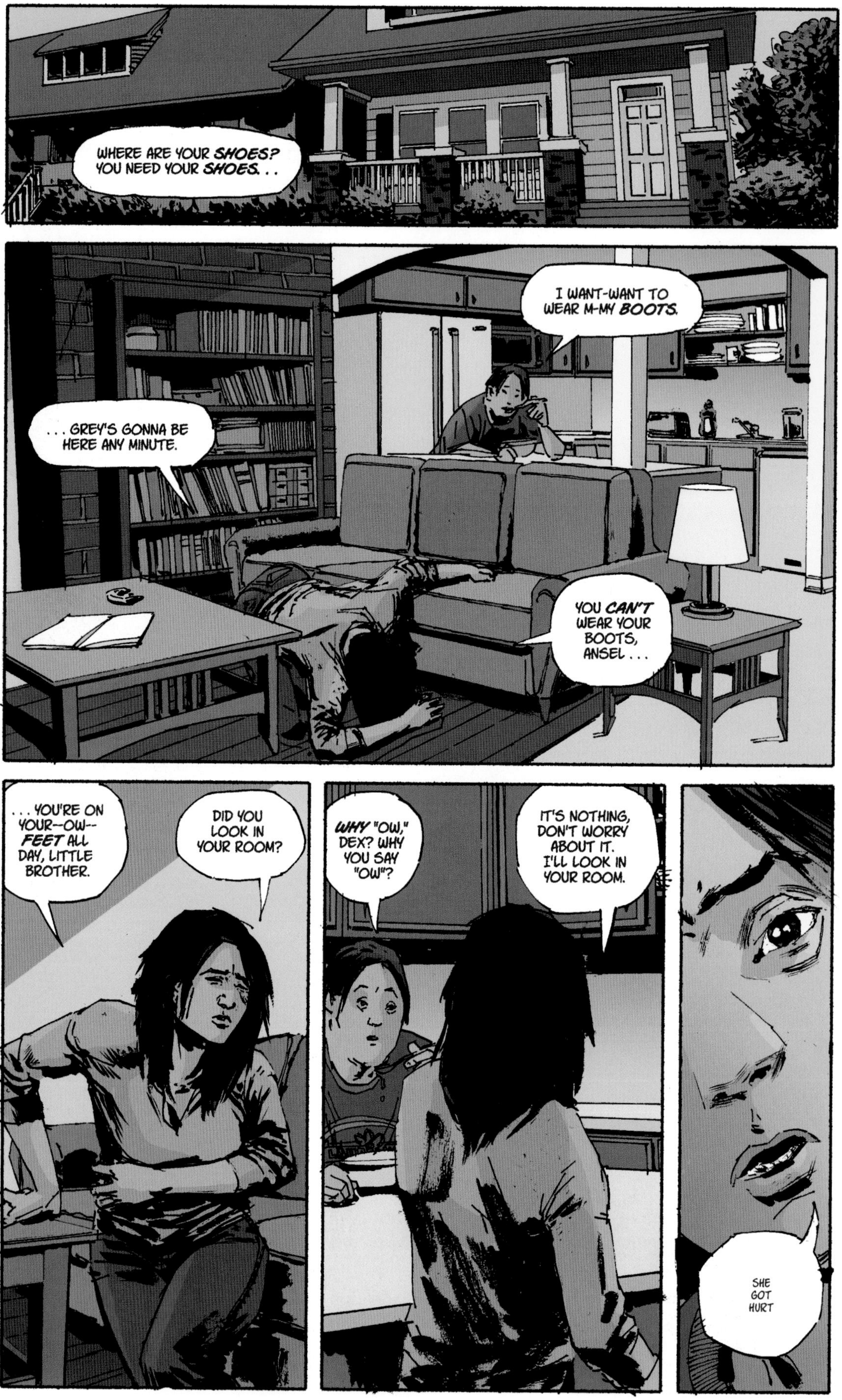

WHERE ARE YOUR SHOES? YOU NEED YOUR SHOES. . .
I WANT-WANT TO WEAR M-MY BOOTS.
. . . GREY'S GONNA BE HERE ANY MINUTE.
YOU CAN'T WEAR YOUR BOOTS, ANSEL . . .
. . . YOU'RE ON YOUR--OW-- FEET ALL DAY, LITTLE BROTHER.
DID YOU LOOK IN YOUR ROOM?
WHY "OW," DEX? WHY YOU SAY "OW"?
IT'S NOTHING, DON'T WORRY ABOUT IT. I'LL LOOK IN YOUR ROOM.
SHE GOT HURT

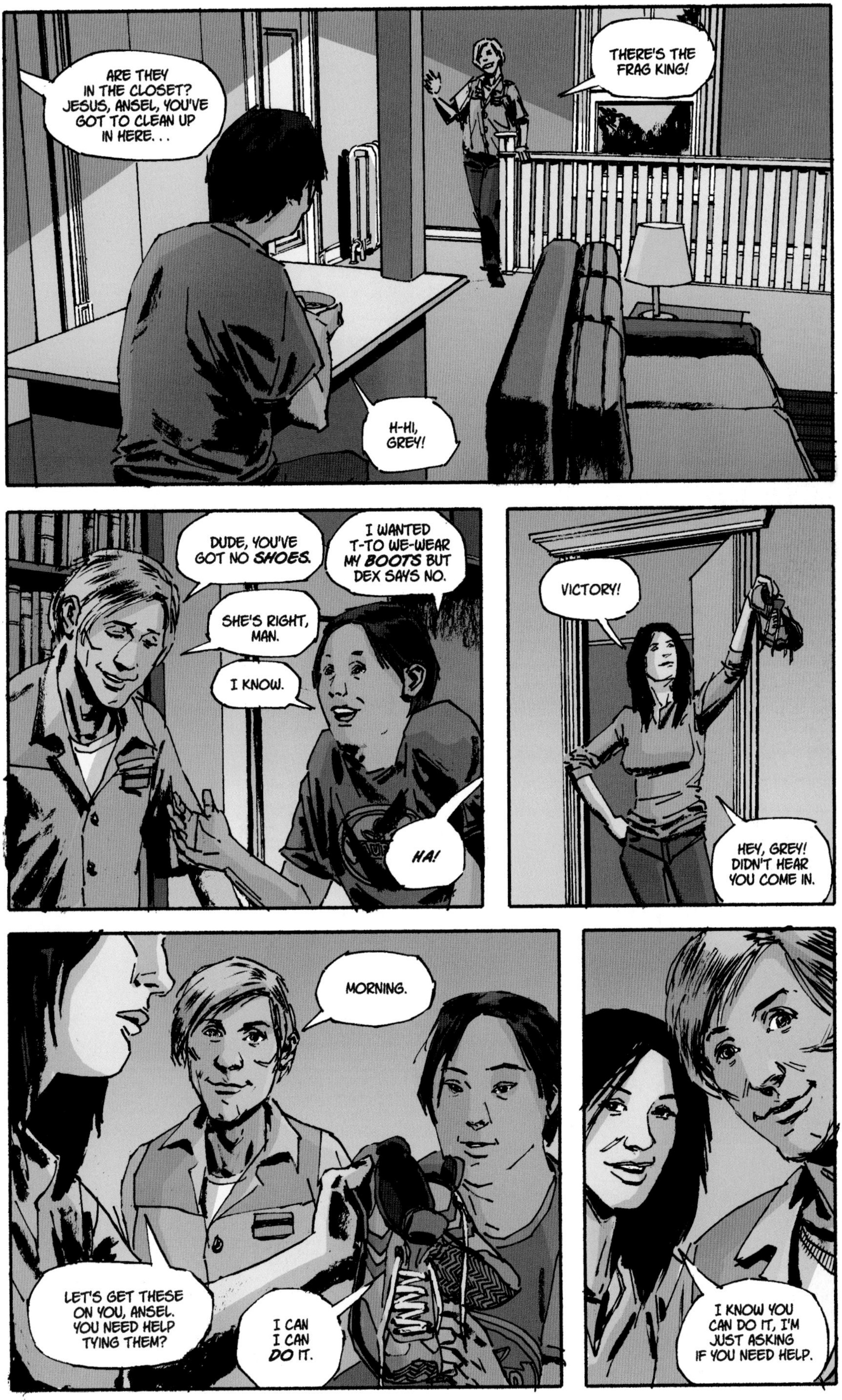
ARE THEY IN THE CLOSET? JESUS, ANSEL, YOU'VE GOT TO CLEAN UP IN HERE. . .
THERE'S THE FRAG KING!
H-HI, GREY!
DUDE, YOU'VE GOT NO *SHOES*.
I WANTED T-TO WE-WEAR MY *BOOTS* BUT DEX SAYS NO.
SHE'S RIGHT, MAN.
I KNOW.
HA!
VICTORY!
HEY, GREY! DIDN'T HEAR YOU COME IN.
MORNING.
LET'S GET THESE ON YOU, ANSEL. YOU NEED HELP TYING THEM?
I CAN I CAN *DO* IT.
I KNOW YOU CAN DO IT, I'M JUST ASKING IF YOU NEED HELP.

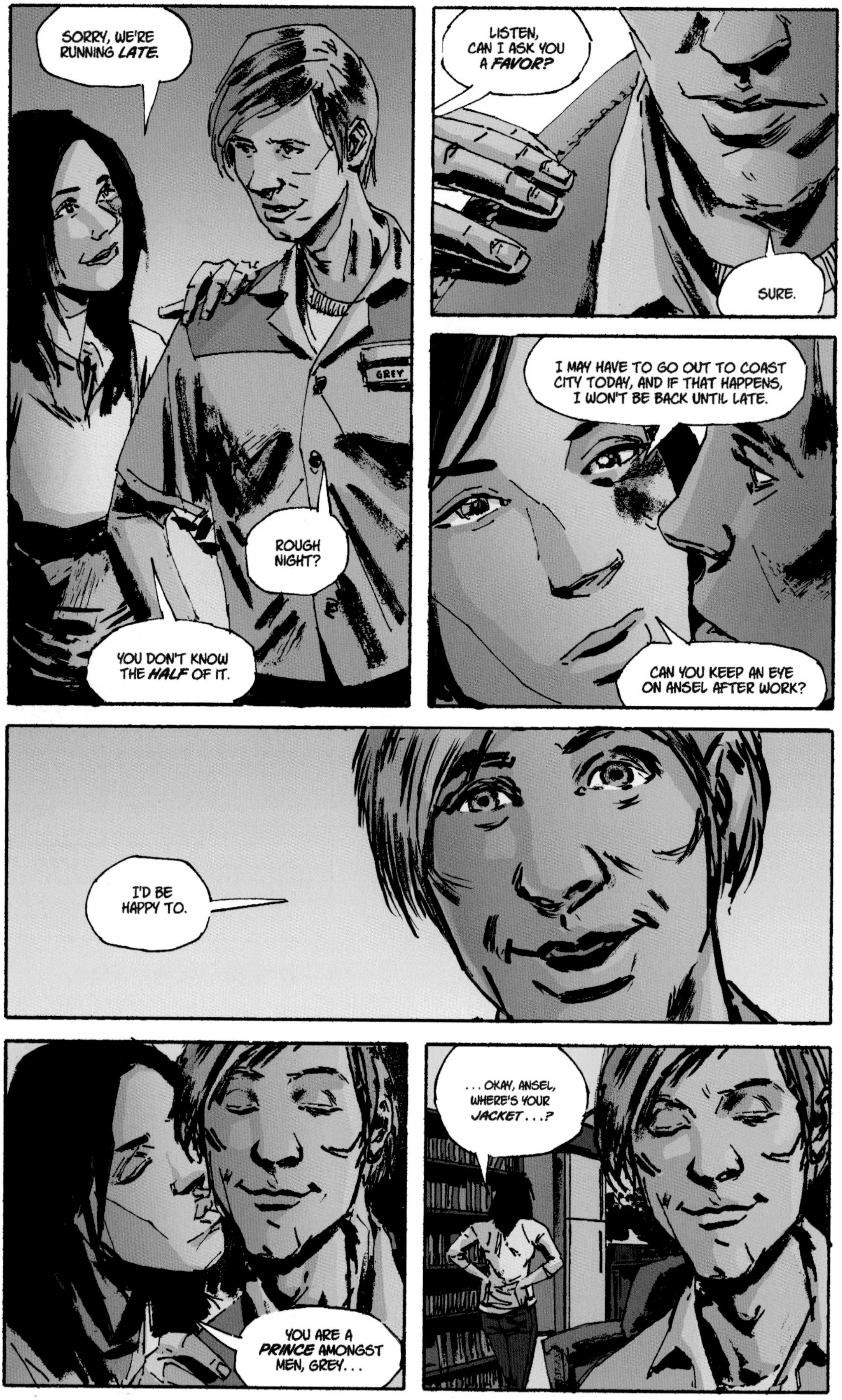
SORRY, WE'RE RUNNING LATE.
GREY
ROUGH NIGHT?
YOU DON'T KNOW THE HALF OF IT.
LISTEN, CAN I ASK YOU A FAVOR?
SURE.
I MAY HAVE TO GO OUT TO COAST CITY TODAY, AND IF THAT HAPPENS, I WON'T BE BACK UNTIL LATE.
CAN YOU KEEP AN EYE ON ANSEL AFTER WORK?
I'D BE HAPPY TO.
YOU ARE A PRINCE AMONGST MEN, GREY . . .
. . . OKAY, ANSEL, WHERE'S YOUR JACKET . . .?

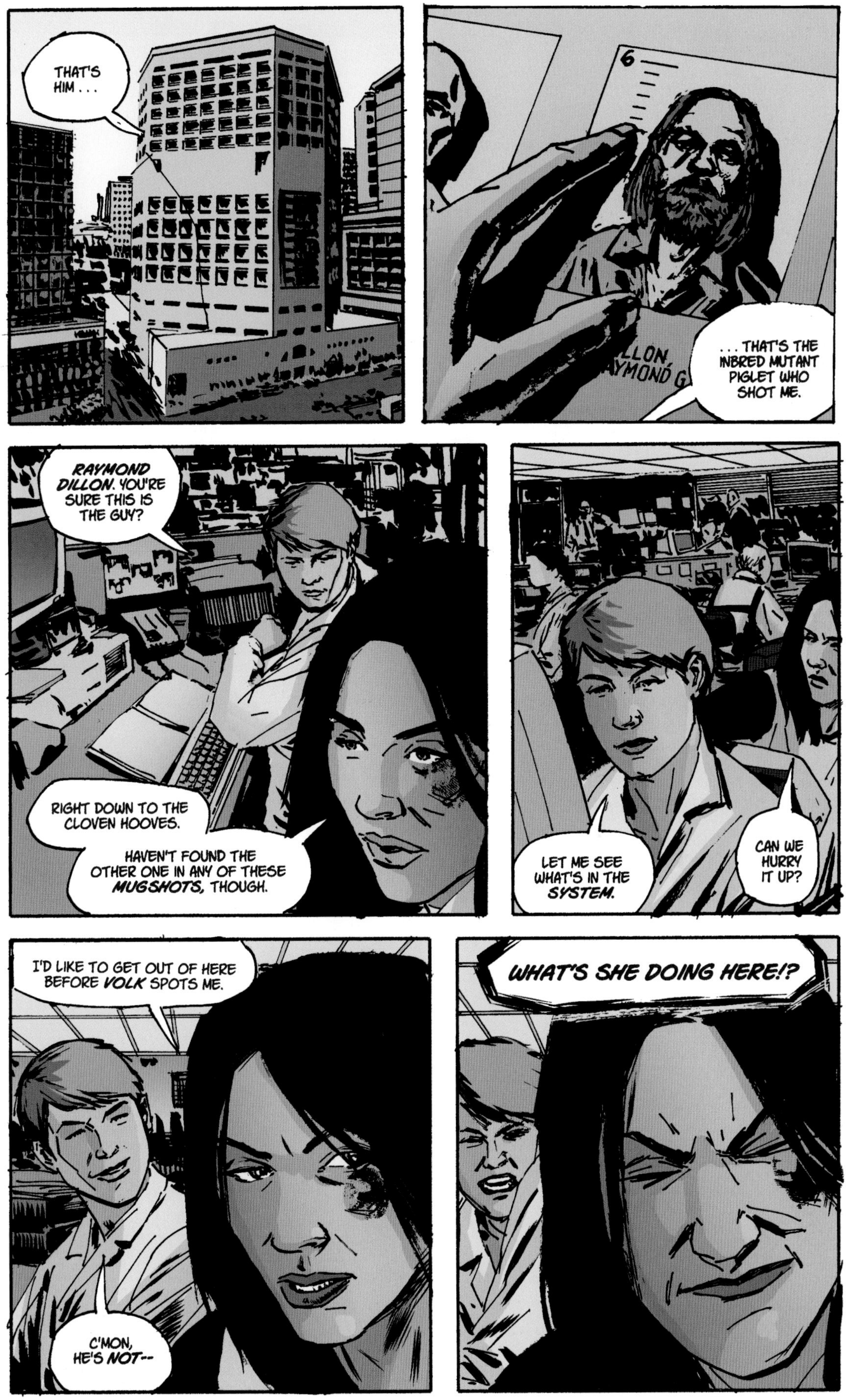
THAT'S HIM . . .
. . . THAT'S THE INBRED MUTANT PIGLET WHO SHOT ME.
DILLON RAYMOND G
RAYMOND DILLON. YOU'RE SURE THIS IS THE GUY?
RIGHT DOWN TO THE CLOVEN HOOVES.
HAVEN'T FOUND THE OTHER ONE IN ANY OF THESE MUGSHOTS, THOUGH.
LET ME SEE WHAT'S IN THE SYSTEM.
CAN WE HURRY IT UP?
I'D LIKE TO GET OUT OF HERE BEFORE VOLK SPOTS ME.
C'MON, HE'S NOT--
WHAT'S SHE DOING HERE!?

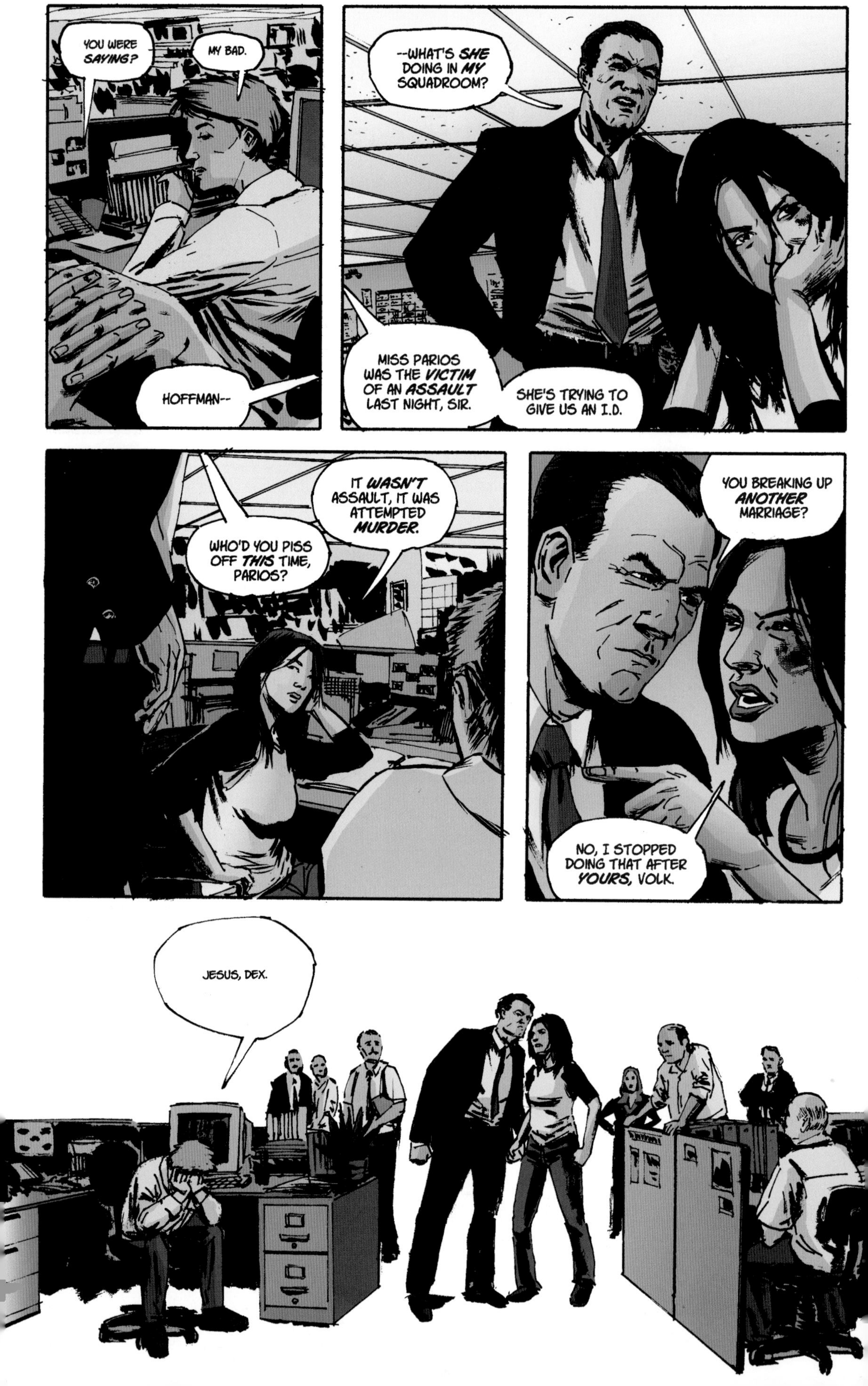
YOU WERE SAYING?
MY BAD.
HOFFMAN--
--WHAT'S SHE DOING IN MY SQUADROOM?
MISS PARIOS WAS THE VICTIM OF AN ASSAULT LAST NIGHT, SIR.
SHE'S TRYING TO GIVE US AN I.D.
WHO'D YOU PISS OFF THIS TIME, PARIOS?
IT WASN'T ASSAULT, IT WAS ATTEMPTED MURDER.
YOU BREAKING UP ANOTHER MARRIAGE?
NO, I STOPPED DOING THAT AFTER YOURS, VOLK.
JESUS, DEX.

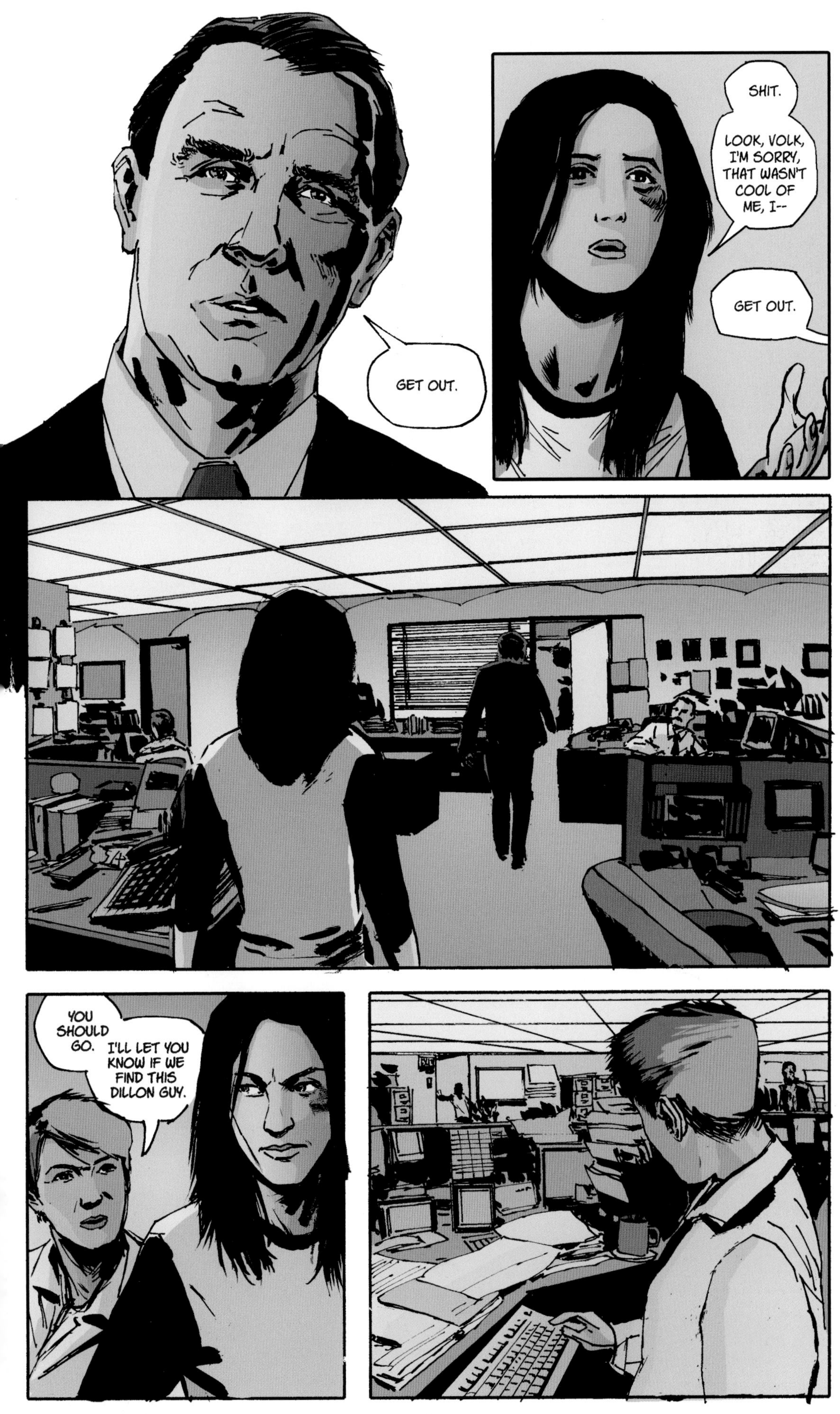
GET OUT.
SHIT.
LOOK, VOLK, I'M SORRY, THAT WASN'T COOL OF ME, I--
GET OUT.
YOU SHOULD GO.
I'LL LET YOU KNOW IF WE FIND THIS DILLON GUY.

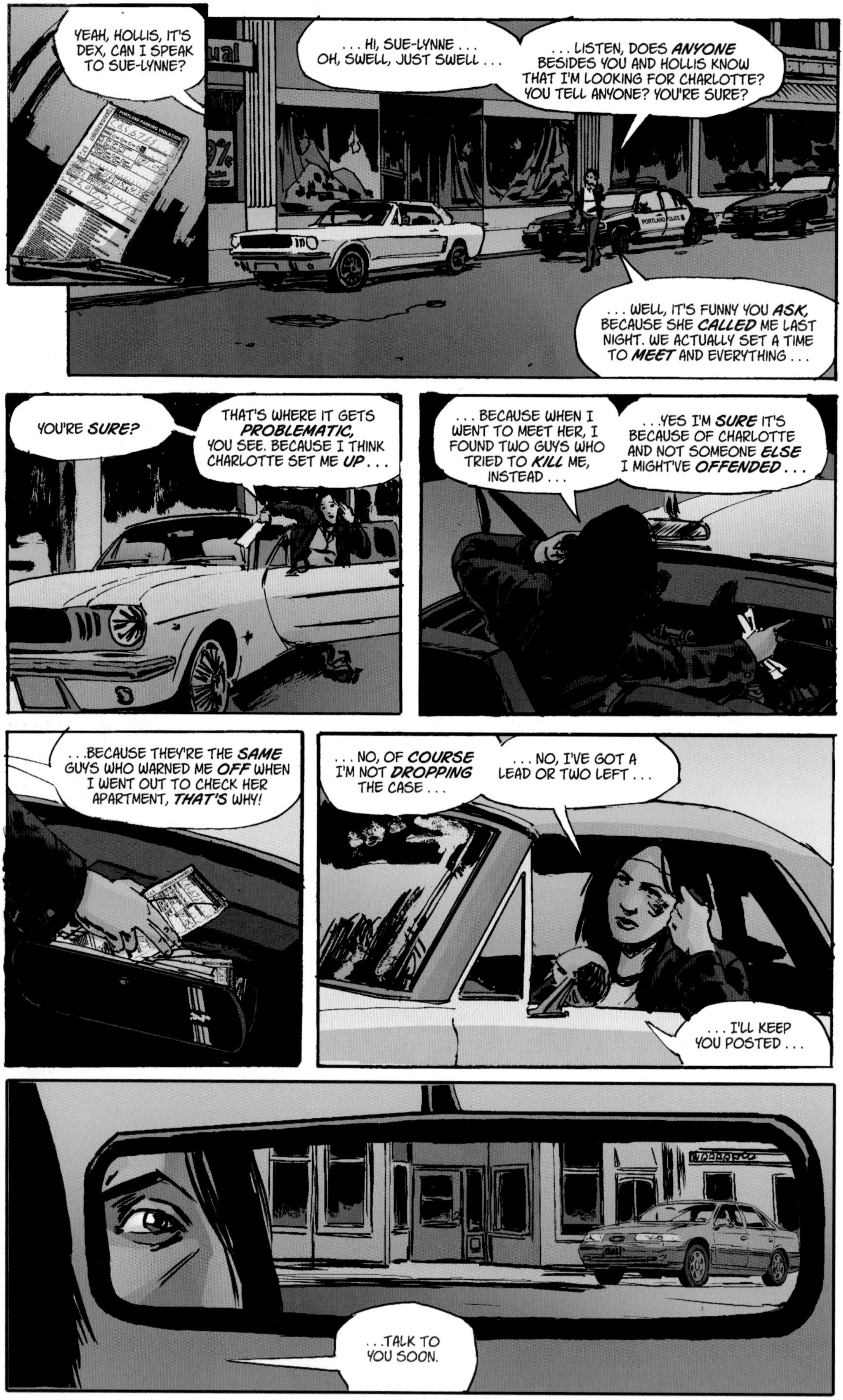
YEAH, HOLLIS, IT'S DEX, CAN I SPEAK TO SUE-LYNNE?
. . . HI, SUE-LYNNE . . . OH, SWELL, JUST SWELL . . .
. . . LISTEN, DOES ANYONE BESIDES YOU AND HOLLIS KNOW THAT I'M LOOKING FOR CHARLOTTE? YOU TELL ANYONE? YOU'RE SURE?
. . . WELL, IT'S FUNNY YOU ASK, BECAUSE SHE CALLED ME LAST NIGHT. WE ACTUALLY SET A TIME TO MEET AND EVERYTHING . . .
YOU'RE SURE?
THAT'S WHERE IT GETS PROBLEMATIC, YOU SEE. BECAUSE I THINK CHARLOTTE SET ME UP . . .
. . . BECAUSE WHEN I WENT TO MEET HER, I FOUND TWO GUYS WHO TRIED TO KILL ME, INSTEAD . . .
. . .YES I'M SURE IT'S BECAUSE OF CHARLOTTE AND NOT SOMEONE ELSE I MIGHT'VE OFFENDED . . .
. . .BECAUSE THEY'RE THE SAME GUYS WHO WARNED ME OFF WHEN I WENT OUT TO CHECK HER APARTMENT, THAT'S WHY!
. . . NO, OF COURSE I'M NOT DROPPING THE CASE . . .
. . . NO, I'VE GOT A LEAD OR TWO LEFT . . .
. . . I'LL KEEP YOU POSTED . . .
. . .TALK TO YOU SOON.

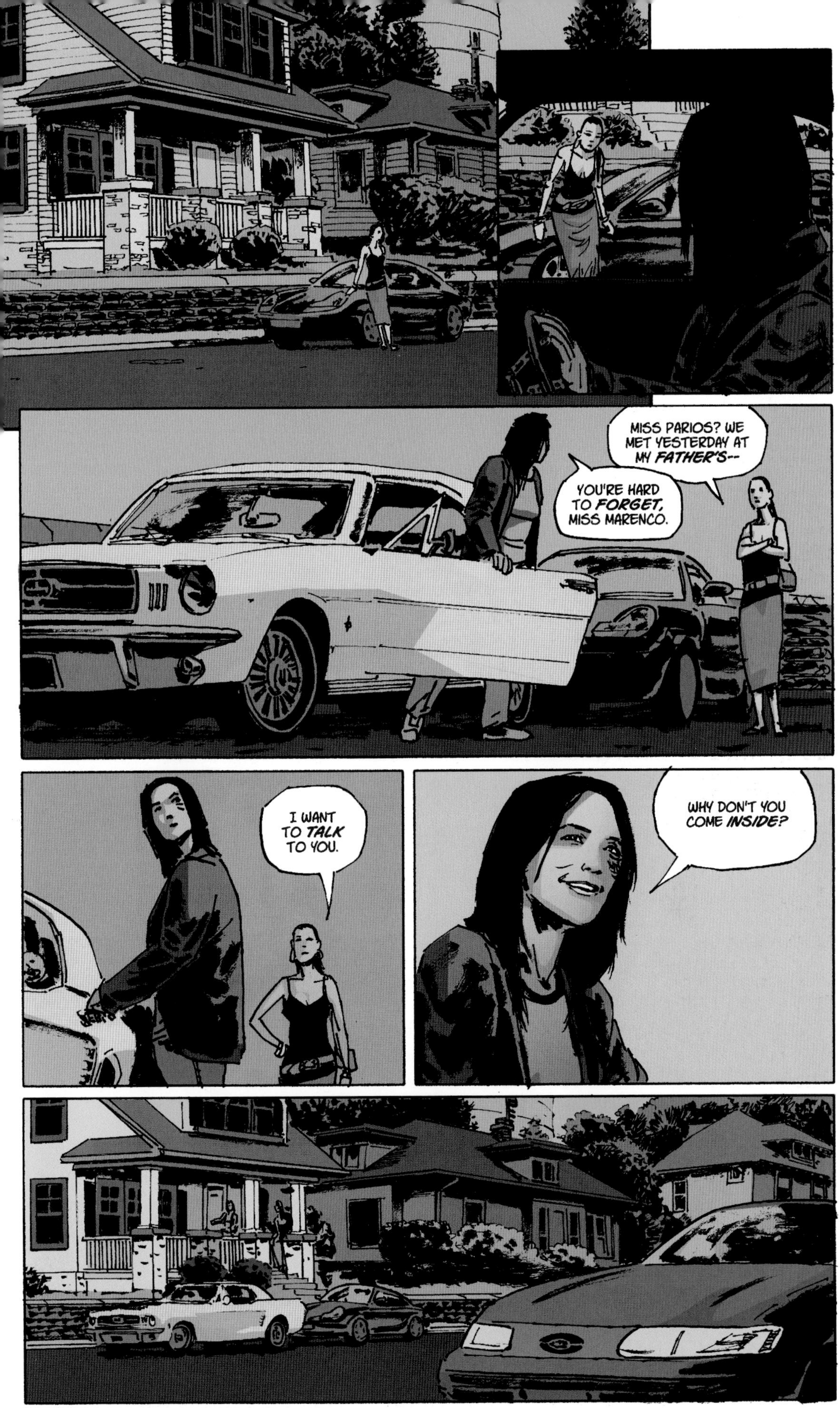
MISS PARIOS? WE MET YESTERDAY AT MY *FATHER'S*--
YOU'RE HARD TO *FORGET,* MISS MARENCO.
I WANT TO *TALK* TO YOU.
WHY DON'T YOU COME *INSIDE?*

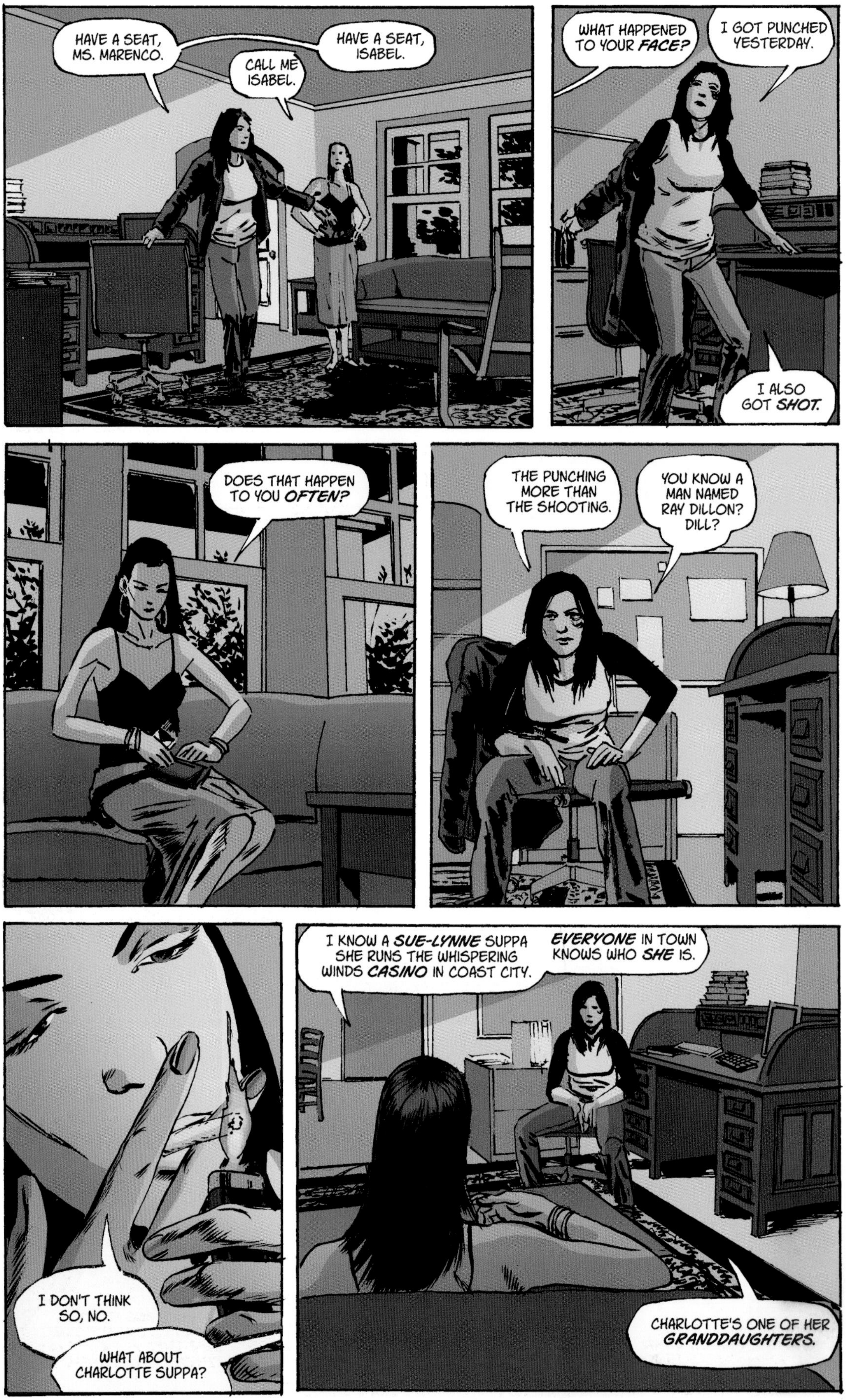
HAVE A SEAT, MS. MARENCO.
CALL ME ISABEL.
HAVE A SEAT, ISABEL.
WHAT HAPPENED TO YOUR FACE?
I GOT PUNCHED YESTERDAY.
I ALSO GOT SHOT.
DOES THAT HAPPEN TO YOU OFTEN?
THE PUNCHING MORE THAN THE SHOOTING.
YOU KNOW A MAN NAMED RAY DILLON? DILL?
I DON'T THINK SO, NO.
WHAT ABOUT CHARLOTTE SUPPA?
I KNOW A SUE-LYNNE SUPPA SHE RUNS THE WHISPERING WINDS CASINO IN COAST CITY.
EVERYONE IN TOWN KNOWS WHO SHE IS.
CHARLOTTE'S ONE OF HER GRANDDAUGHTERS.

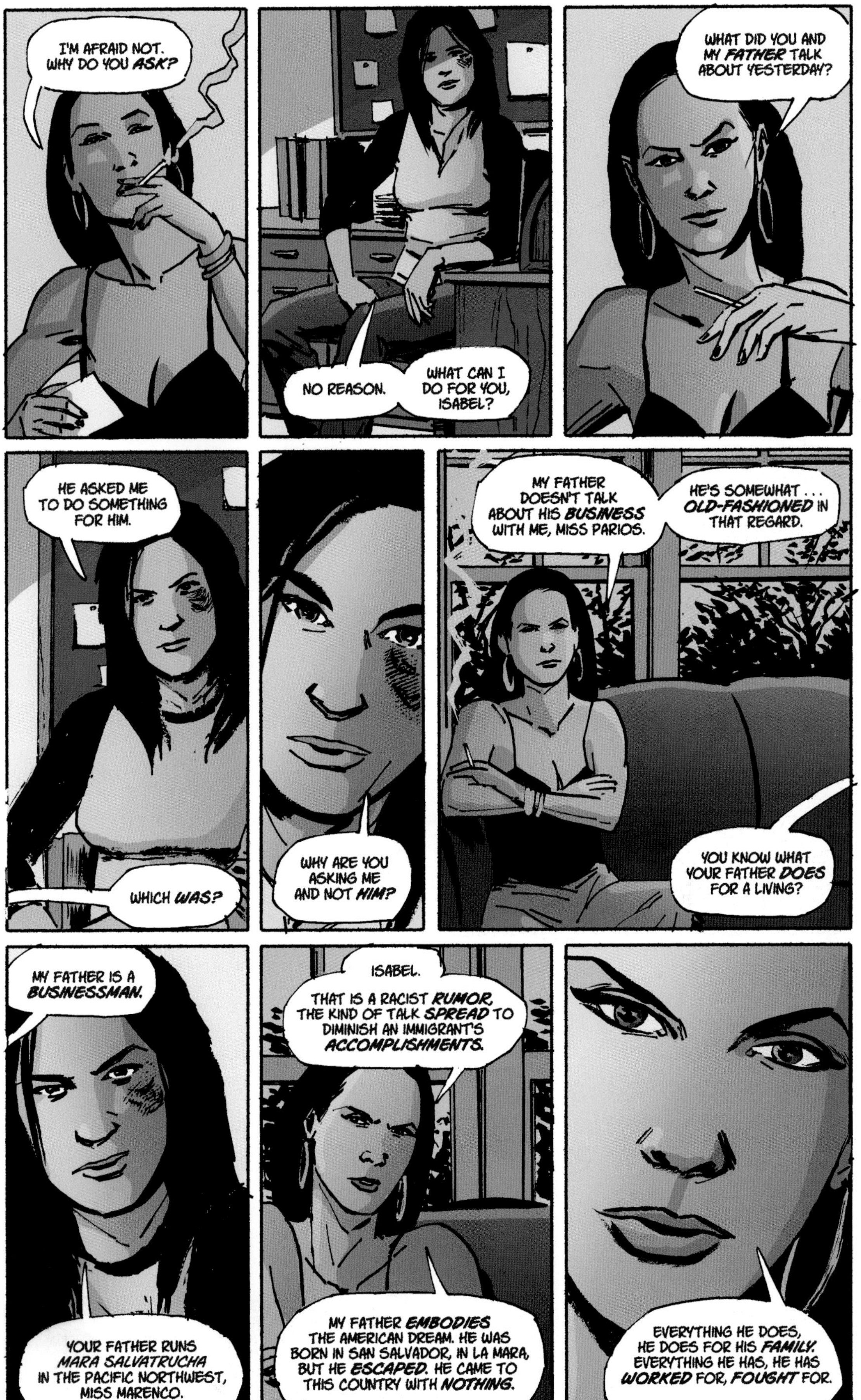

I'M AFRAID NOT. WHY DO YOU ASK?
NO REASON.
WHAT CAN I DO FOR YOU, ISABEL?
WHAT DID YOU AND MY FATHER TALK ABOUT YESTERDAY?
HE ASKED ME TO DO SOMETHING FOR HIM.
WHICH WAS?
WHY ARE YOU ASKING ME AND NOT HIM?
MY FATHER DOESN'T TALK ABOUT HIS BUSINESS WITH ME, MISS PARIOS.
HE'S SOMEWHAT . . . OLD-FASHIONED IN THAT REGARD.
YOU KNOW WHAT YOUR FATHER DOES FOR A LIVING?
MY FATHER IS A BUSINESSMAN.
YOUR FATHER RUNS MARA SALVATRUCHA IN THE PACIFIC NORTHWEST, MISS MARENCO.
ISABEL.
THAT IS A RACIST RUMOR, THE KIND OF TALK SPREAD TO DIMINISH AN IMMIGRANT'S ACCOMPLISHMENTS.
MY FATHER EMBODIES THE AMERICAN DREAM. HE WAS BORN IN SAN SALVADOR, IN LA MARA, BUT HE ESCAPED. HE CAME TO THIS COUNTRY WITH NOTHING.
EVERYTHING HE DOES, HE DOES FOR HIS FAMILY. EVERYTHING HE HAS, HE HAS WORKED FOR, FOUGHT FOR.

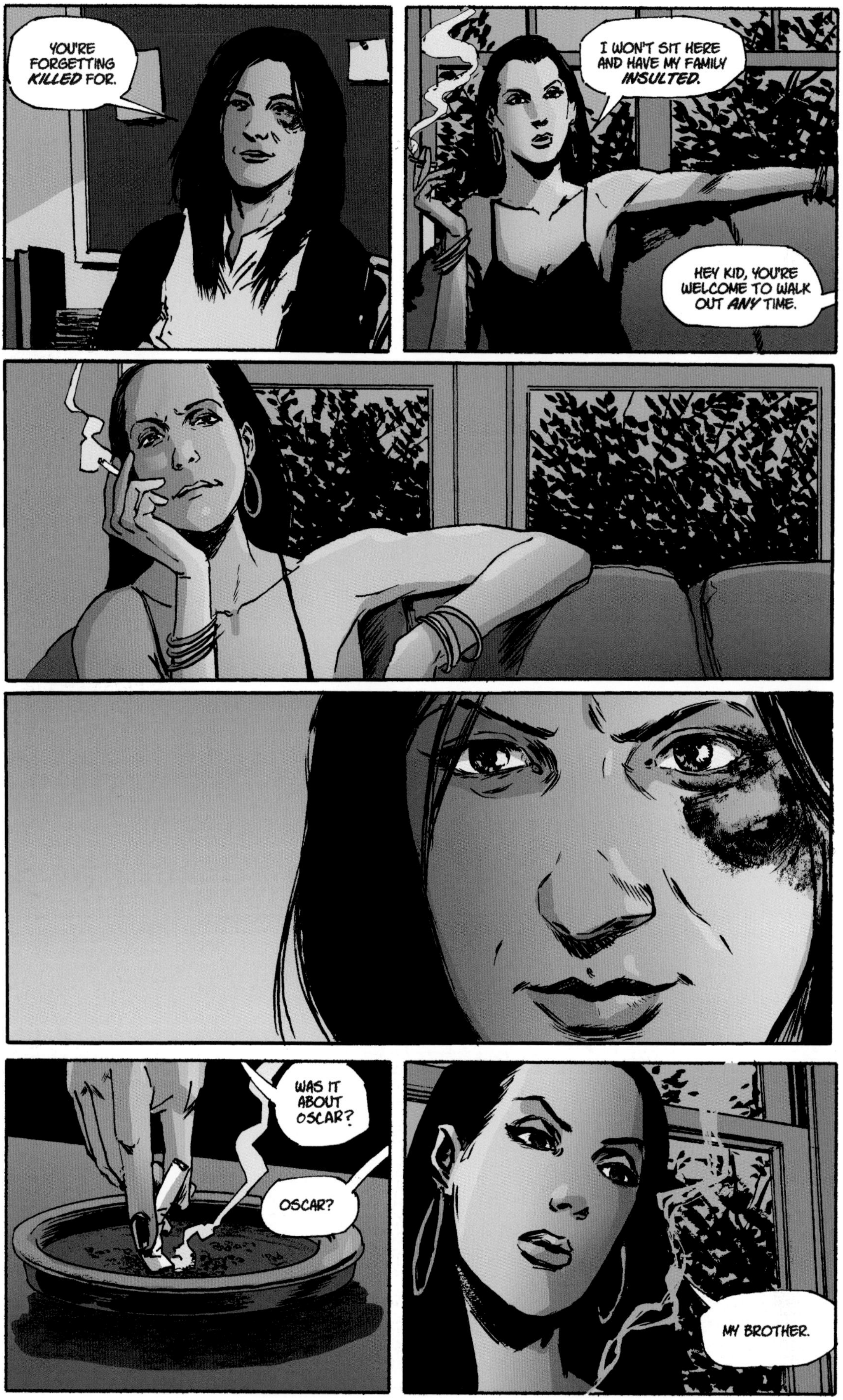
YOU'RE FORGETTING KILLED FOR.
I WON'T SIT HERE AND HAVE MY FAMILY INSULTED.
HEY KID, YOU'RE WELCOME TO WALK OUT ANY TIME.
WAS IT ABOUT OSCAR?
OSCAR?
MY BROTHER.

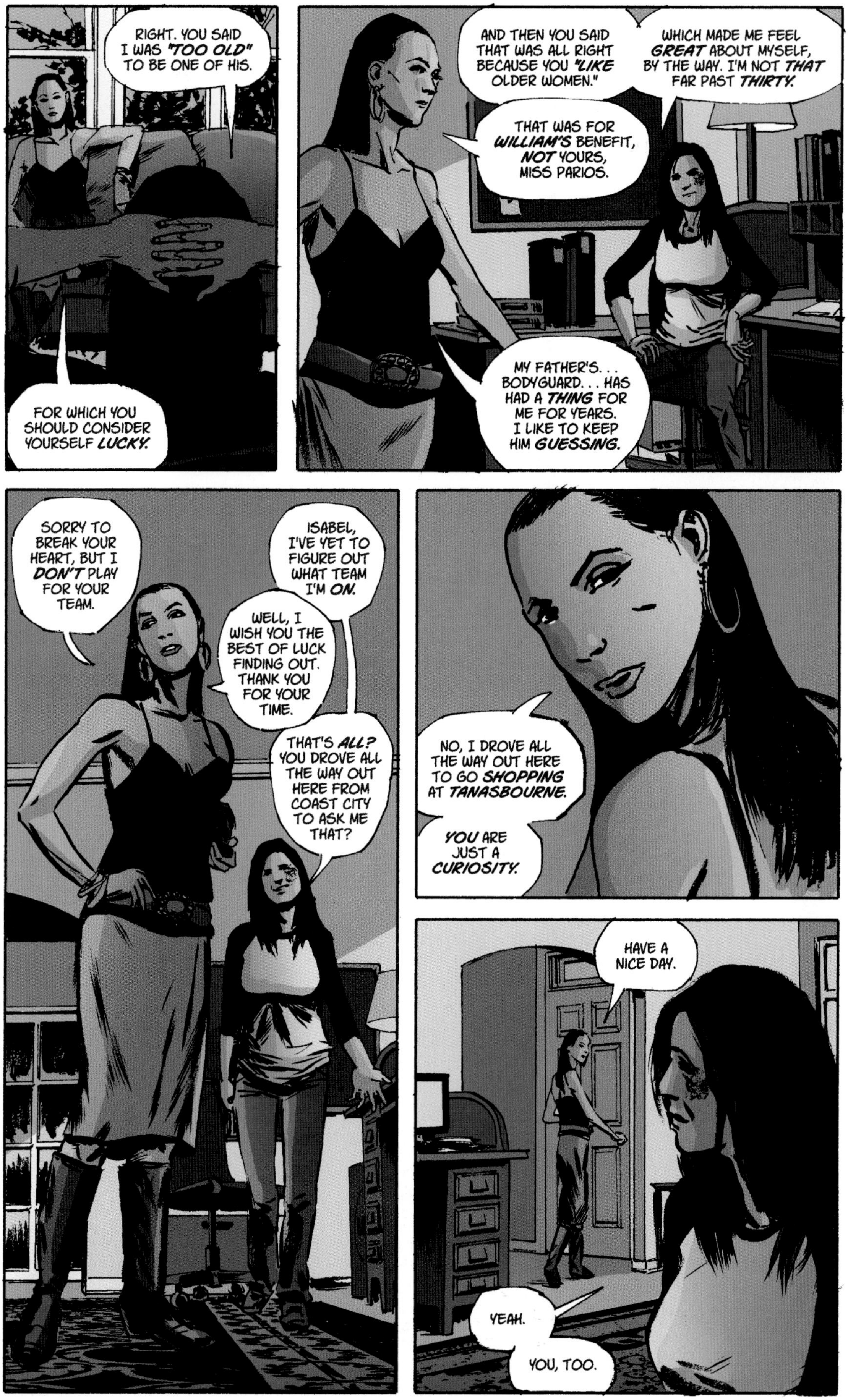
RIGHT. YOU SAID I WAS "TOO OLD" TO BE ONE OF HIS.
FOR WHICH YOU SHOULD CONSIDER YOURSELF LUCKY.
AND THEN YOU SAID THAT WAS ALL RIGHT BECAUSE YOU "LIKE OLDER WOMEN."
WHICH MADE ME FEEL GREAT ABOUT MYSELF, BY THE WAY. I'M NOT THAT FAR PAST THIRTY.
THAT WAS FOR WILLIAM'S BENEFIT, NOT YOURS, MISS PARIOS.
MY FATHER'S. . . BODYGUARD. . . HAS HAD A THING FOR ME FOR YEARS. I LIKE TO KEEP HIM GUESSING.
SORRY TO BREAK YOUR HEART, BUT I DON'T PLAY FOR YOUR TEAM.
ISABEL, I'VE YET TO FIGURE OUT WHAT TEAM I'M ON.
WELL, I WISH YOU THE BEST OF LUCK FINDING OUT. THANK YOU FOR YOUR TIME.
THAT'S ALL? YOU DROVE ALL THE WAY OUT HERE FROM COAST CITY TO ASK ME THAT?
NO, I DROVE ALL THE WAY OUT HERE TO GO SHOPPING AT TANASBOURNE.
YOU ARE JUST A CURIOSITY.
HAVE A NICE DAY.
YEAH.
YOU, TOO.

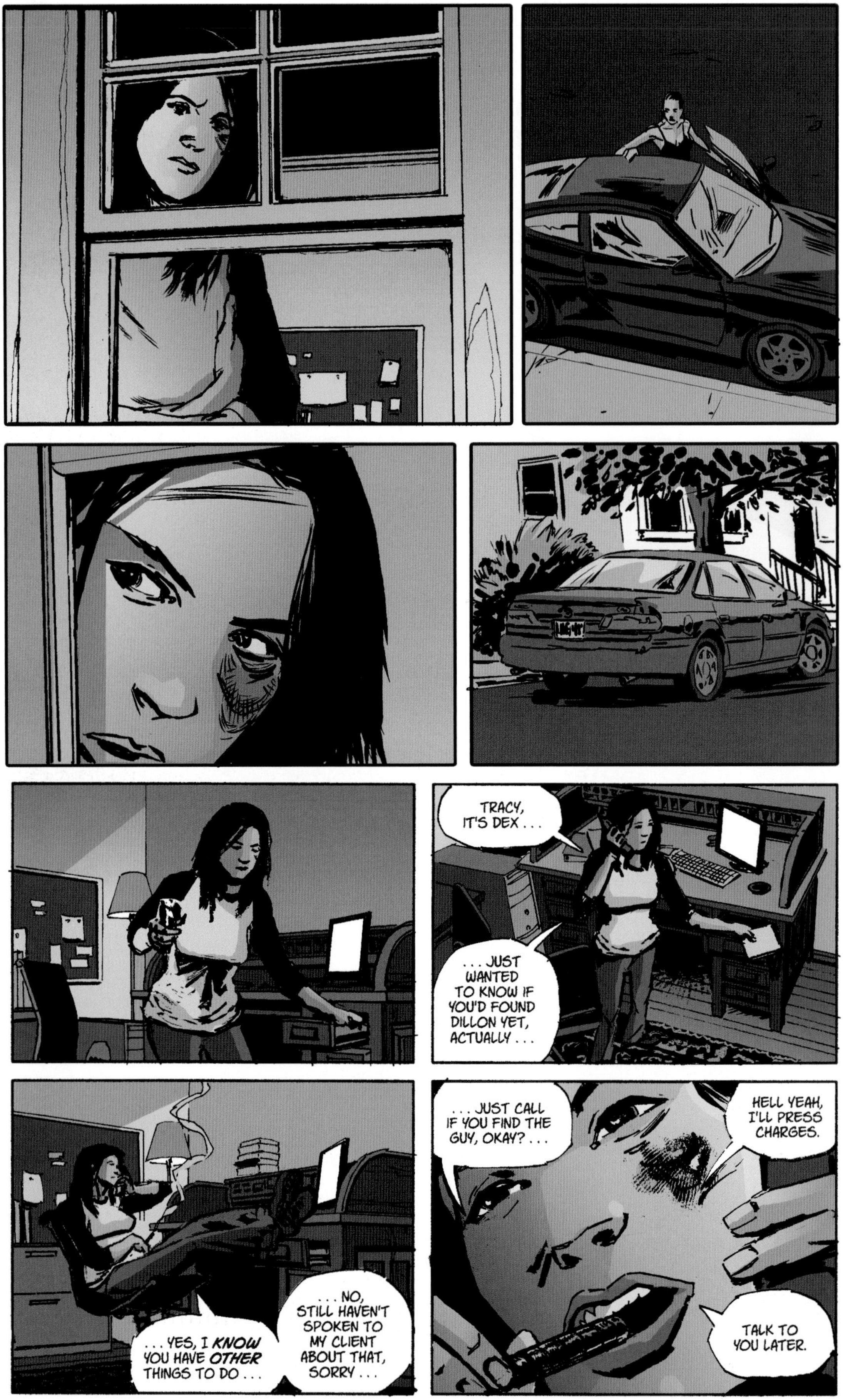
TRACY, IT'S DEX . . .
. . . JUST WANTED TO KNOW IF YOU'D FOUND DILLON YET, ACTUALLY . . .
. . . YES, I KNOW YOU HAVE OTHER THINGS TO DO . . .
. . . NO, STILL HAVEN'T SPOKEN TO MY CLIENT ABOUT THAT, SORRY . . .
. . . JUST CALL IF YOU FIND THE GUY, OKAY? . . .
HELL YEAH, I'LL PRESS CHARGES.
TALK TO YOU LATER.

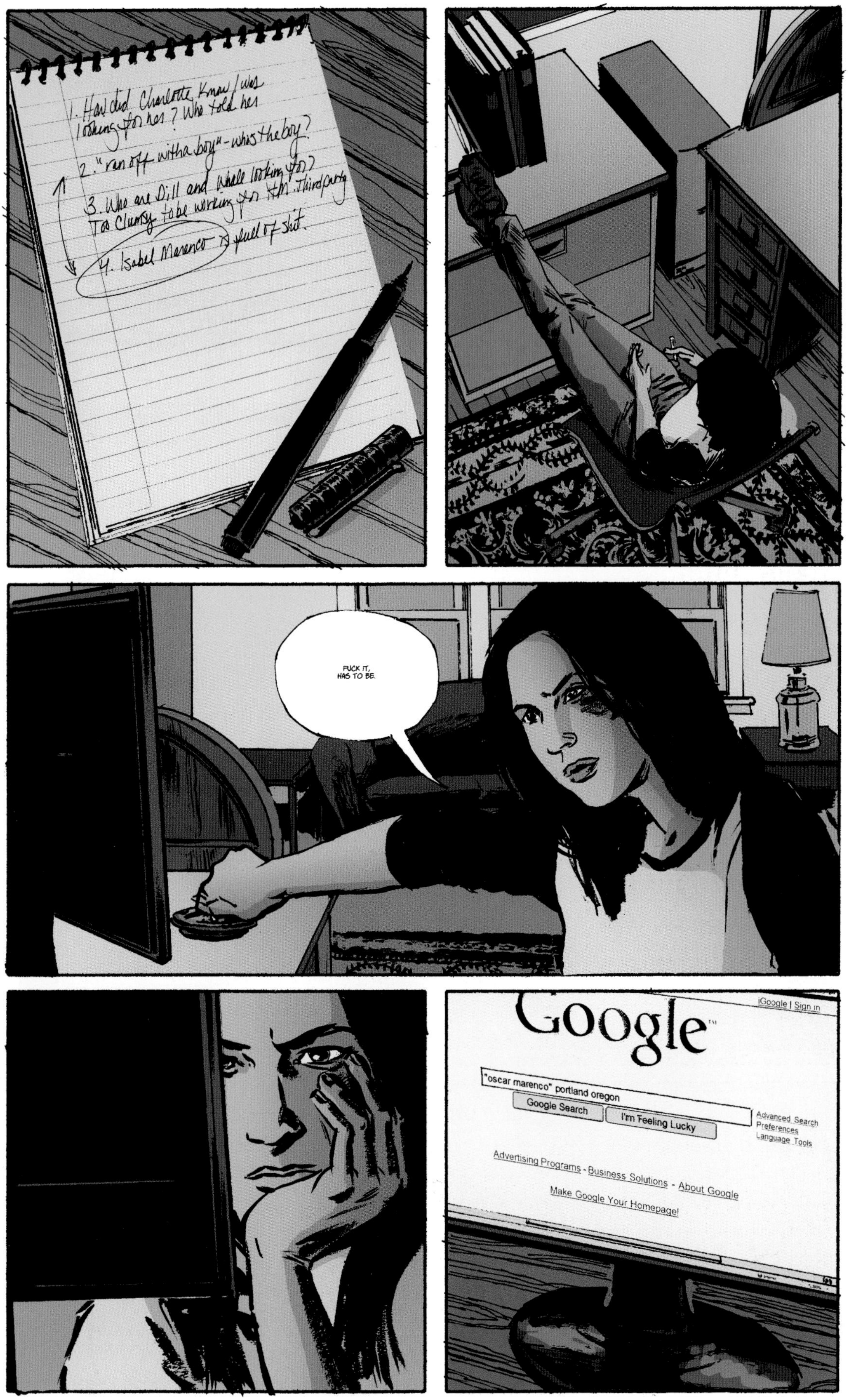
1. How did Charlotte Know I was looking for her? Who told her
2. "ran off with a boy" - who's the boy?
3. Who are Dill and Whale looking for? Too Clumsy to be working for HM. Third party
4. Isabel Marenco is full of shit.
FUCK IT, HAS TO BE.
Google
iGoogle | Sign in
"oscar marenco" portland oregon
Google Search
I'm Feeling Lucky
Advanced Search
Preferences
Language Tools
Advertising Programs - Business Solutions - About Google
Make Google Your Homepage!

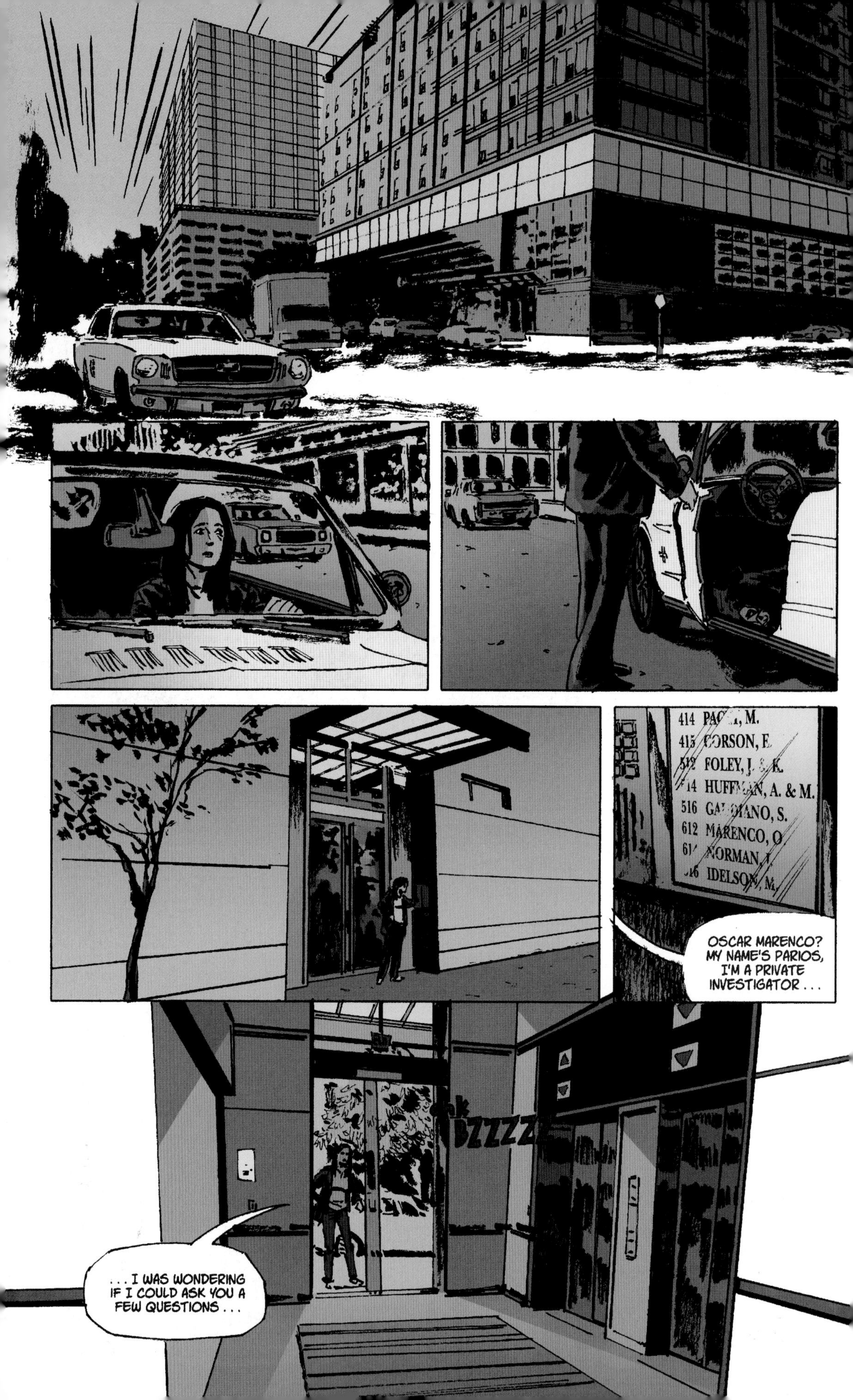

612 MARENCO, O
OSCAR MARENCO? MY NAME'S PARIOS, I'M A PRIVATE INVESTIGATOR . . .
BZZZZZ
. . . I WAS WONDERING IF I COULD ASK YOU A FEW QUESTIONS . . .

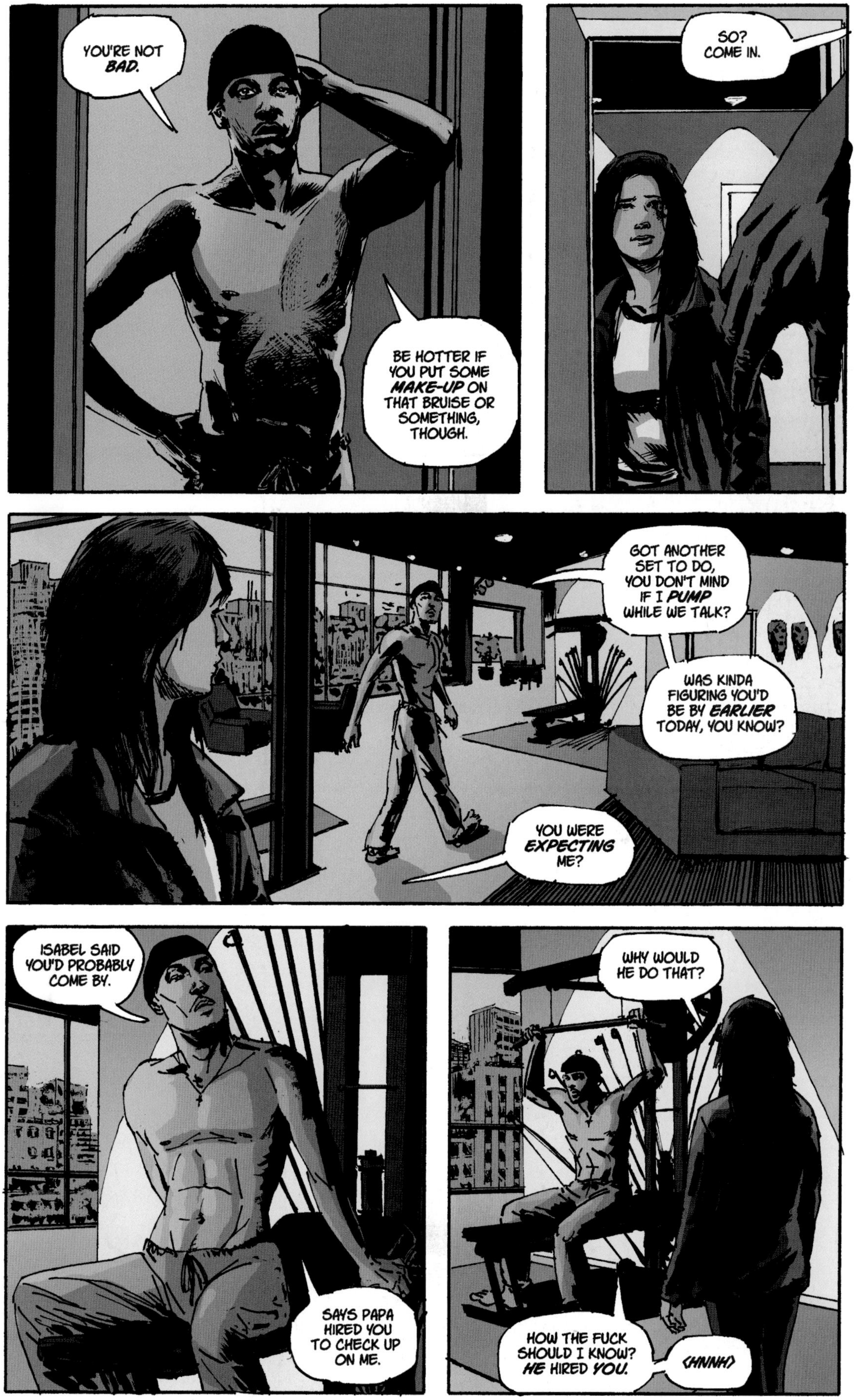

YOU'RE NOT *BAD.*
BE HOTTER IF YOU PUT SOME *MAKE-UP* ON THAT BRUISE OR SOMETHING, THOUGH.
SO? COME IN.
GOT ANOTHER SET TO DO, YOU DON'T MIND IF I *PUMP* WHILE WE TALK?
WAS KINDA FIGURING YOU'D BE BY *EARLIER* TODAY, YOU KNOW?
YOU WERE *EXPECTING* ME?
ISABEL SAID YOU'D PROBABLY COME BY.
SAYS PAPA HIRED YOU TO CHECK UP ON ME.
WHY WOULD HE DO THAT?
HOW THE FUCK SHOULD I KNOW? *HE* HIRED *YOU.*
<HNNH>

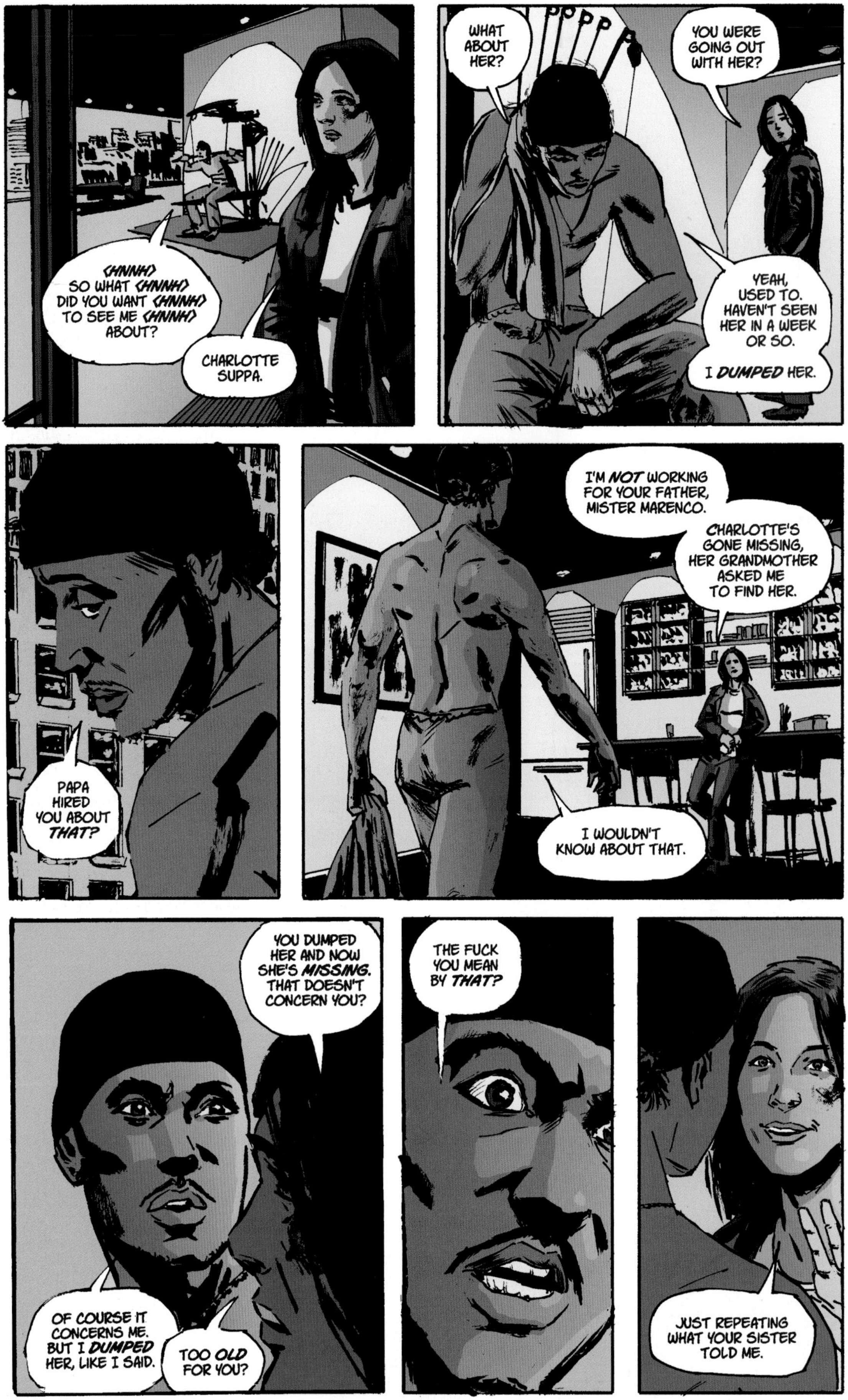
⟨HNNH⟩ SO WHAT ⟨HNNH⟩ DID YOU WANT ⟨HNNH⟩ TO SEE ME ⟨HNNH⟩ ABOUT?
CHARLOTTE SUPPA.
WHAT ABOUT HER?
YOU WERE GOING OUT WITH HER?
YEAH, USED TO. HAVEN'T SEEN HER IN A WEEK OR SO.
I *DUMPED* HER.
PAPA HIRED YOU ABOUT *THAT?*
I'M *NOT* WORKING FOR YOUR FATHER, MISTER MARENCO.
CHARLOTTE'S GONE MISSING, HER GRANDMOTHER ASKED ME TO FIND HER.
I WOULDN'T KNOW ABOUT THAT.
YOU DUMPED HER AND NOW SHE'S *MISSING*. THAT DOESN'T CONCERN YOU?
OF COURSE IT CONCERNS ME. BUT I *DUMPED* HER, LIKE I SAID.
TOO *OLD* FOR YOU?
THE FUCK YOU MEAN BY *THAT?*
JUST REPEATING WHAT YOUR SISTER TOLD ME.

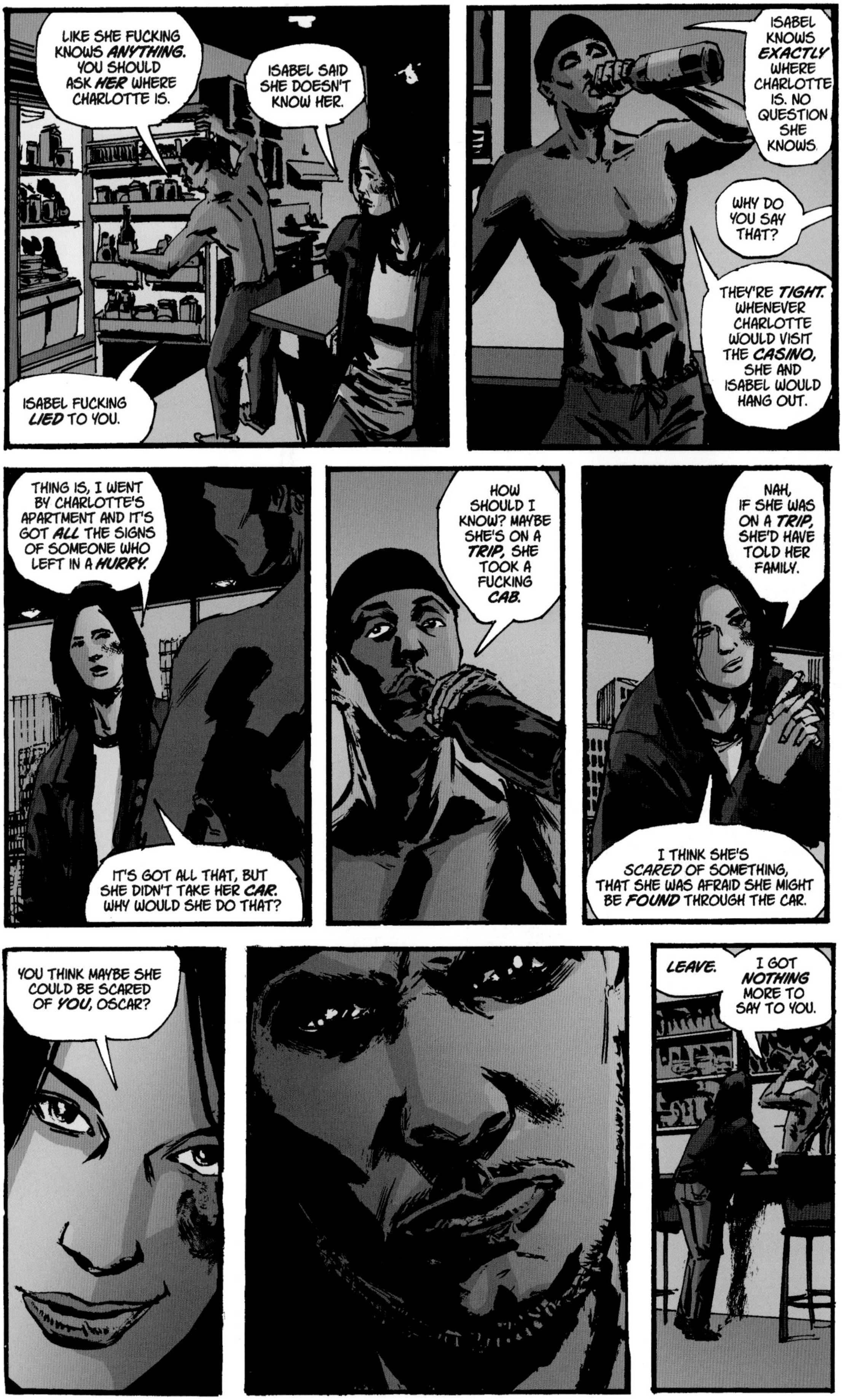
LIKE SHE FUCKING KNOWS ANYTHING. YOU SHOULD ASK HER WHERE CHARLOTTE IS.
ISABEL SAID SHE DOESN'T KNOW HER.
ISABEL FUCKING LIED TO YOU.
ISABEL KNOWS EXACTLY WHERE CHARLOTTE IS. NO QUESTION SHE KNOWS.
WHY DO YOU SAY THAT?
THEY'RE TIGHT. WHENEVER CHARLOTTE WOULD VISIT THE CASINO, SHE AND ISABEL WOULD HANG OUT.
THING IS, I WENT BY CHARLOTTE'S APARTMENT AND IT'S GOT ALL THE SIGNS OF SOMEONE WHO LEFT IN A HURRY.
IT'S GOT ALL THAT, BUT SHE DIDN'T TAKE HER CAR. WHY WOULD SHE DO THAT?
HOW SHOULD I KNOW? MAYBE SHE'S ON A TRIP, SHE TOOK A FUCKING CAB.
NAH, IF SHE WAS ON A TRIP, SHE'D HAVE TOLD HER FAMILY.
I THINK SHE'S SCARED OF SOMETHING, THAT SHE WAS AFRAID SHE MIGHT BE FOUND THROUGH THE CAR.
YOU THINK MAYBE SHE COULD BE SCARED OF YOU, OSCAR?
LEAVE.
I GOT NOTHING MORE TO SAY TO YOU.

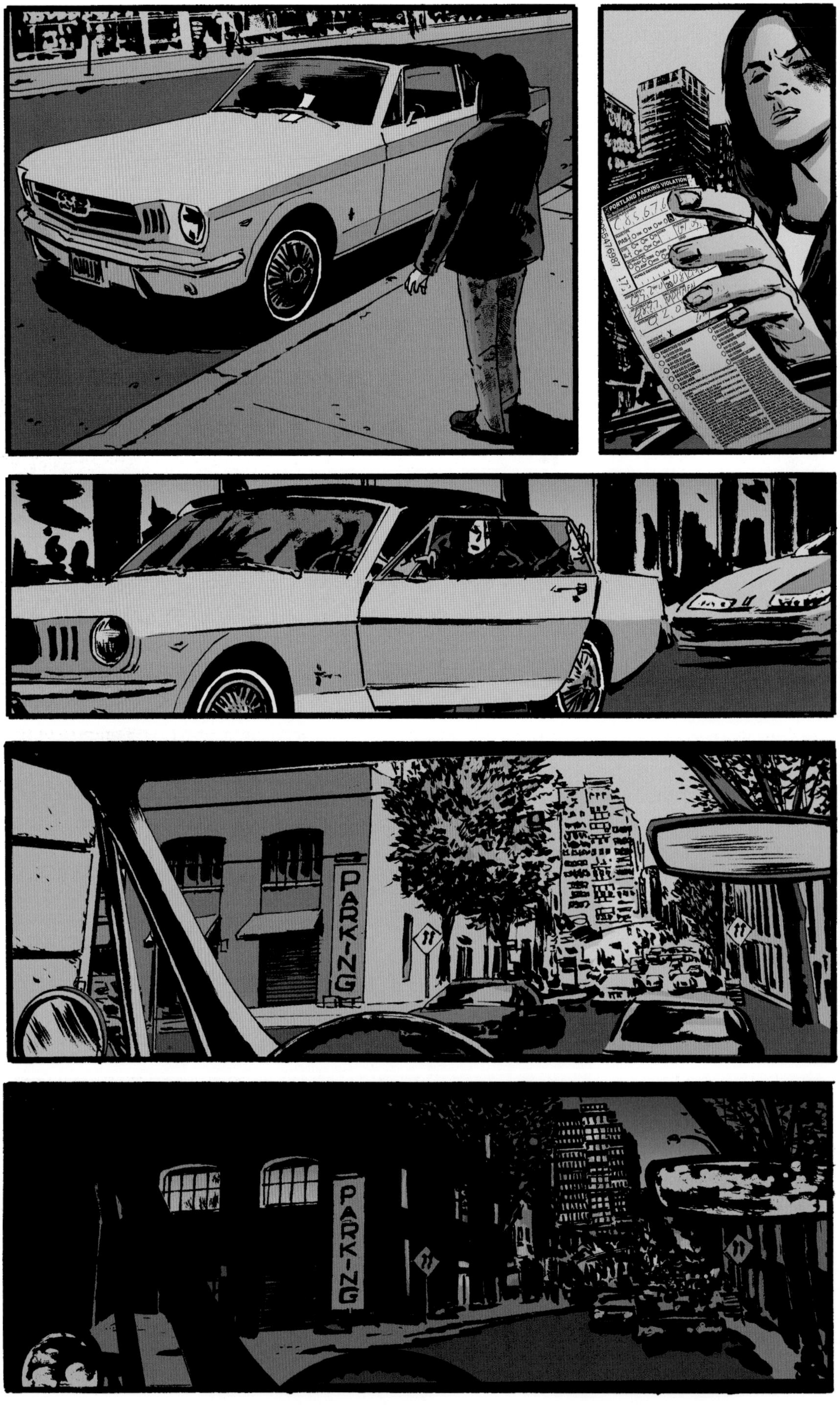
PORTLAND PARKING VIOLATION
PARKING
PARKING

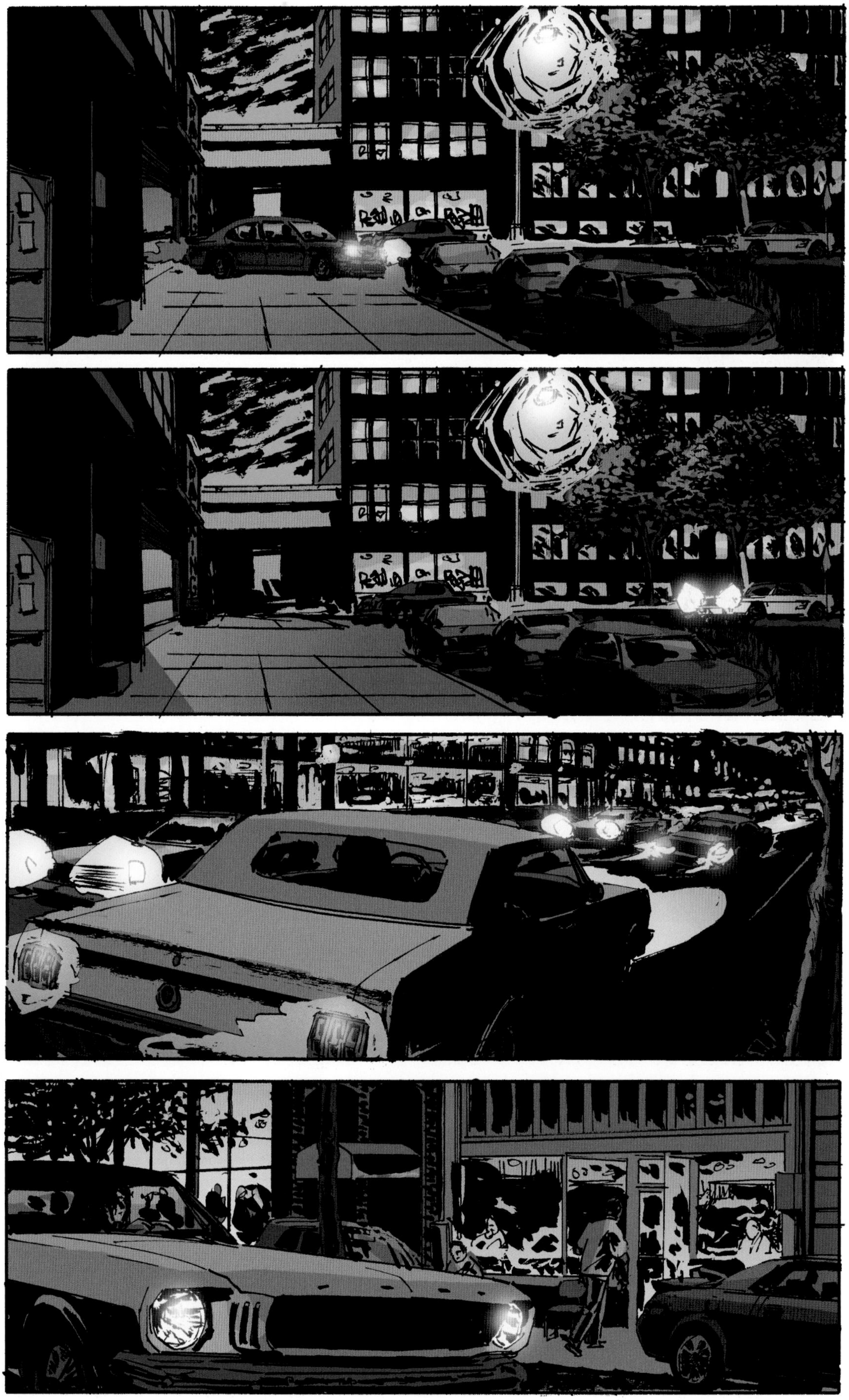

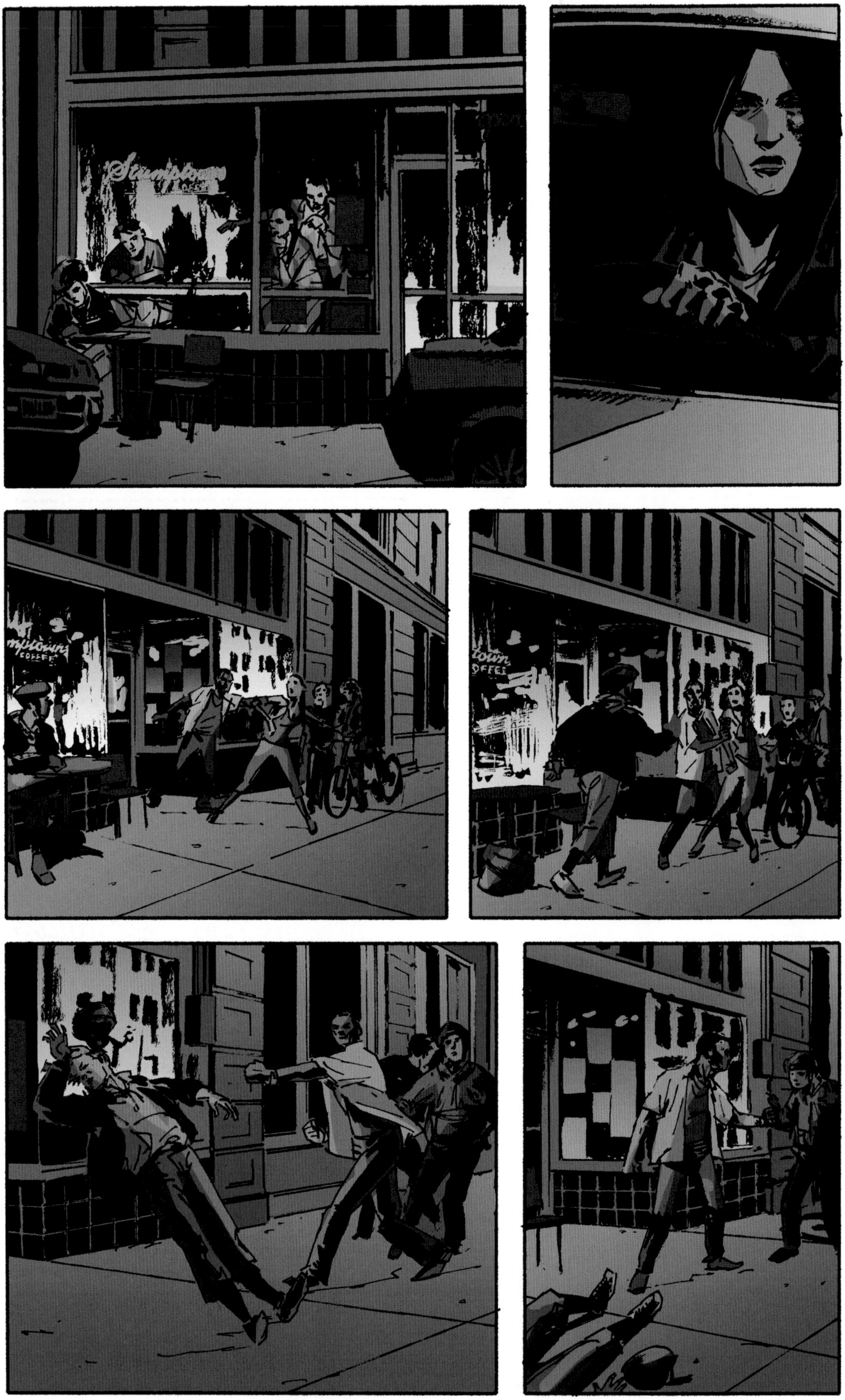
COFFEE

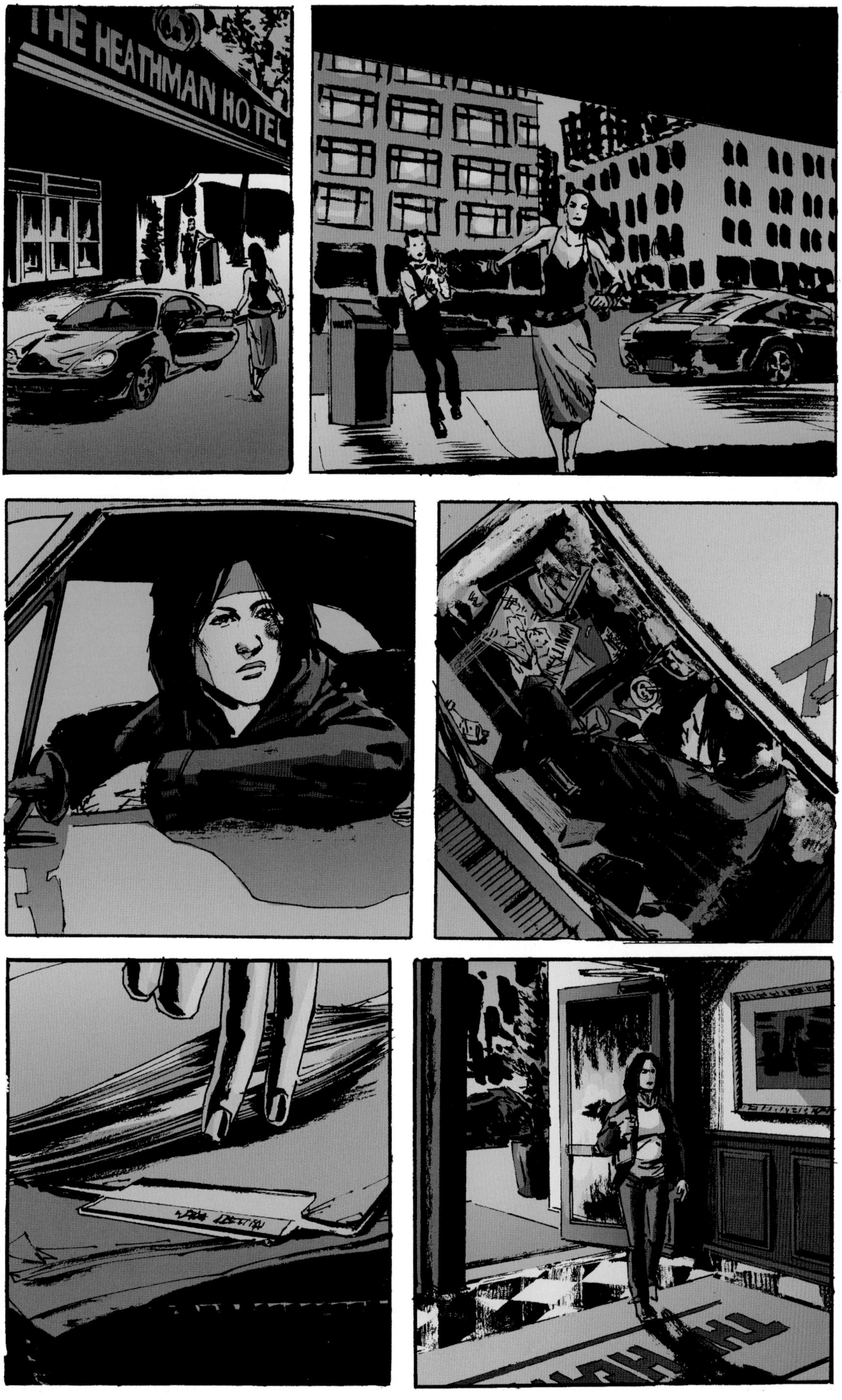
THE HEATHMAN HOTEL

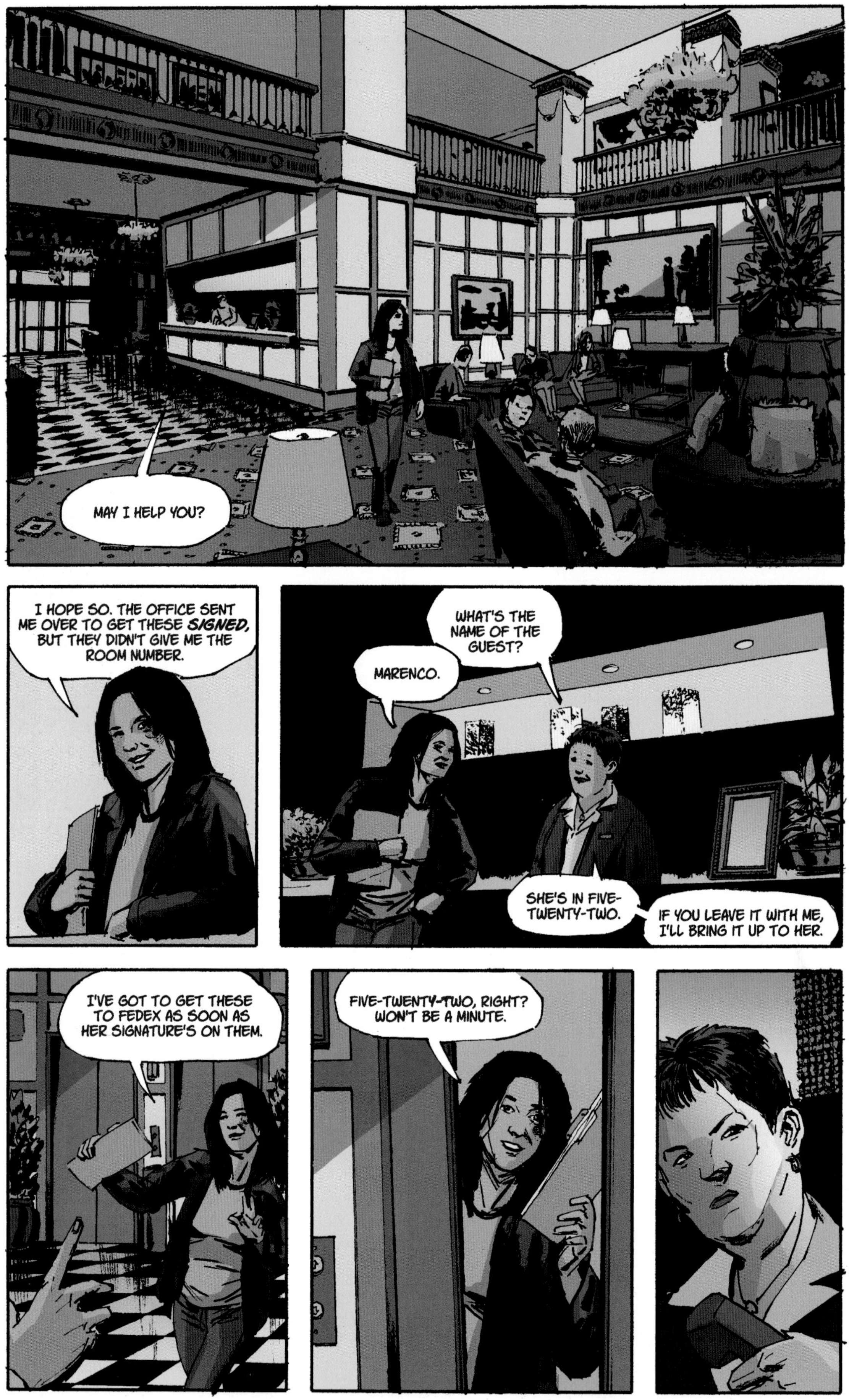
MAY I HELP YOU?
I HOPE SO. THE OFFICE SENT ME OVER TO GET THESE *SIGNED,* BUT THEY DIDN'T GIVE ME THE ROOM NUMBER.
WHAT'S THE NAME OF THE GUEST?
MARENCO.
SHE'S IN FIVE-TWENTY-TWO.
IF YOU LEAVE IT WITH ME, I'LL BRING IT UP TO HER.
I'VE GOT TO GET THESE TO FEDEX AS SOON AS HER SIGNATURE'S ON THEM.
FIVE-TWENTY-TWO, RIGHT? WON'T BE A MINUTE.

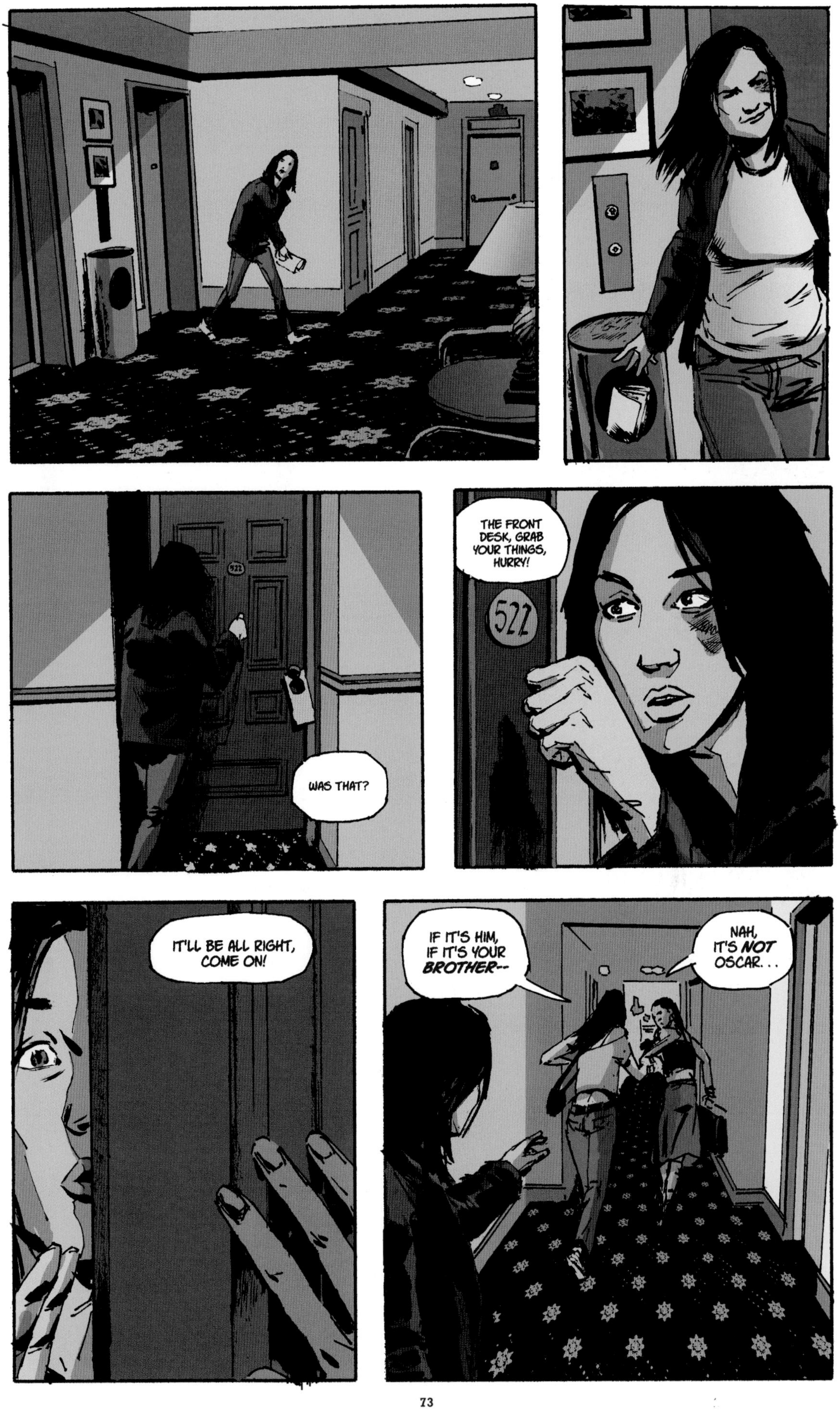
WAS THAT?
THE FRONT DESK, GRAB YOUR THINGS, HURRY!
IT'LL BE ALL RIGHT, COME ON!
IF IT'S HIM, IF IT'S YOUR *BROTHER--*
NAH, IT'S *NOT* OSCAR...

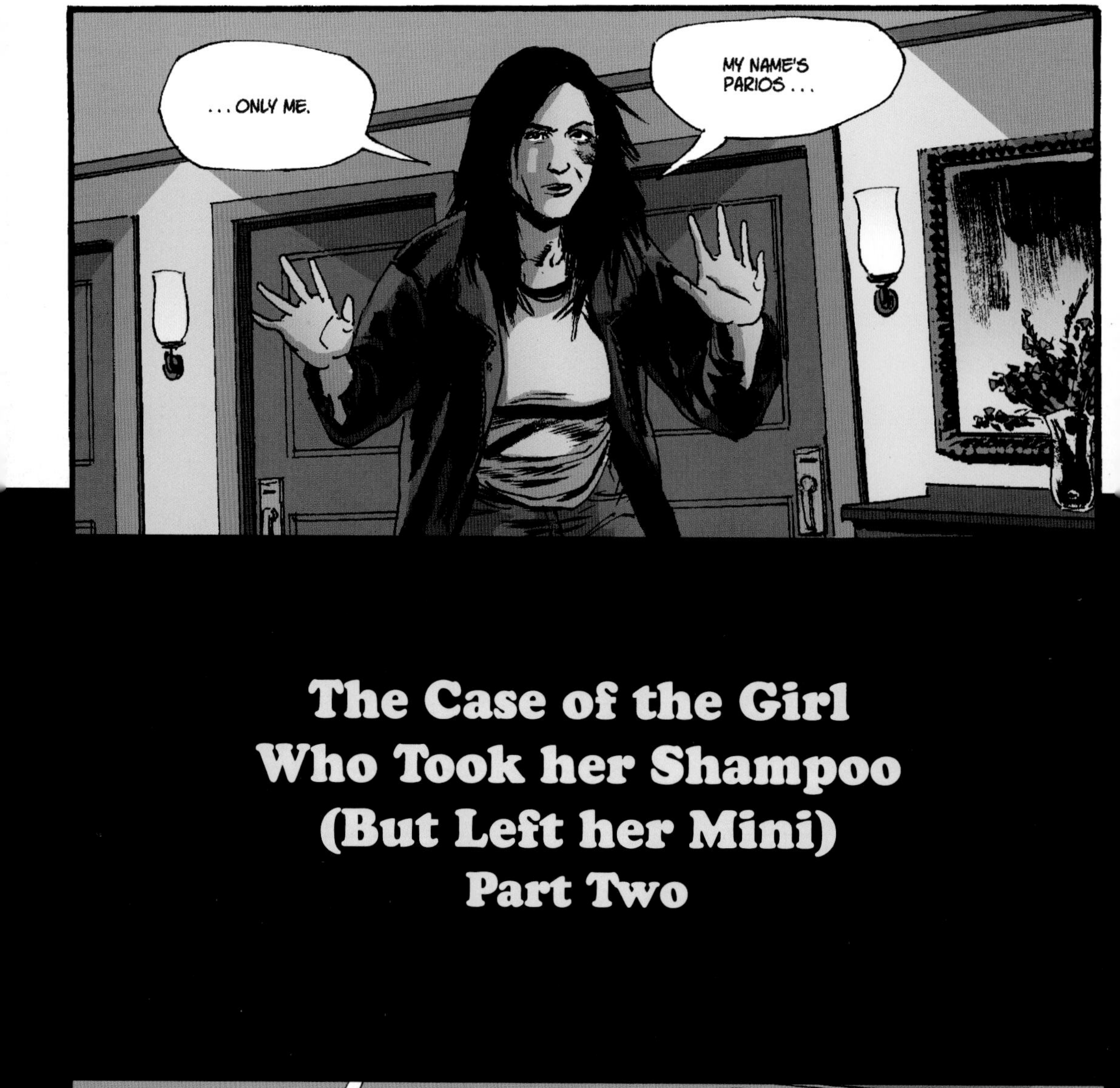
. . . ONLY ME.
MY NAME'S PARIOS . . .

The Case of the Girl Who Took her Shampoo (But Left her Mini) Part Two

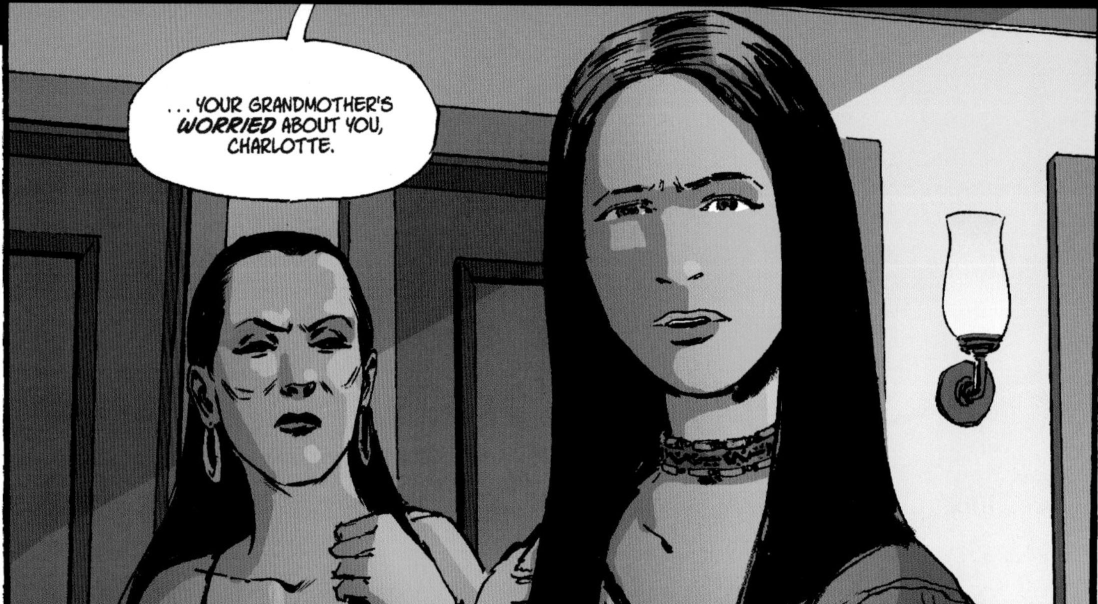
. . . YOUR GRANDMOTHER'S *WORRIED* ABOUT YOU, CHARLOTTE.

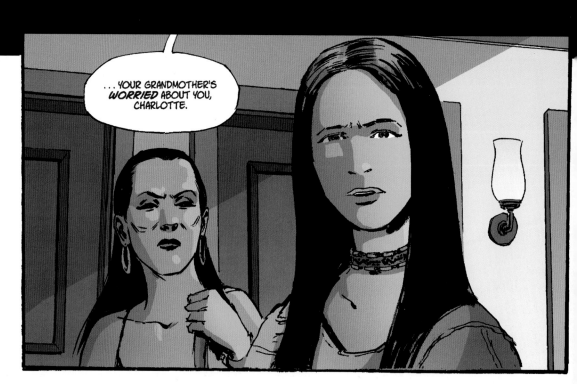

Chapter Three

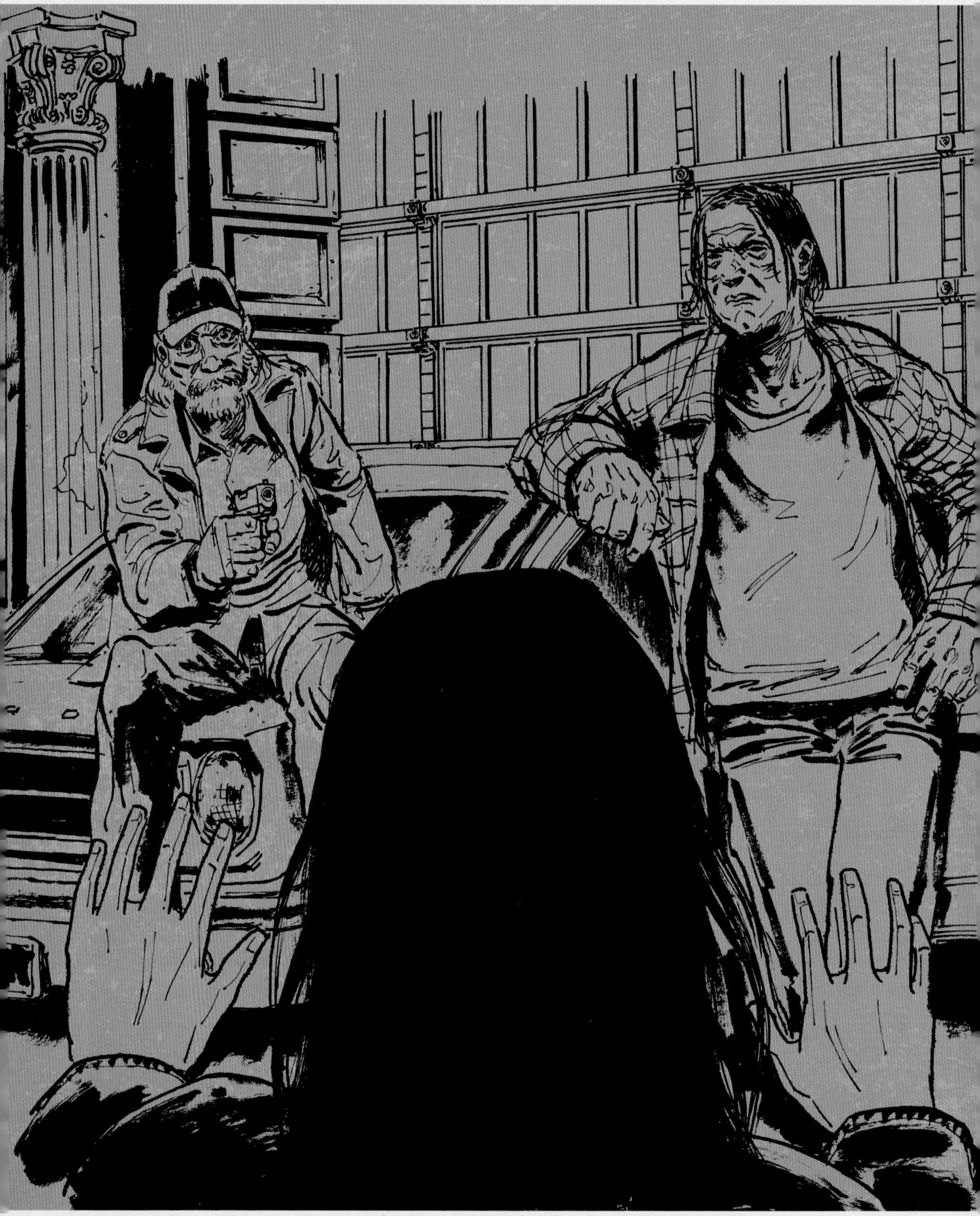

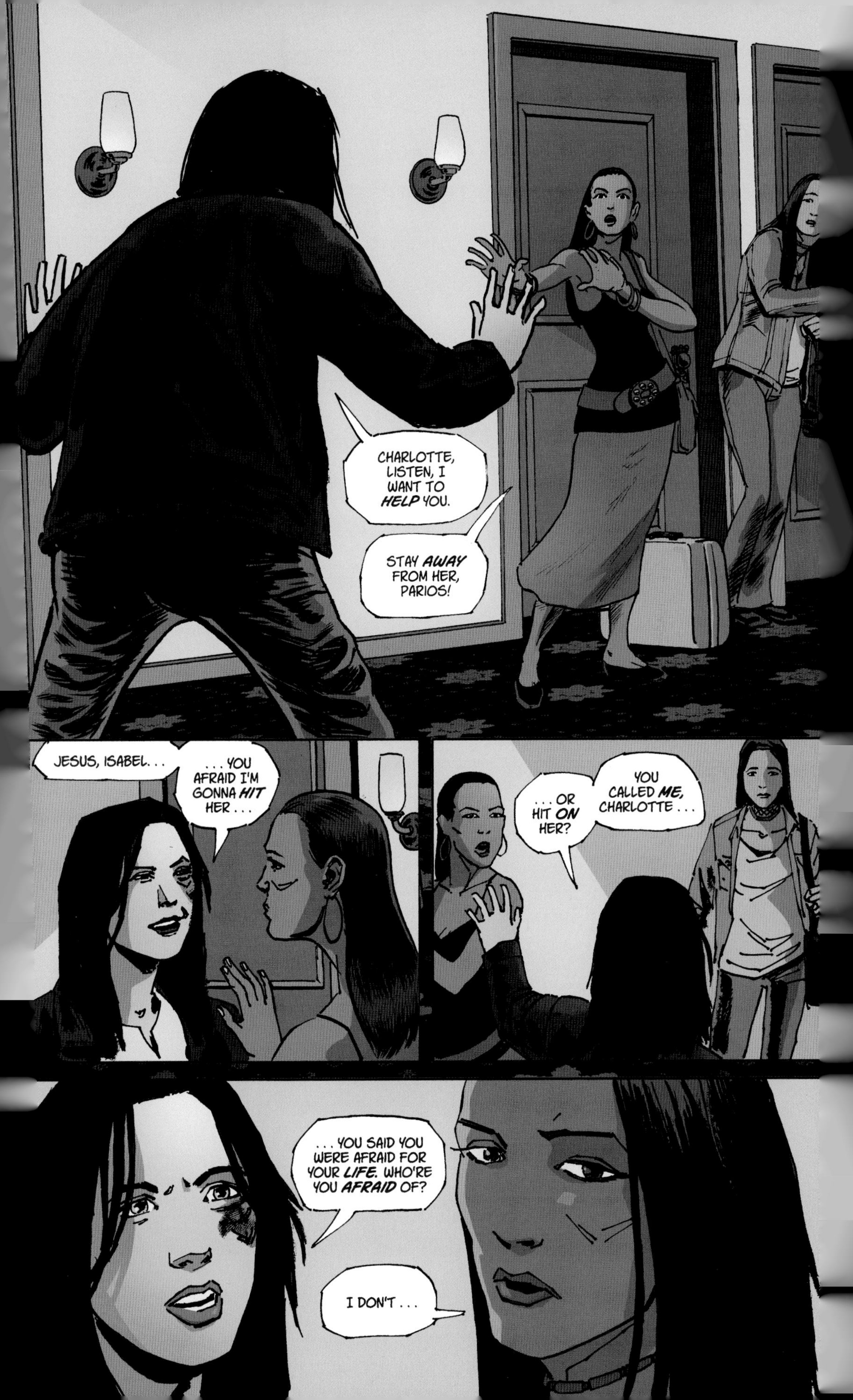
CHARLOTTE, LISTEN, I WANT TO **HELP** YOU.
STAY **AWAY** FROM HER, PARIOS!
JESUS, ISABEL. . .
. . . YOU AFRAID I'M GONNA **HIT** HER . . .
. . . OR HIT **ON** HER?
YOU CALLED **ME,** CHARLOTTE . . .
. . . YOU SAID YOU WERE AFRAID FOR YOUR **LIFE.** WHO'RE YOU **AFRAID** OF?
I DON'T . . .

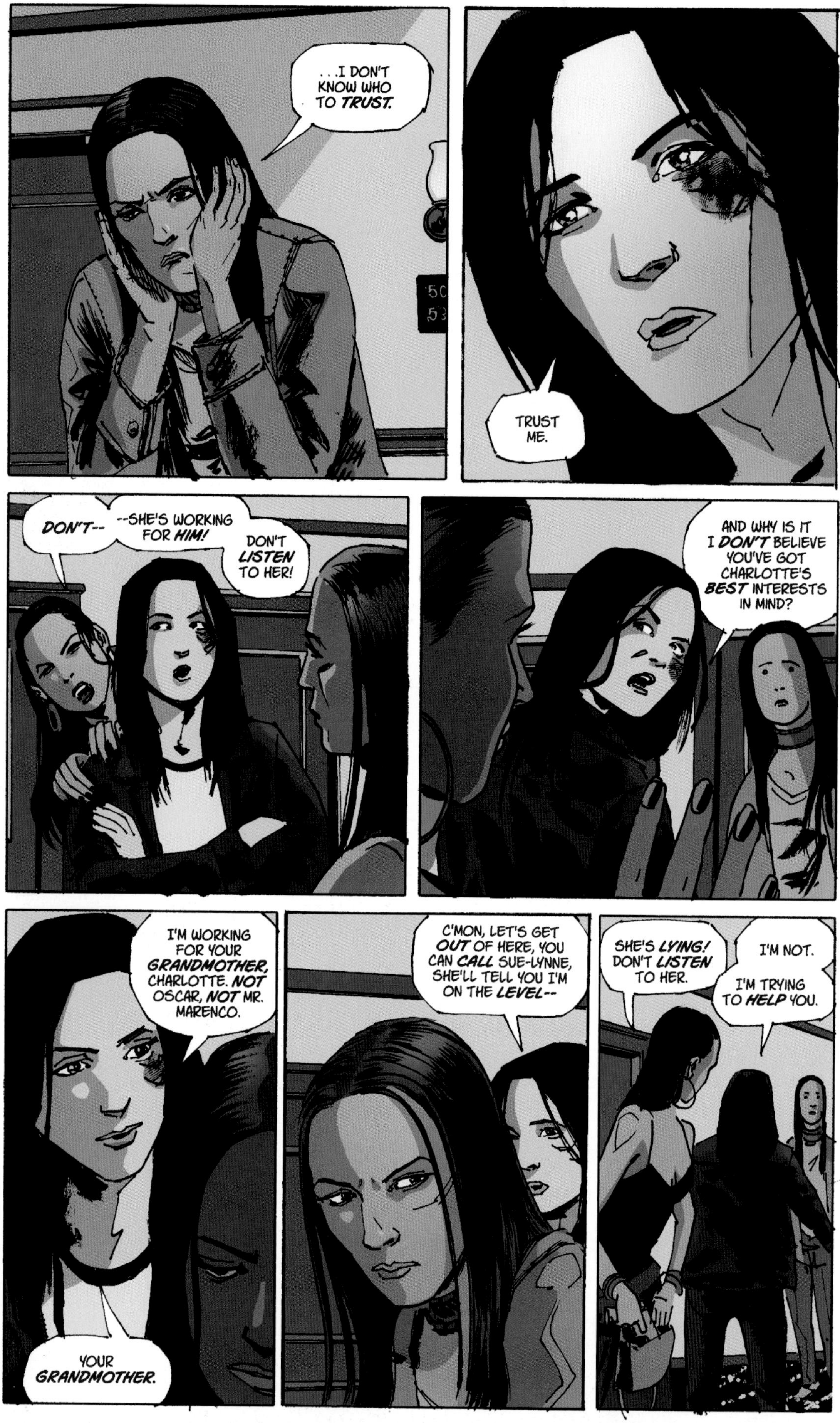

. . .I DON'T KNOW WHO TO TRUST.
TRUST ME.
DON'T--
--SHE'S WORKING FOR HIM!
DON'T LISTEN TO HER!
AND WHY IS IT I DON'T BELIEVE YOU'VE GOT CHARLOTTE'S BEST INTERESTS IN MIND?
I'M WORKING FOR YOUR GRANDMOTHER, CHARLOTTE. NOT OSCAR, NOT MR. MARENCO.
YOUR GRANDMOTHER.
C'MON, LET'S GET OUT OF HERE, YOU CAN CALL SUE-LYNNE, SHE'LL TELL YOU I'M ON THE LEVEL--
SHE'S LYING! DON'T LISTEN TO HER.
I'M NOT.
I'M TRYING TO HELP YOU.

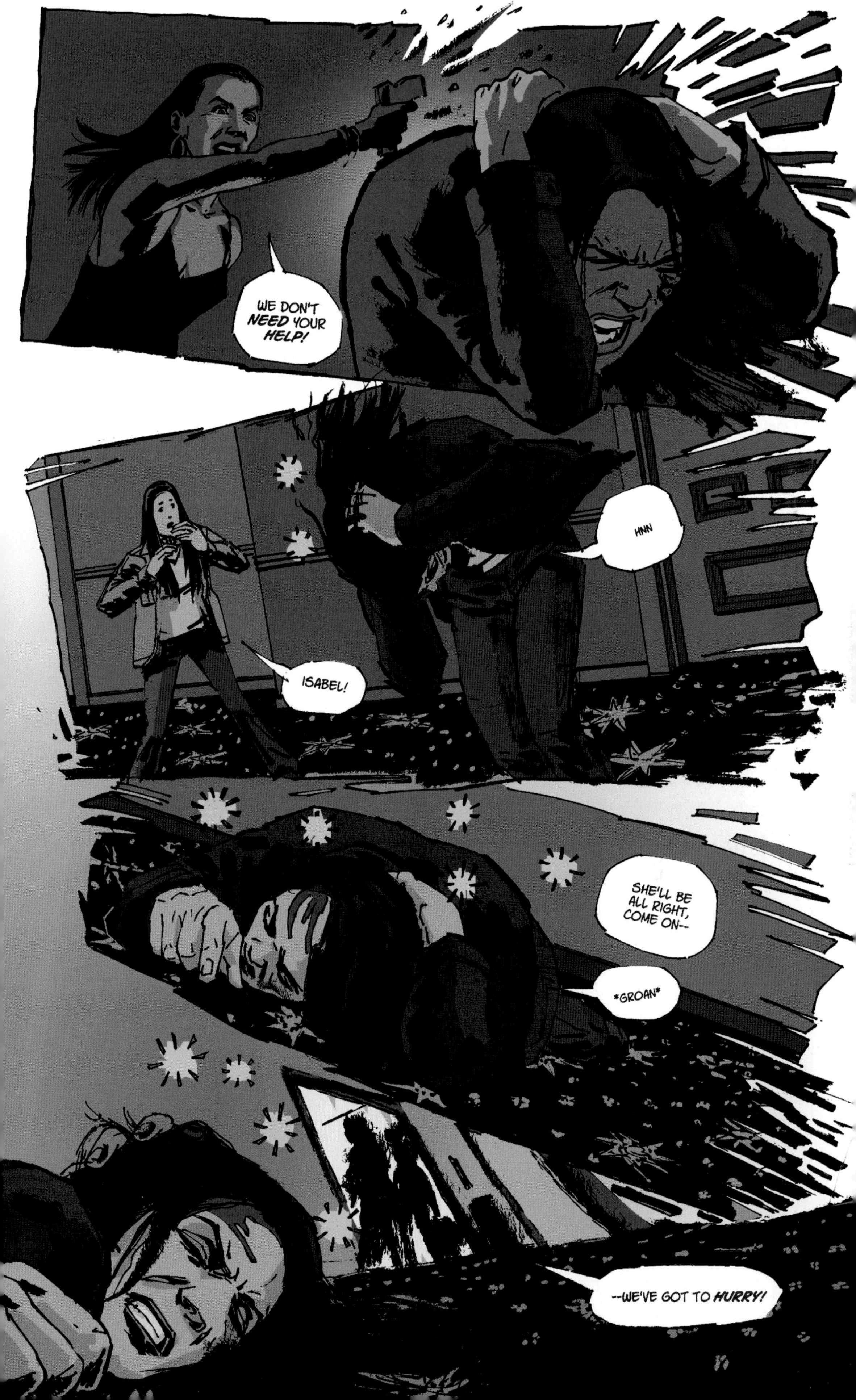
WE DON'T NEED YOUR HELP!
HNN
ISABEL!
SHE'LL BE ALL RIGHT, COME ON--
GROAN
--WE'VE GOT TO HURRY!

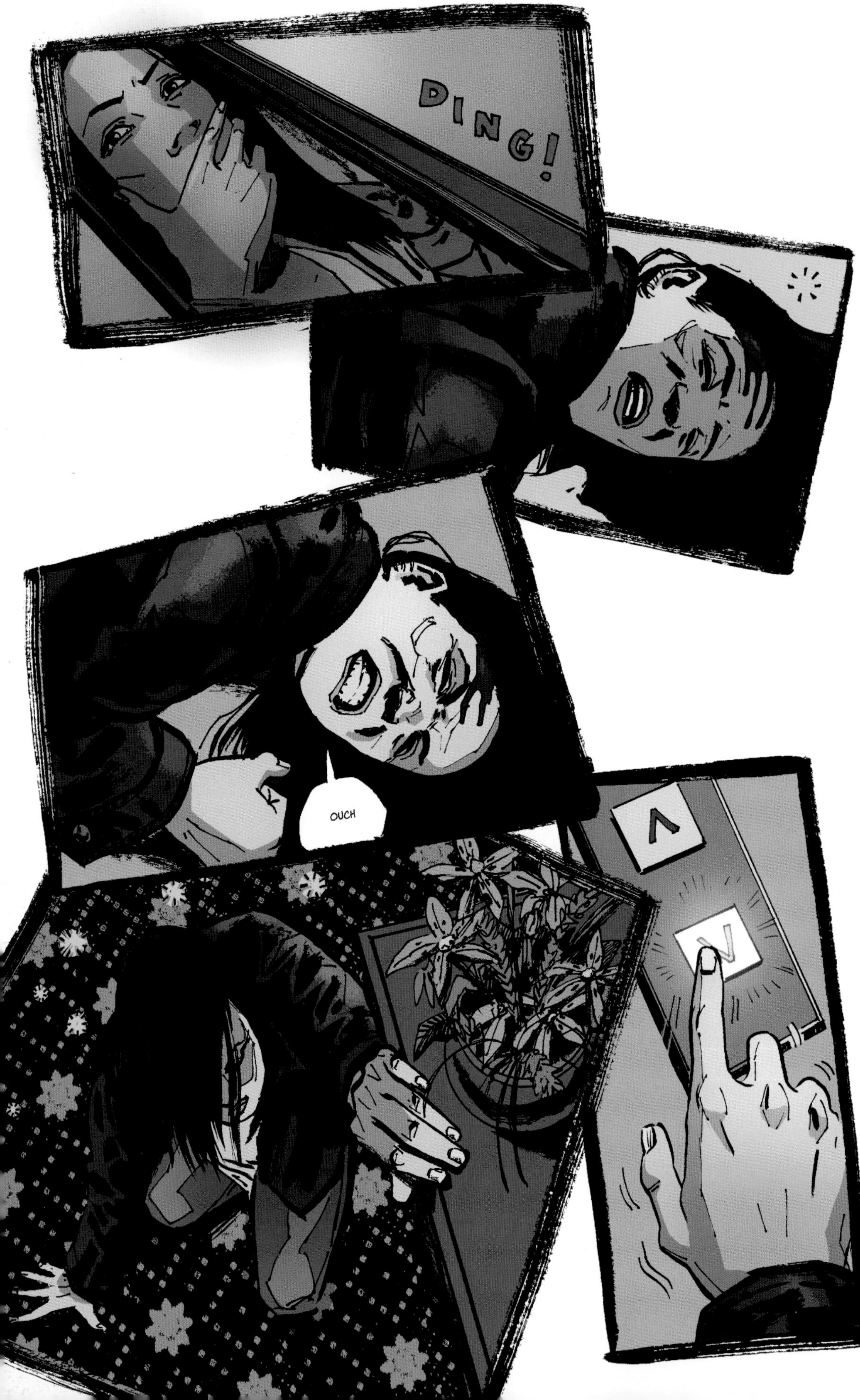
DING!
OUCH

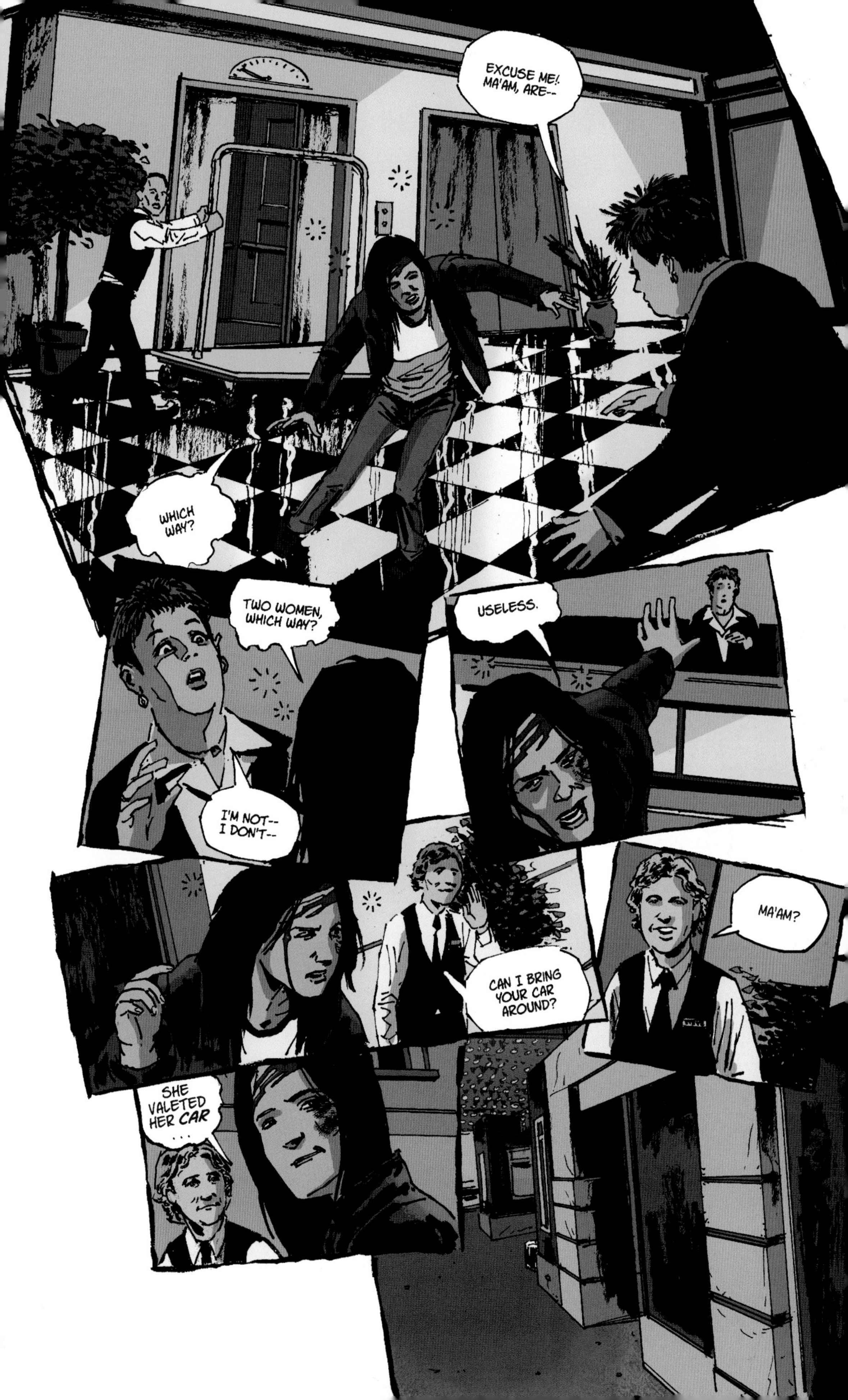
EXCUSE ME!. MA'AM, ARE--
WHICH WAY?
TWO WOMEN, WHICH WAY?
I'M NOT-- I DON'T--
USELESS.
CAN I BRING YOUR CAR AROUND?
MA'AM?
SHE VALETED HER CAR . . .

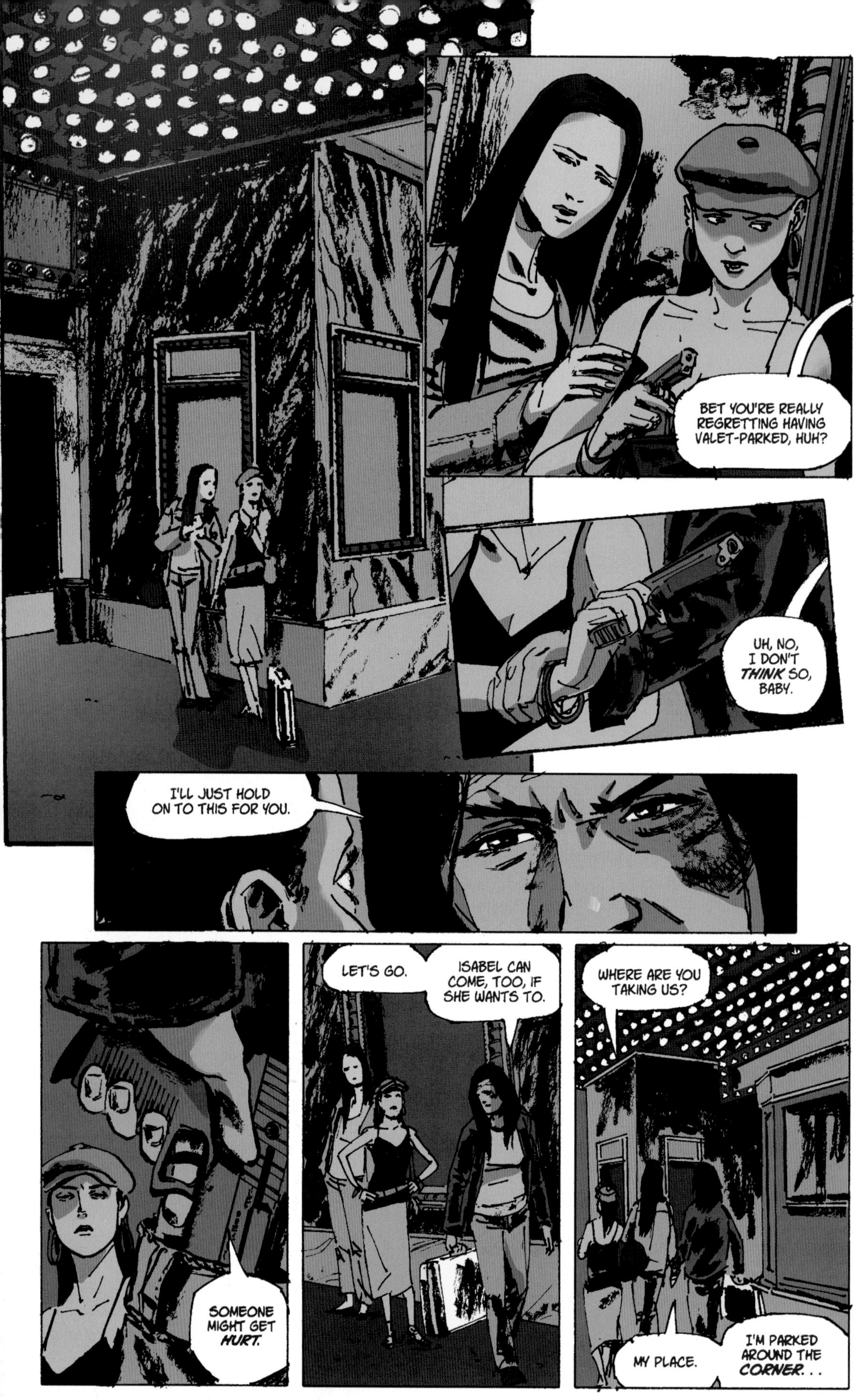
BET YOU'RE REALLY REGRETTING HAVING VALET-PARKED, HUH?
UH, NO, I DON'T *THINK* SO, BABY.
I'LL JUST HOLD ON TO THIS FOR YOU.
SOMEONE MIGHT GET *HURT.*
LET'S GO.
ISABEL CAN COME, TOO, IF SHE WANTS TO.
WHERE ARE YOU TAKING US?
MY PLACE.
I'M PARKED AROUND THE *CORNER*. . .

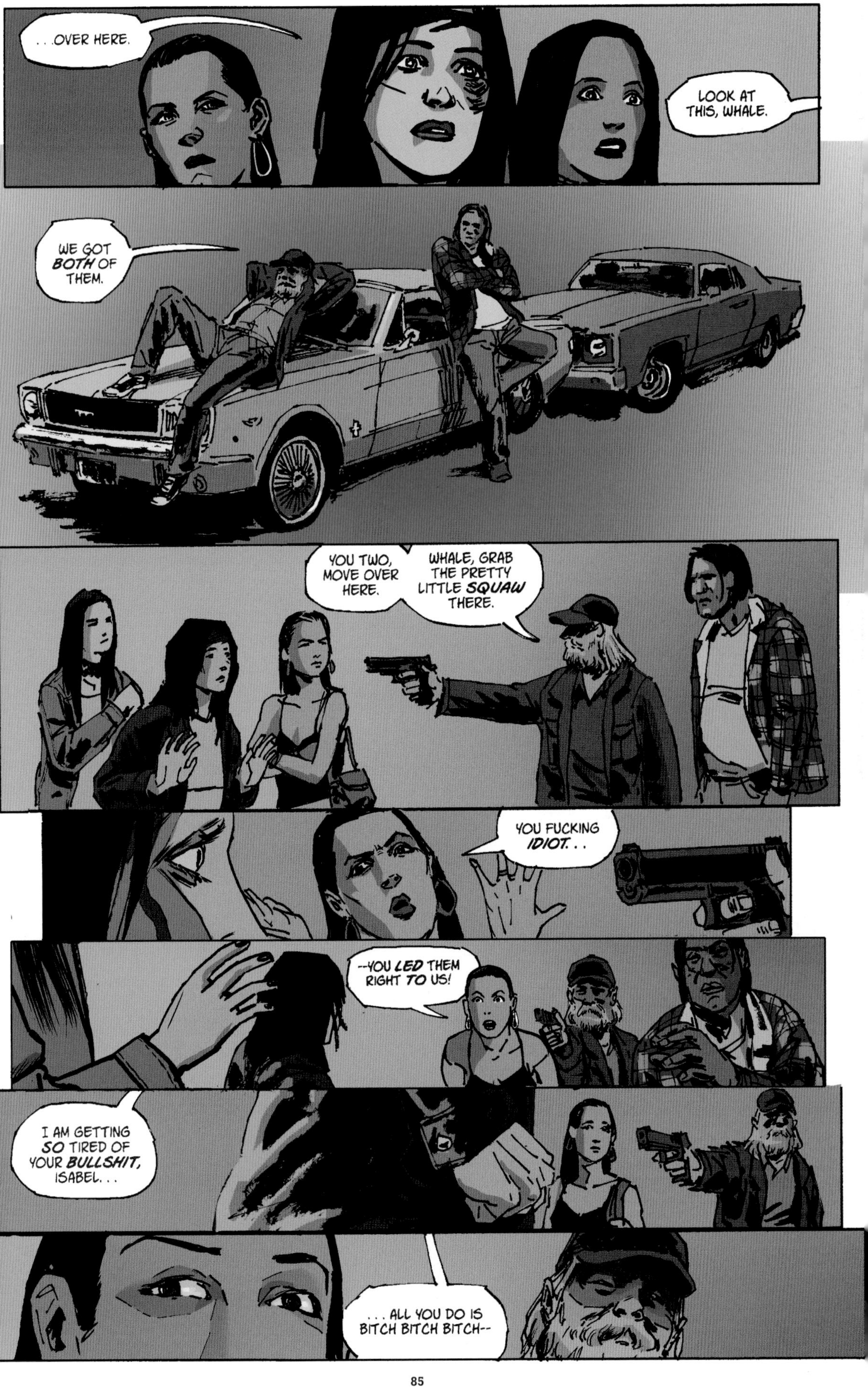
. . .OVER HERE.
LOOK AT THIS, WHALE.
WE GOT *BOTH* OF THEM.
YOU TWO, MOVE OVER HERE.
WHALE, GRAB THE PRETTY LITTLE *SQUAW* THERE.
YOU FUCKING *IDIOT*. . .
--YOU *LED* THEM RIGHT *TO* US!
I AM GETTING *SO* TIRED OF YOUR *BULLSHIT*, ISABEL. . .
. . . ALL YOU DO IS BITCH BITCH BITCH--

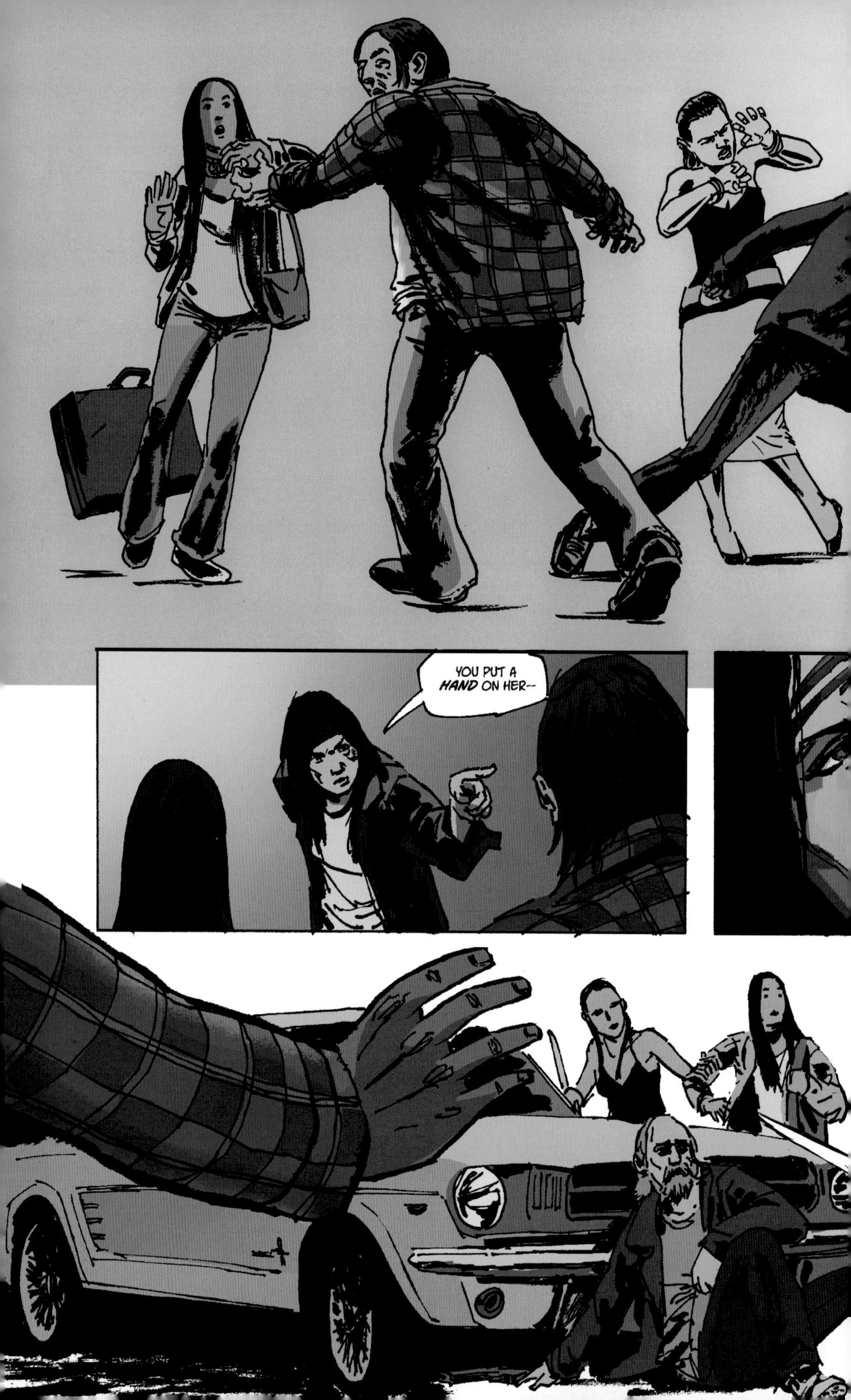
YOU PUT A *HAND* ON HER--

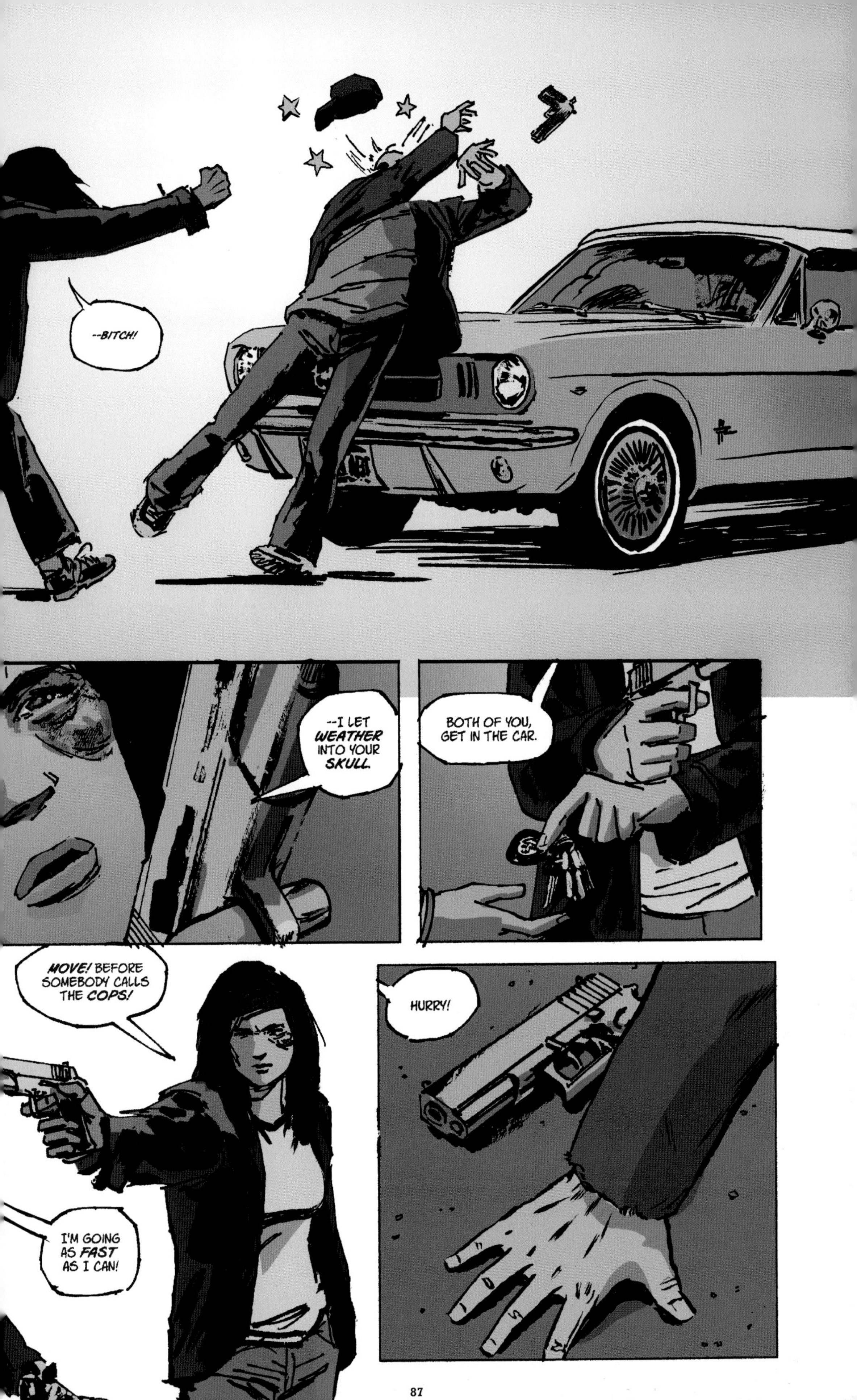
--BITCH!
--I LET WEATHER INTO YOUR SKULL.
BOTH OF YOU, GET IN THE CAR.
MOVE! BEFORE SOMEBODY CALLS THE COPS!
HURRY!
I'M GOING AS FAST AS I CAN!

OH, *PLEASE* GO FOR IT.

I ACTUALLY *WANT* TO SHOOT *YOU*.

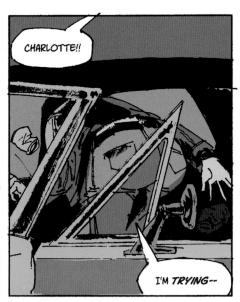

CHARLOTTE!!

I'M *TRYING*--

--THERE'S NO ≤HFF≥ *ROOM!*

YEAH, IT'S KINDA A MESS, I APOLOGIZE.

HOLD ON A SECOND...

...DON'T WANT YOU FOLLOWING US.

CLK

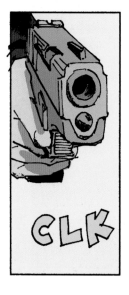

CLK

CLK

CLK

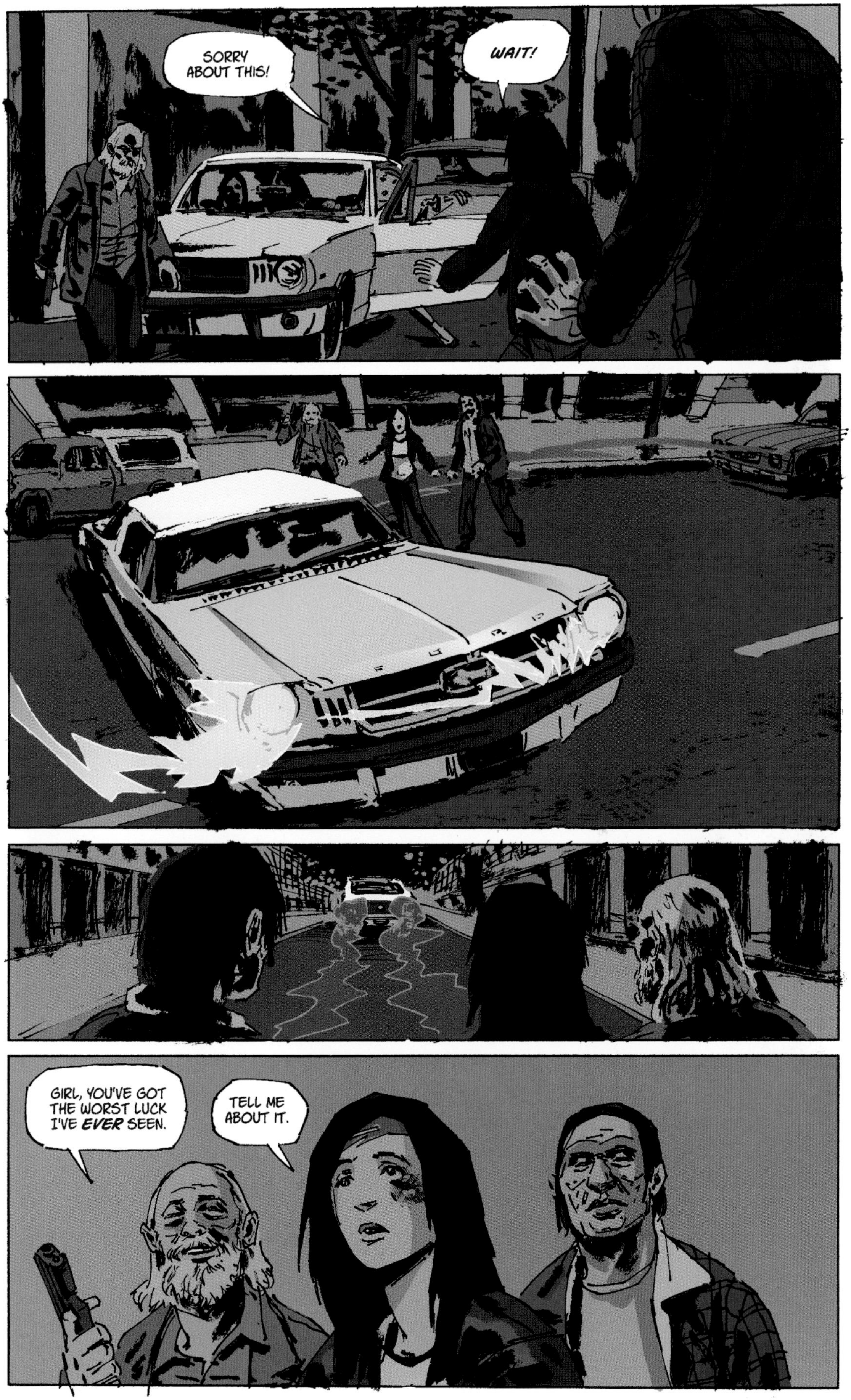
SORRY ABOUT THIS!
WAIT!
GIRL, YOU'VE GOT THE WORST LUCK I'VE EVER SEEN.
TELL ME ABOUT IT.

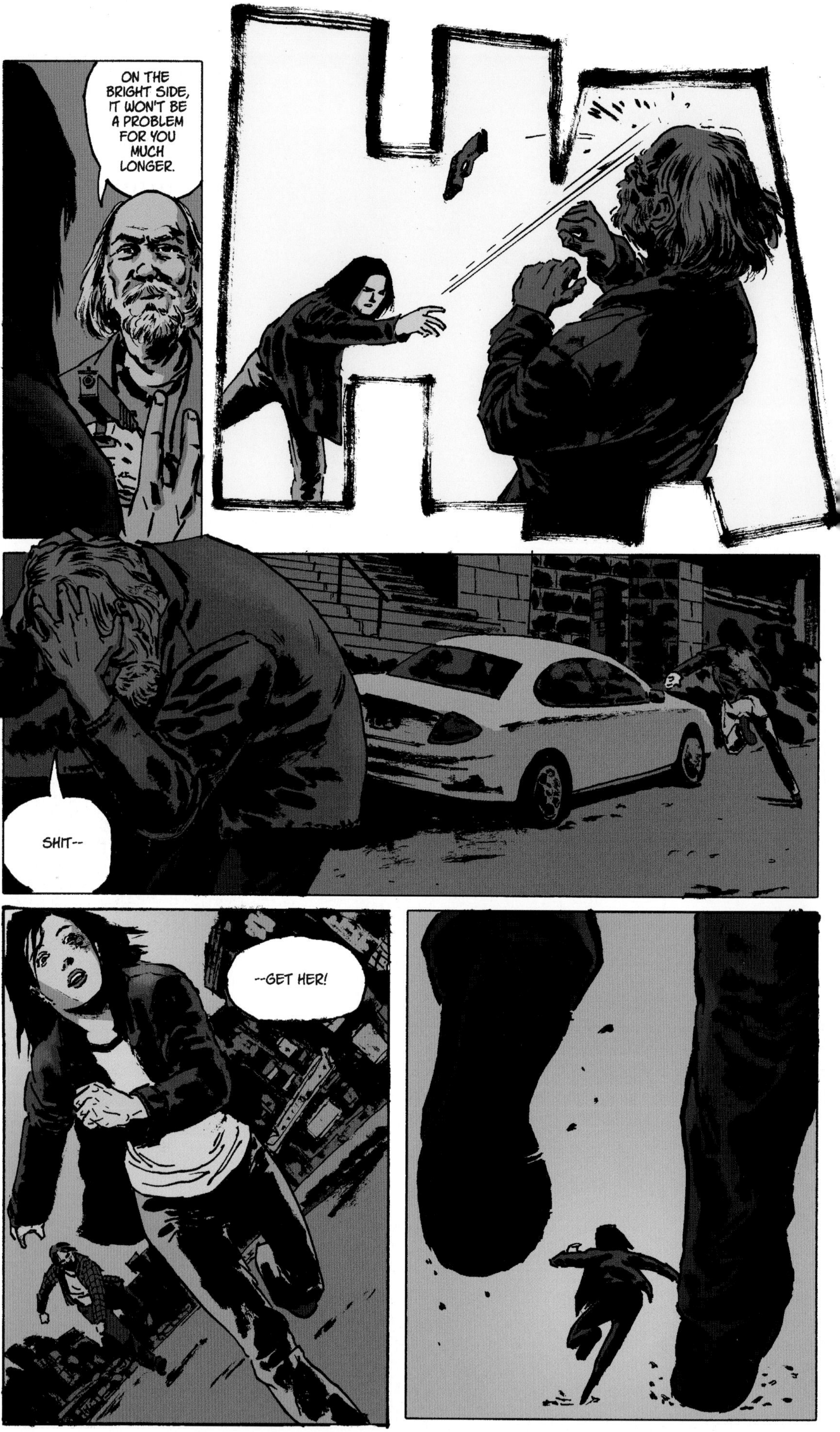

ON THE BRIGHT SIDE, IT WON'T BE A PROBLEM FOR YOU MUCH LONGER.
SHIT--
--GET HER!

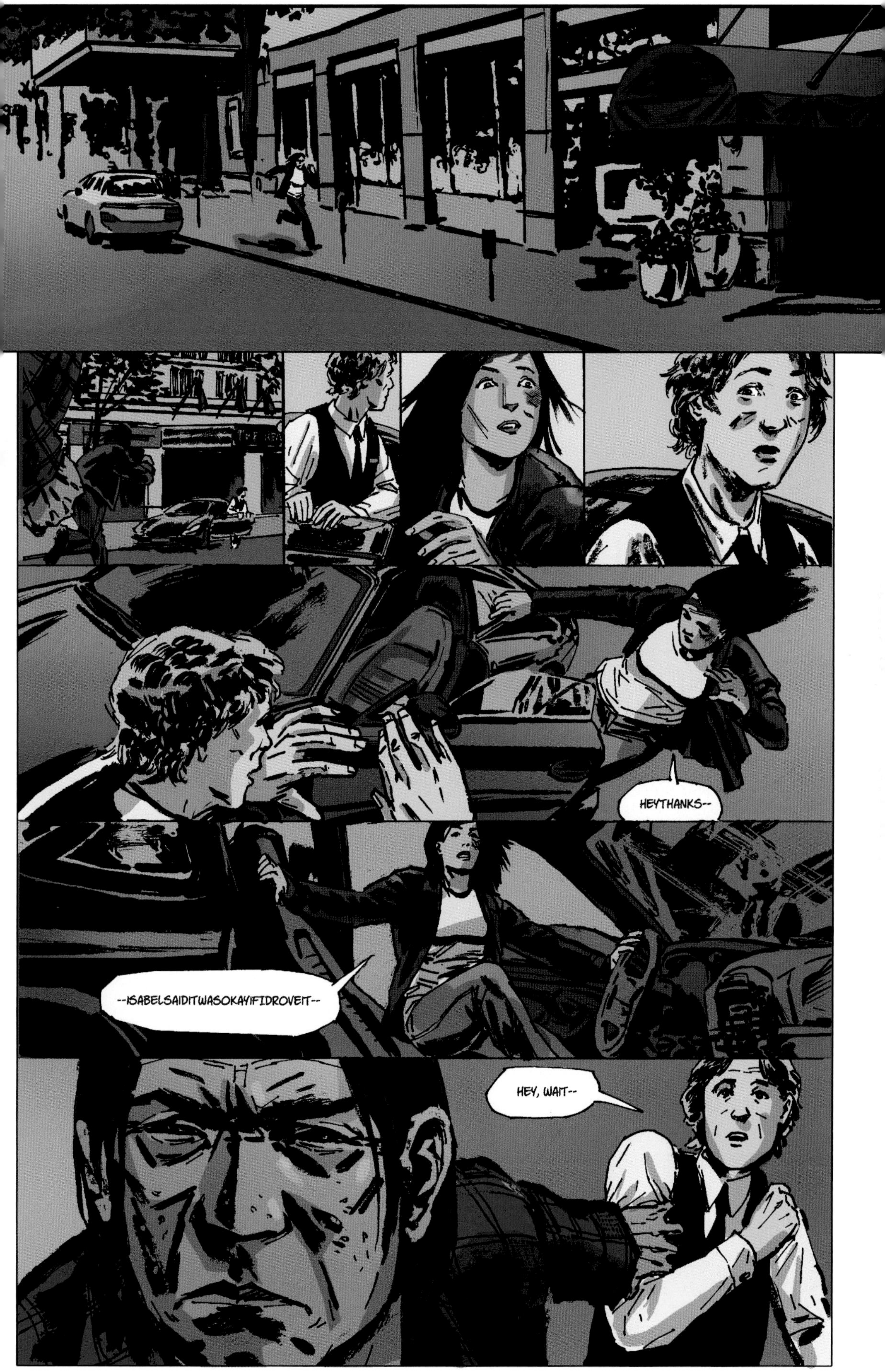
HEYTHANKS--
--ISABELSAIDITWASOKAYIFIDROVEIT--
HEY, WAIT--

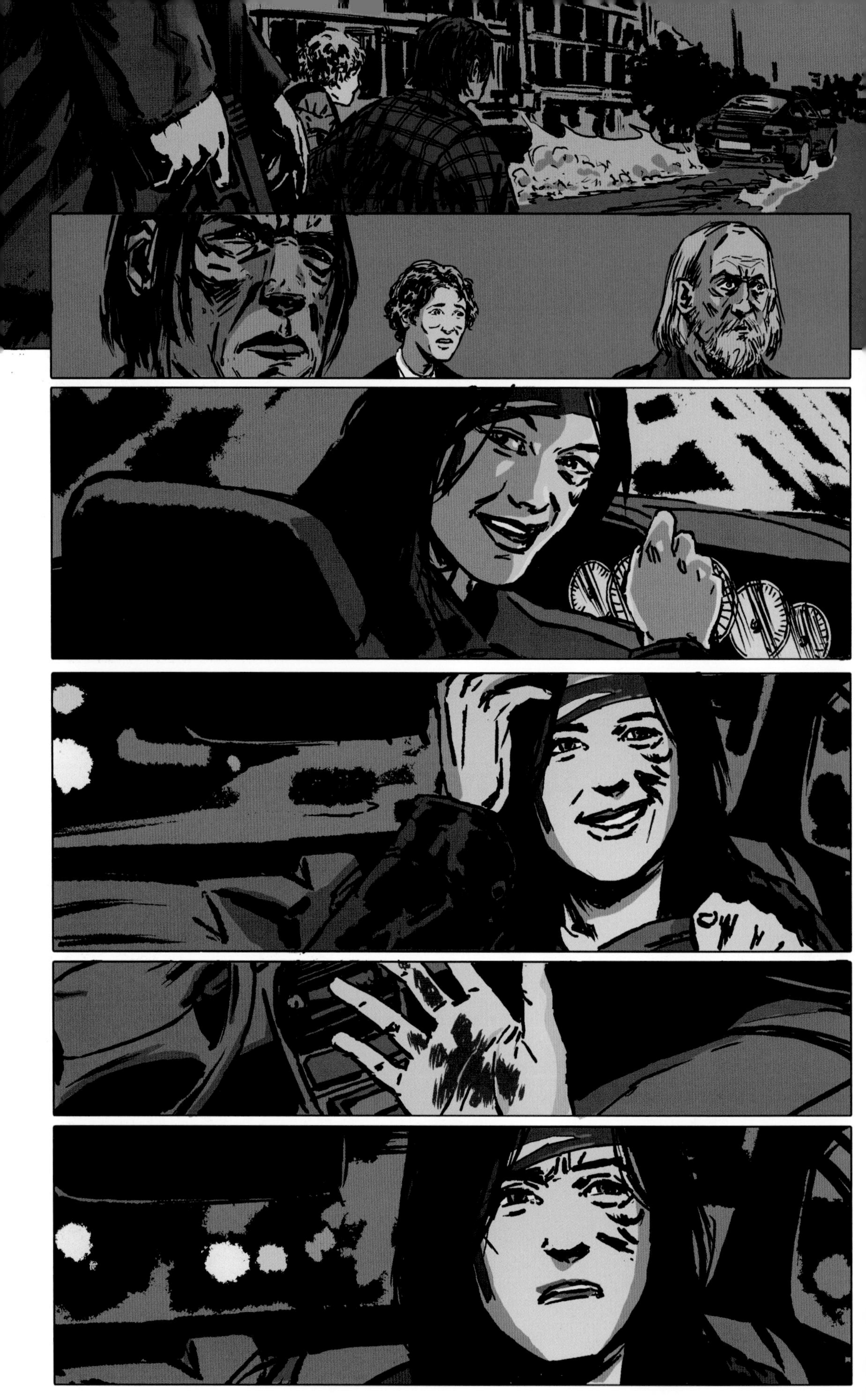

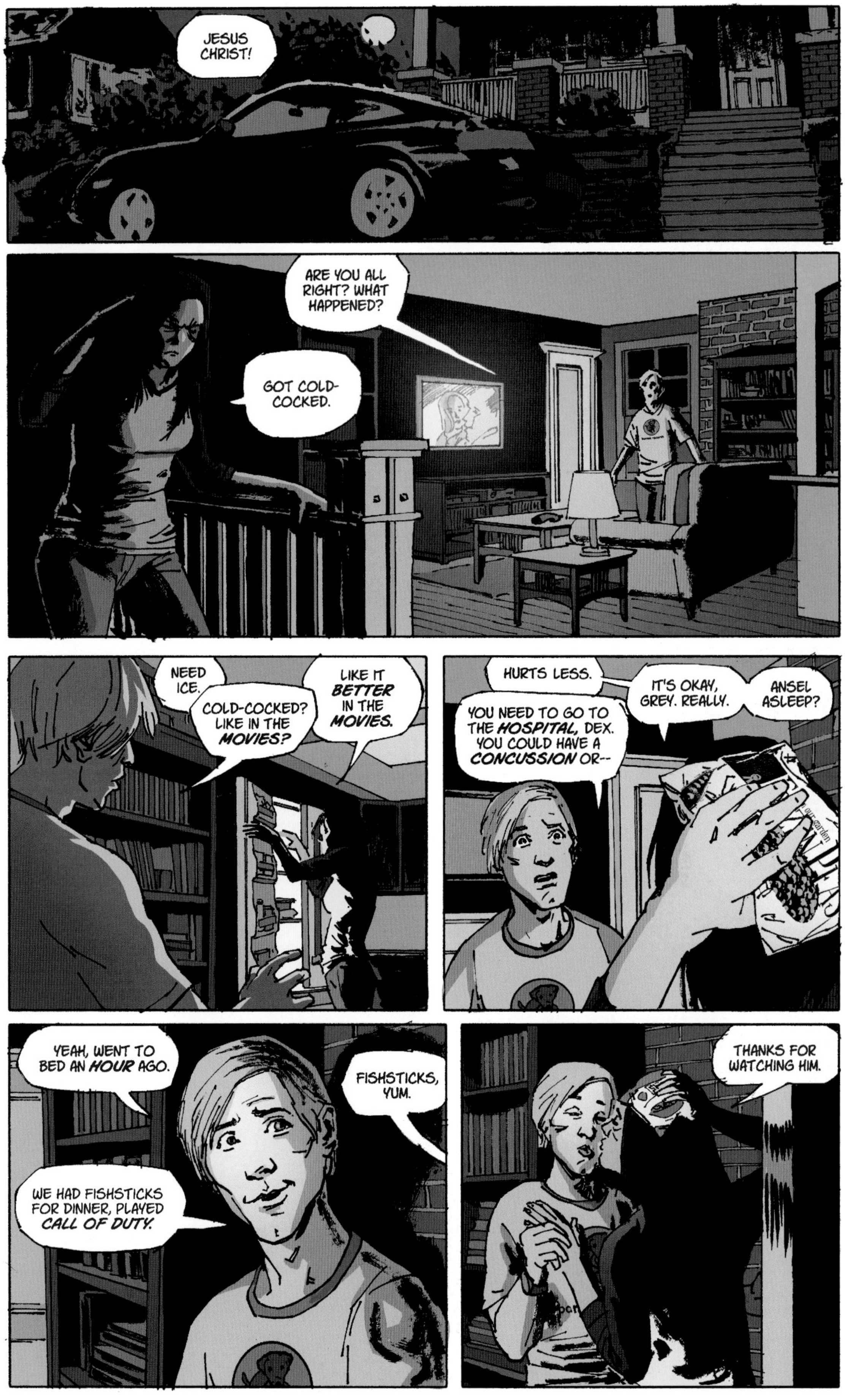
JESUS CHRIST!
ARE YOU ALL RIGHT? WHAT HAPPENED?
GOT COLD-COCKED.
NEED ICE.
COLD-COCKED? LIKE IN THE MOVIES?
LIKE IT BETTER IN THE MOVIES.
HURTS LESS.
YOU NEED TO GO TO THE HOSPITAL, DEX. YOU COULD HAVE A CONCUSSION OR--
IT'S OKAY, GREY. REALLY.
ANSEL ASLEEP?
YEAH, WENT TO BED AN HOUR AGO.
WE HAD FISHSTICKS FOR DINNER, PLAYED CALL OF DUTY.
FISHSTICKS, YUM.
THANKS FOR WATCHING HIM.

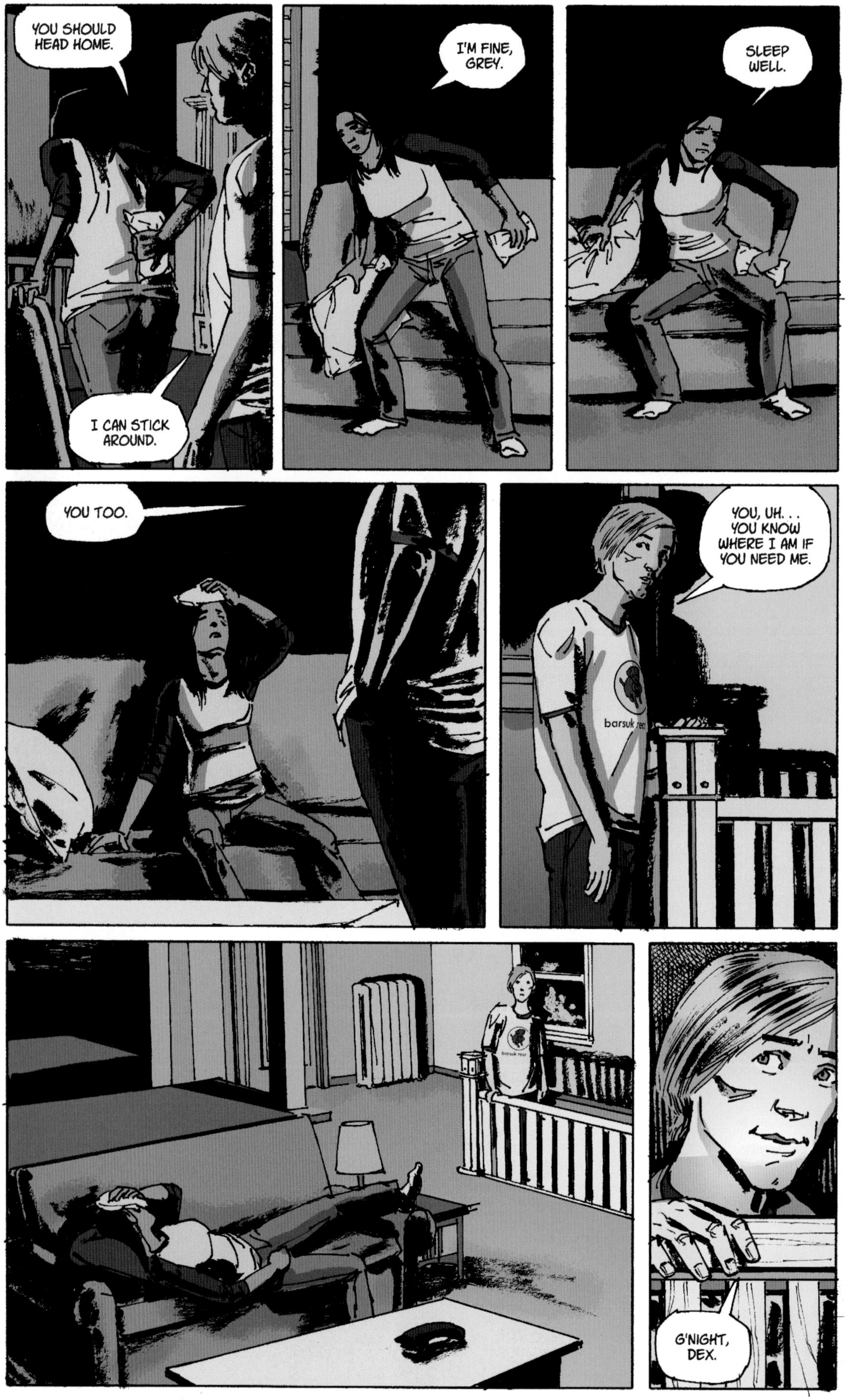
YOU SHOULD HEAD HOME.
I CAN STICK AROUND.
I'M FINE, GREY.
SLEEP WELL.
YOU TOO.
YOU, UH. . . YOU KNOW WHERE I AM IF YOU NEED ME.
barsuk rec
barsuk recr
G'NIGHT, DEX.

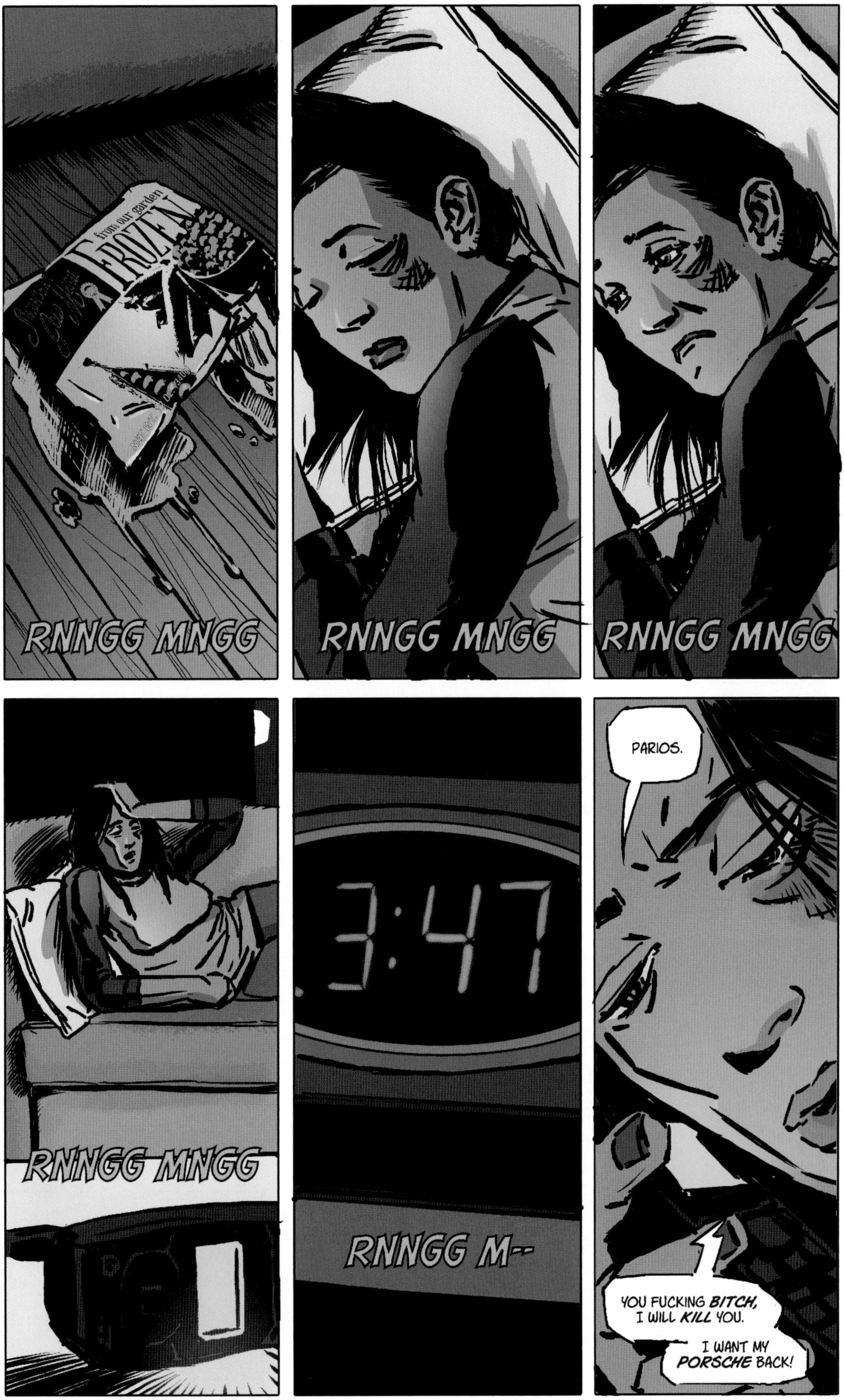

RNNGG MNGG
RNNGG MNGG
RNNGG MNGG
RNNGG MNGG
3:47
RNNGG M--
PARIOS.
YOU FUCKING BITCH, I WILL KILL YOU.
I WANT MY PORSCHE BACK!

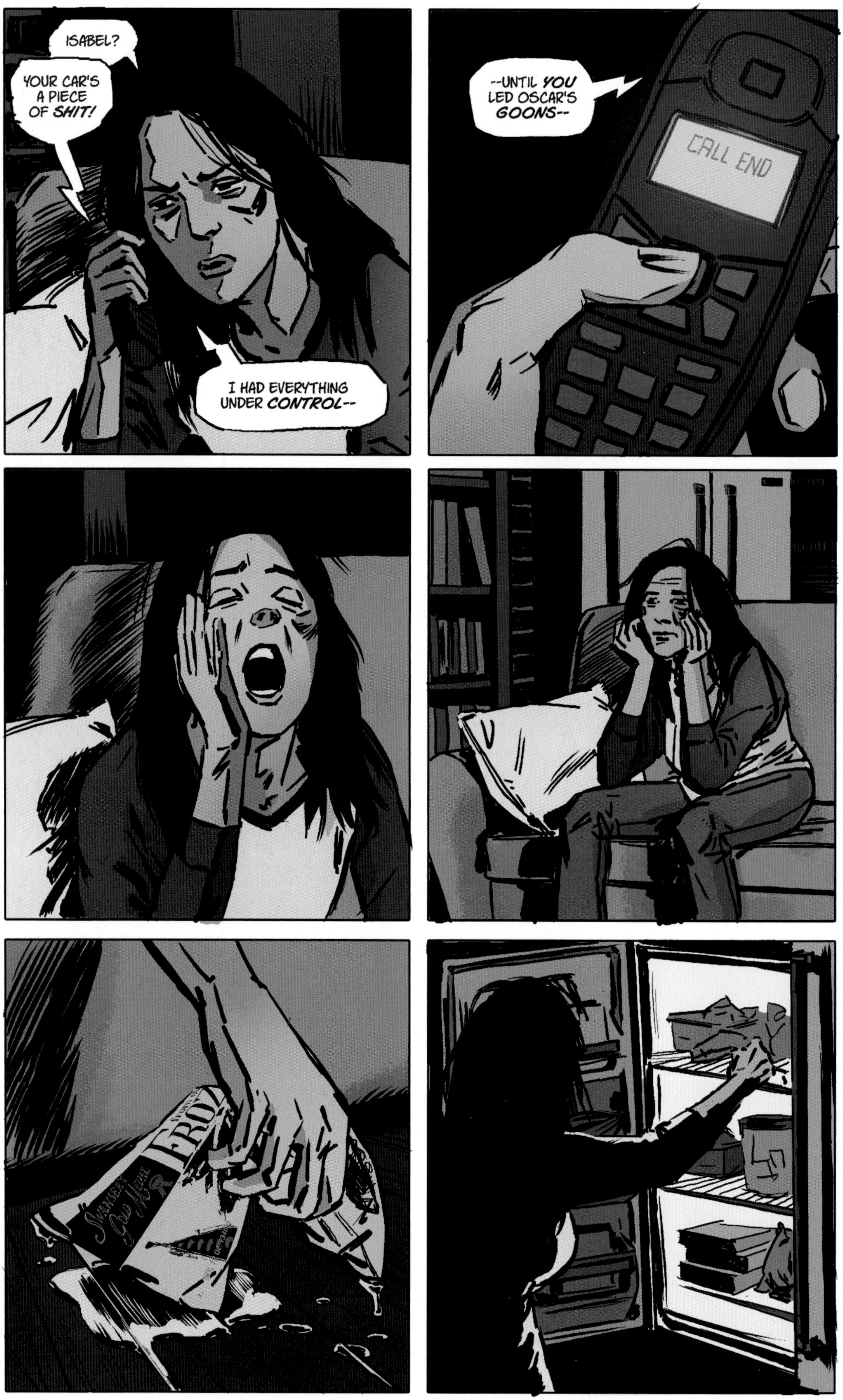
ISABEL?
YOUR CAR'S A PIECE OF SHIT!
I HAD EVERYTHING UNDER CONTROL--
--UNTIL YOU LED OSCAR'S GOONS--
CALL END

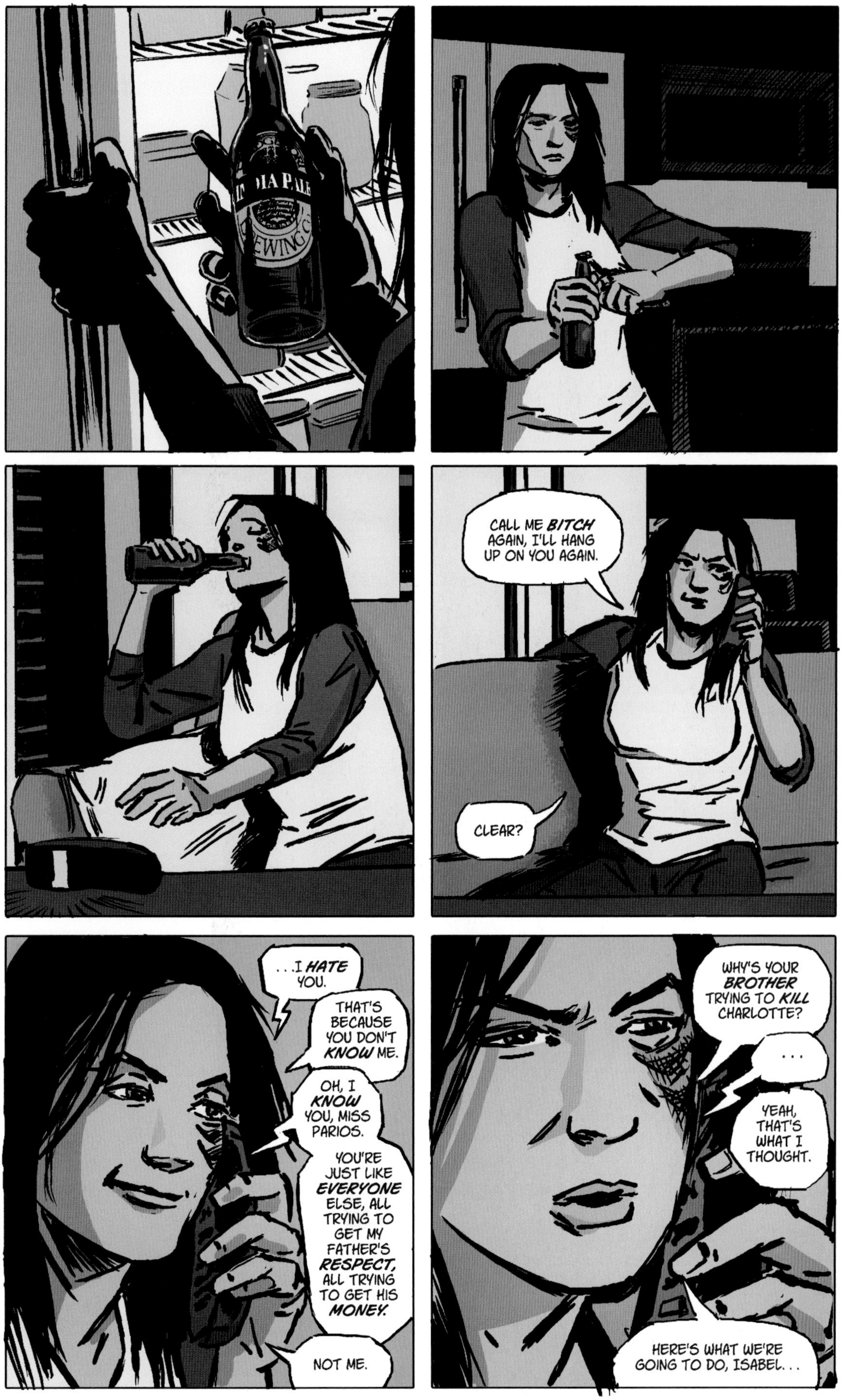
CALL ME BITCH AGAIN, I'LL HANG UP ON YOU AGAIN.
CLEAR?
. . . I HATE YOU.
THAT'S BECAUSE YOU DON'T KNOW ME.
OH, I KNOW YOU, MISS PARIOS.
YOU'RE JUST LIKE EVERYONE ELSE, ALL TRYING TO GET MY FATHER'S RESPECT, ALL TRYING TO GET HIS MONEY.
NOT ME.
WHY'S YOUR BROTHER TRYING TO KILL CHARLOTTE?
. . .
YEAH, THAT'S WHAT I THOUGHT.
HERE'S WHAT WE'RE GOING TO DO, ISABEL. . .

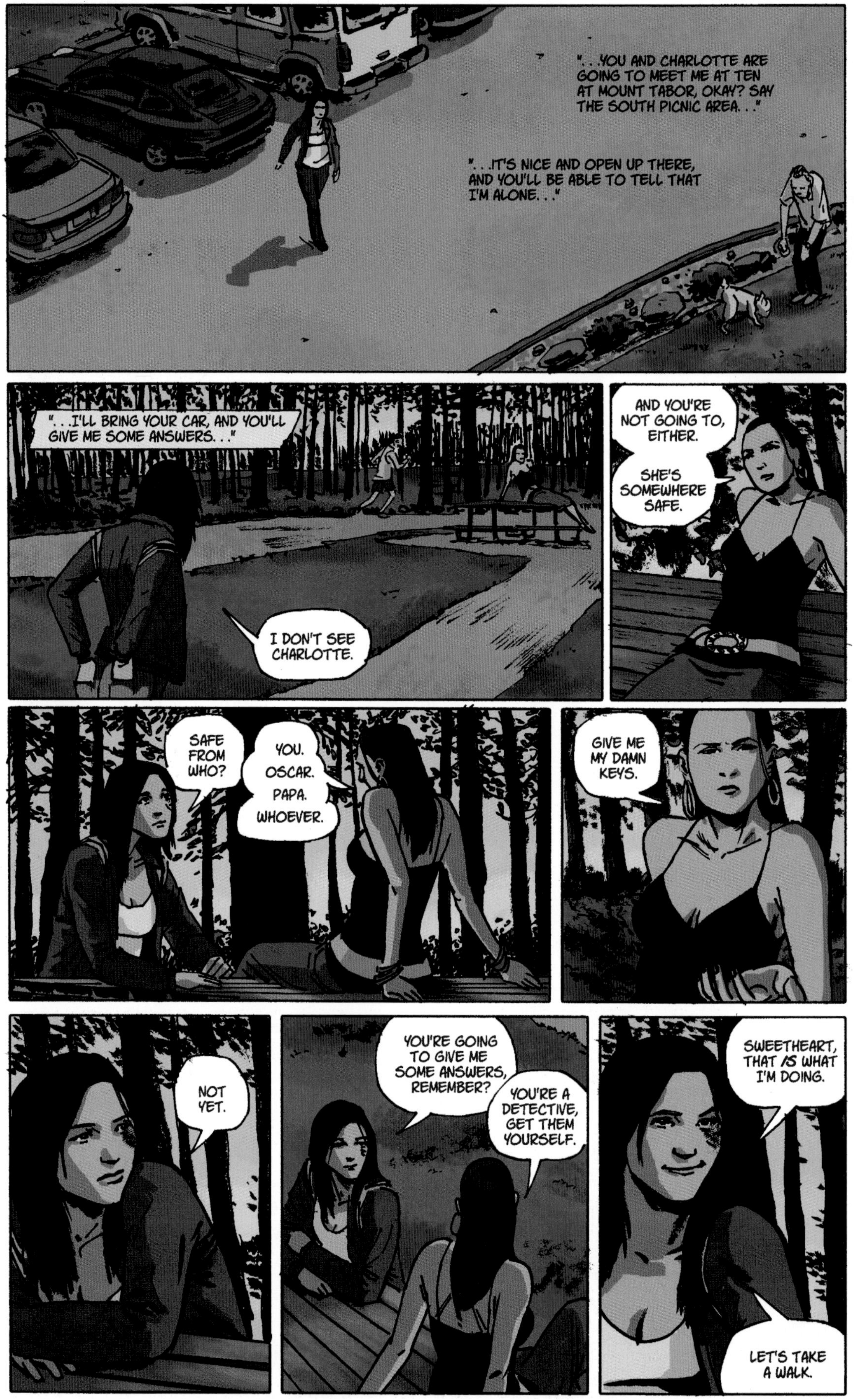
". . .YOU AND CHARLOTTE ARE GOING TO MEET ME AT TEN AT MOUNT TABOR, OKAY? SAY THE SOUTH PICNIC AREA. . ."
". . .IT'S NICE AND OPEN UP THERE, AND YOU'LL BE ABLE TO TELL THAT I'M ALONE. . ."
". . .I'LL BRING YOUR CAR, AND YOU'LL GIVE ME SOME ANSWERS. . ."
I DON'T SEE CHARLOTTE.
AND YOU'RE NOT GOING TO, EITHER.
SHE'S SOMEWHERE SAFE.
SAFE FROM WHO?
YOU. OSCAR. PAPA. WHOEVER.
GIVE ME MY DAMN KEYS.
NOT YET.
YOU'RE GOING TO GIVE ME SOME ANSWERS, REMEMBER?
YOU'RE A DETECTIVE, GET THEM YOURSELF.
SWEETHEART, THAT IS WHAT I'M DOING.
LET'S TAKE A WALK.

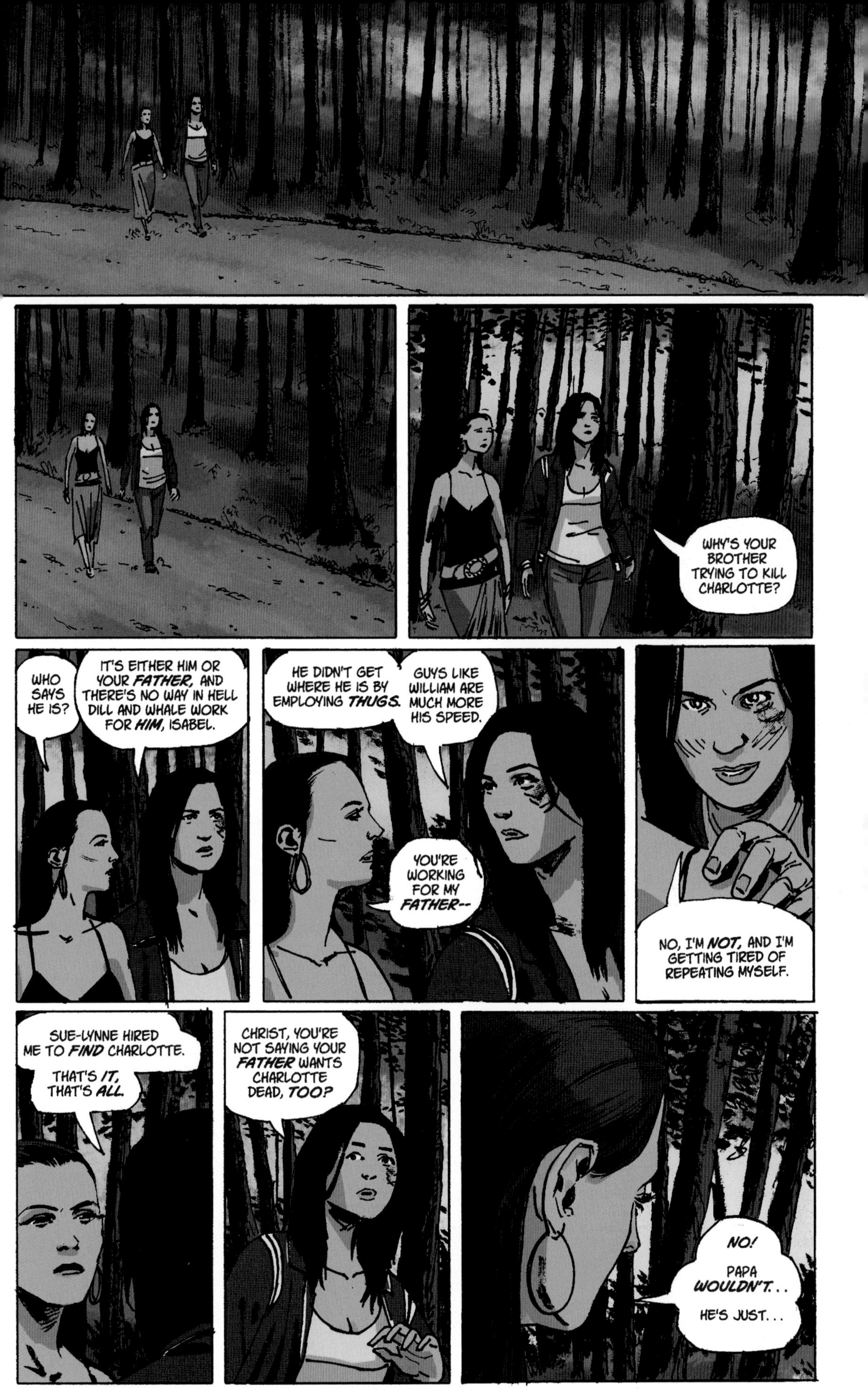
WHY'S YOUR BROTHER TRYING TO KILL CHARLOTTE?
WHO SAYS HE IS?
IT'S EITHER HIM OR YOUR FATHER, AND THERE'S NO WAY IN HELL DILL AND WHALE WORK FOR HIM, ISABEL.
HE DIDN'T GET WHERE HE IS BY EMPLOYING THUGS.
GUYS LIKE WILLIAM ARE MUCH MORE HIS SPEED.
YOU'RE WORKING FOR MY FATHER--
NO, I'M NOT, AND I'M GETTING TIRED OF REPEATING MYSELF.
SUE-LYNNE HIRED ME TO FIND CHARLOTTE.
THAT'S IT, THAT'S ALL.
CHRIST, YOU'RE NOT SAYING YOUR FATHER WANTS CHARLOTTE DEAD, TOO?
NO!
PAPA WOULDN'T. . .
HE'S JUST. . .

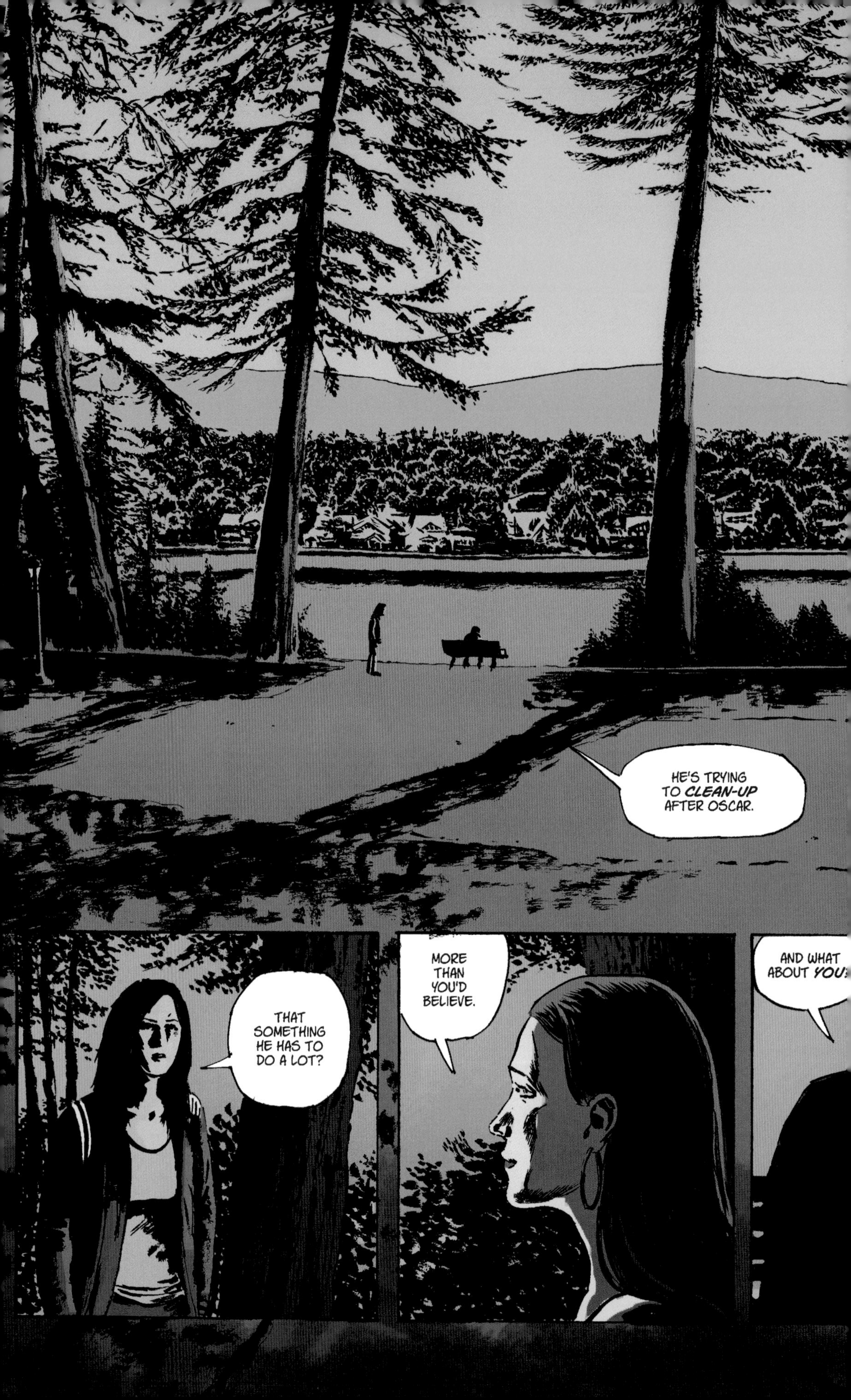
HE'S TRYING TO ***CLEAN-UP*** AFTER OSCAR.
THAT SOMETHING HE HAS TO DO A LOT?
MORE THAN YOU'D BELIEVE.
AND WHAT ABOUT ***YOU***

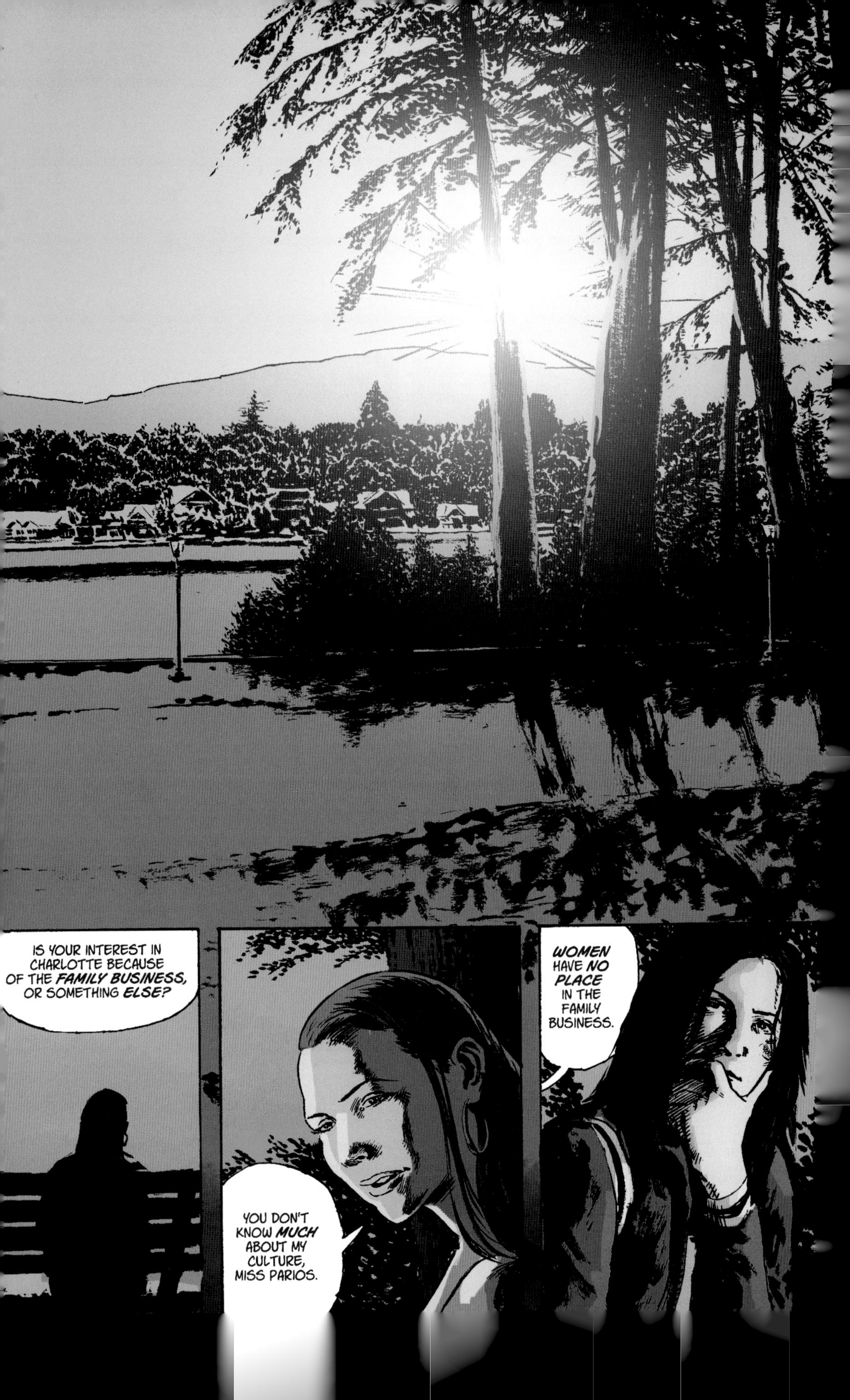
IS YOUR INTEREST IN CHARLOTTE BECAUSE OF THE FAMILY BUSINESS, OR SOMETHING ELSE?
YOU DON'T KNOW MUCH ABOUT MY CULTURE, MISS PARIOS.
WOMEN HAVE NO PLACE IN THE FAMILY BUSINESS.

WHAT DO YOU *MEAN* BY THAT?

THE THING BETWEEN YOU AND CHARLOTTE, IT'S *PERSONAL*--

SO IT'S A *PERSONAL* INVOLVEMENT..

THERE'S NO *"THING"* BETWEEN US. SHE'S MY *FRIEND.*

SURE.

WE'RE FRIENDS, THAT'S *ALL.*

SURE.

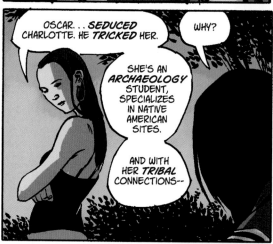

OSCAR... *SEDUCED* CHARLOTTE. HE *TRICKED* HER.

WHY?

SHE'S AN *ARCHAEOLOGY* STUDENT, SPECIALIZES IN NATIVE AMERICAN SITES.

AND WITH HER *TRIBAL* CONNECTIONS--

HE WAS USING HER TO GET AT THE *DIG SITES.*

THEN HE'D *ROB* THE SITES AND *SELL* WHAT HE STOLE.

SHE DIDN'T *KNOW?*

NOT AT FIRST.

AND SHE TOLD *YOU,* AND YOU SAW A WAY TO *SCREW* YOUR BROTHER OVER.

NICE WAY TO HELP A *FRIEND,* ISABEL.

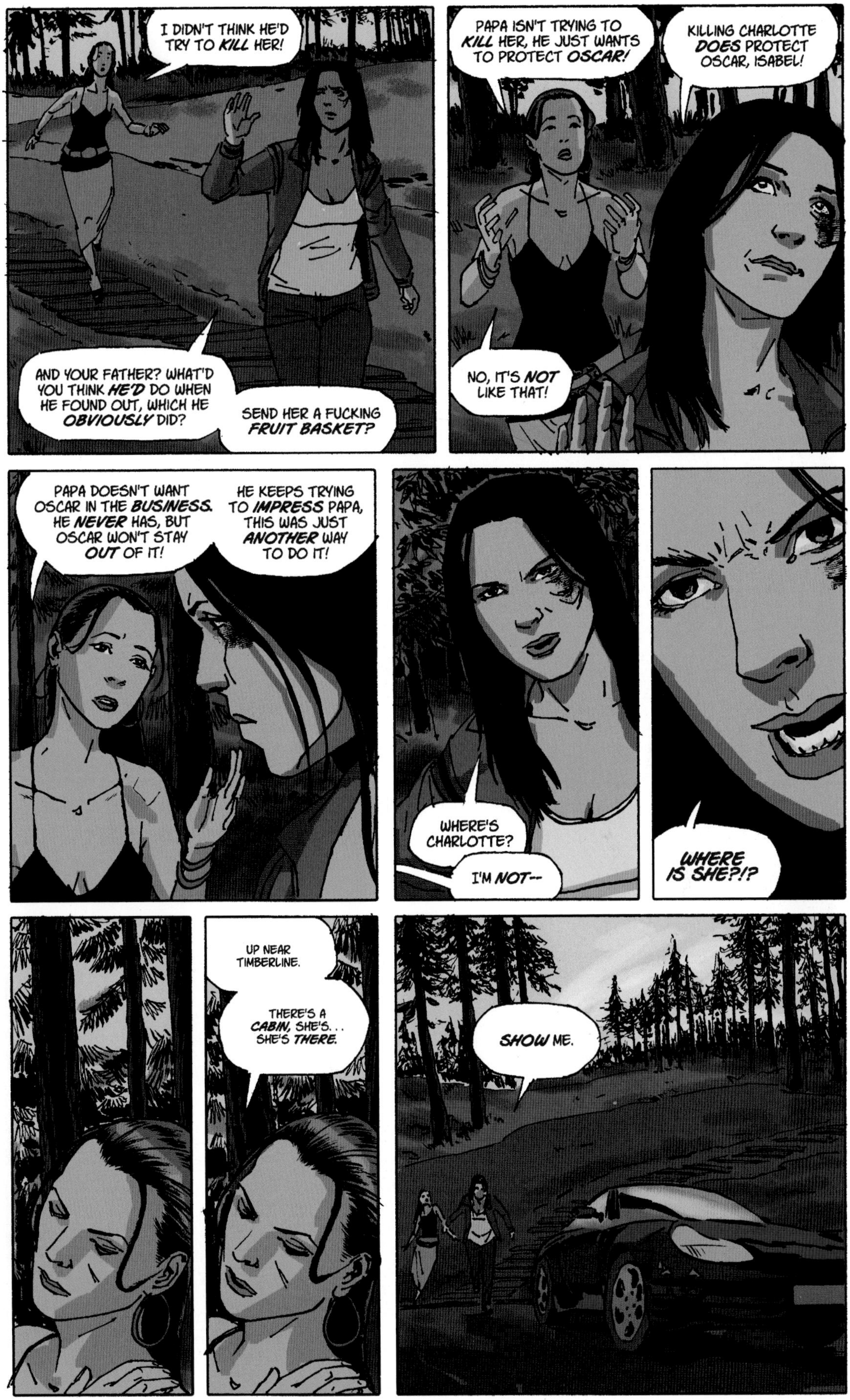
I DIDN'T THINK HE'D TRY TO KILL HER!
AND YOUR FATHER? WHAT'D YOU THINK HE'D DO WHEN HE FOUND OUT, WHICH HE OBVIOUSLY DID?
SEND HER A FUCKING FRUIT BASKET?
PAPA ISN'T TRYING TO KILL HER, HE JUST WANTS TO PROTECT OSCAR!
KILLING CHARLOTTE DOES PROTECT OSCAR, ISABEL!
NO, IT'S NOT LIKE THAT!
PAPA DOESN'T WANT OSCAR IN THE BUSINESS. HE NEVER HAS, BUT OSCAR WON'T STAY OUT OF IT!
HE KEEPS TRYING TO IMPRESS PAPA, THIS WAS JUST ANOTHER WAY TO DO IT!
WHERE'S CHARLOTTE?
I'M NOT--
WHERE IS SHE?!?
UP NEAR TIMBERLINE.
THERE'S A CABIN, SHE'S... SHE'S THERE.
SHOW ME.

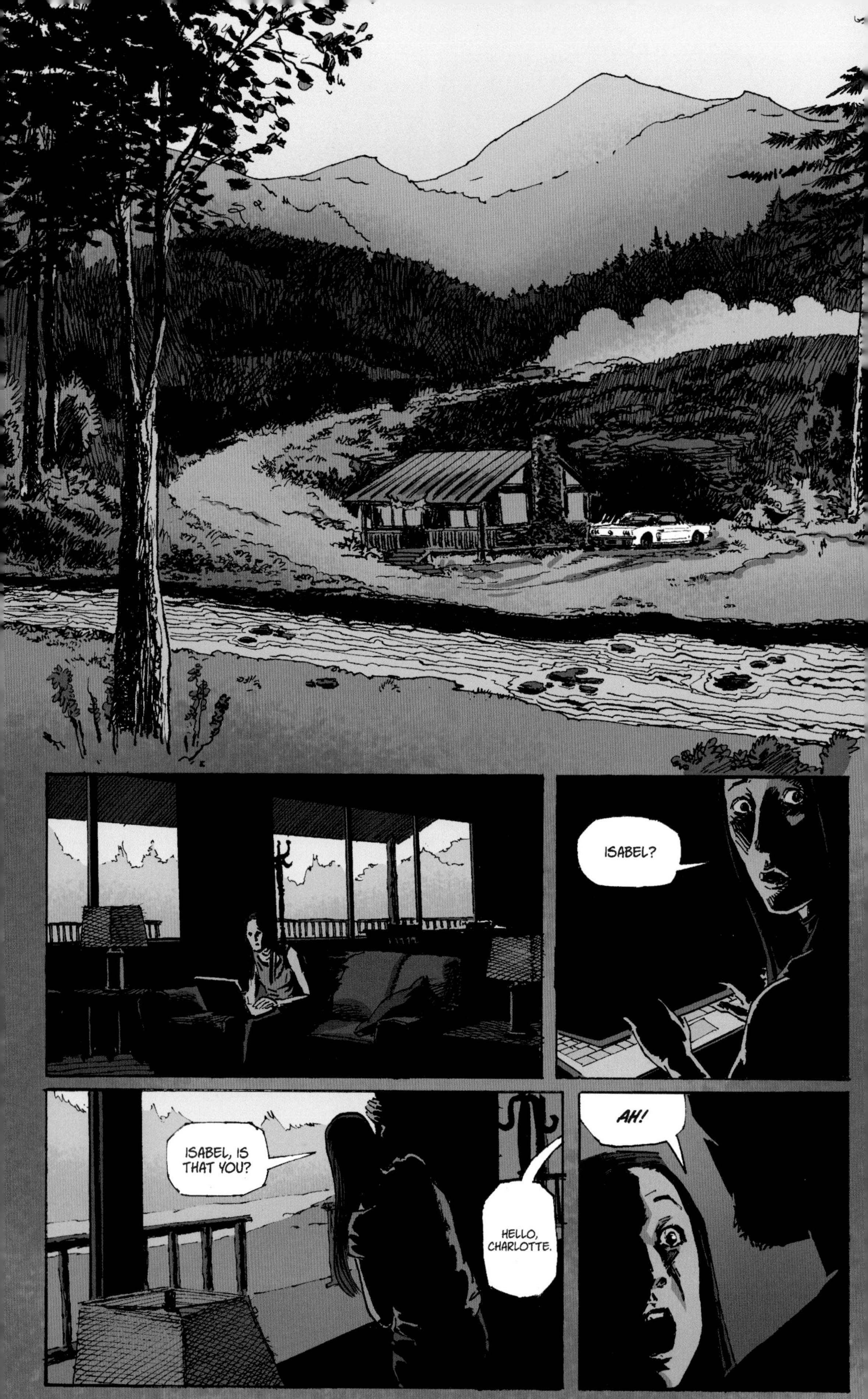
ISABEL?
ISABEL, IS THAT YOU?
HELLO, CHARLOTTE.
AH!

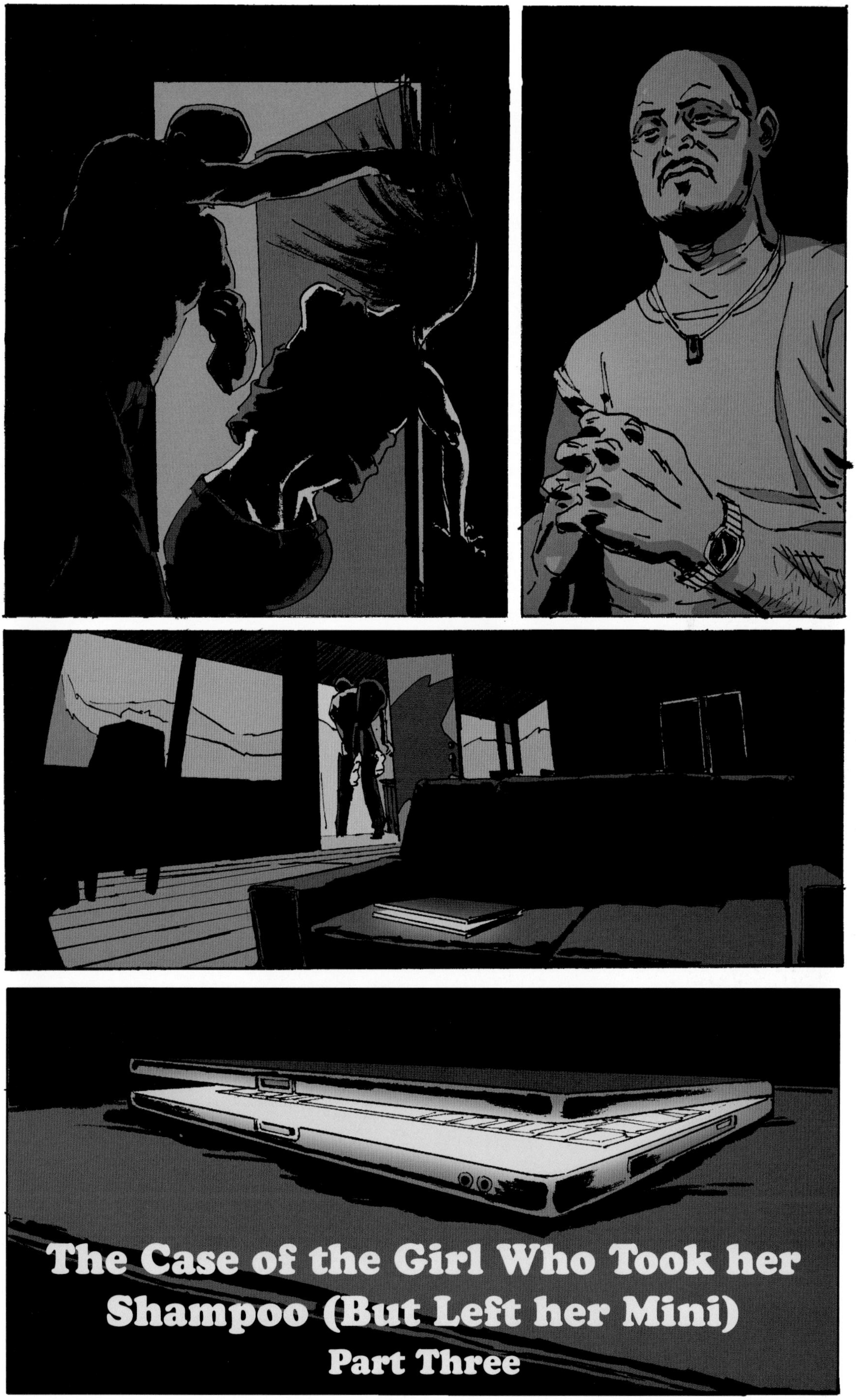
The Case of the Girl Who Took her
Shampoo (But Left her Mini)
Part Three

Chapter Four

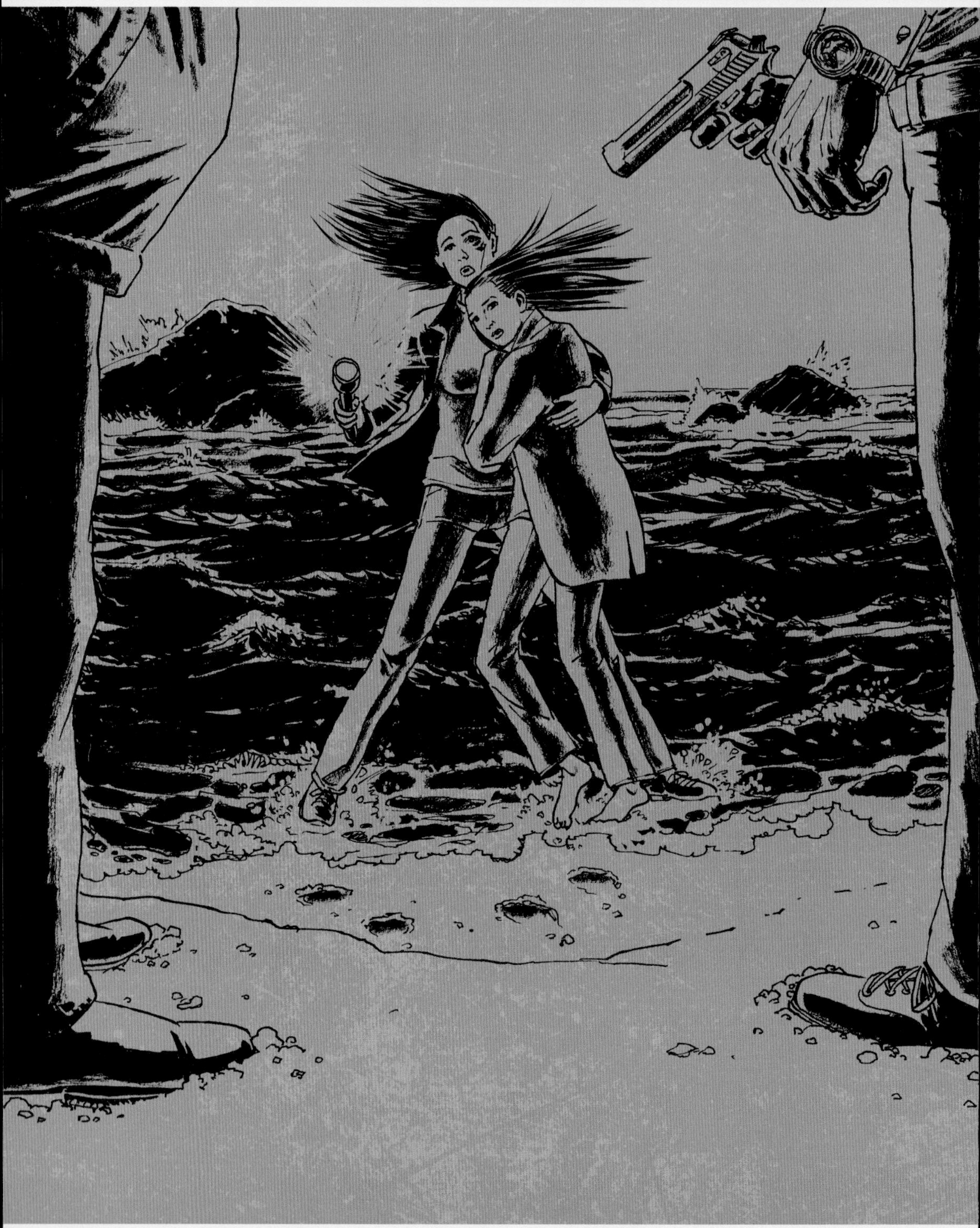

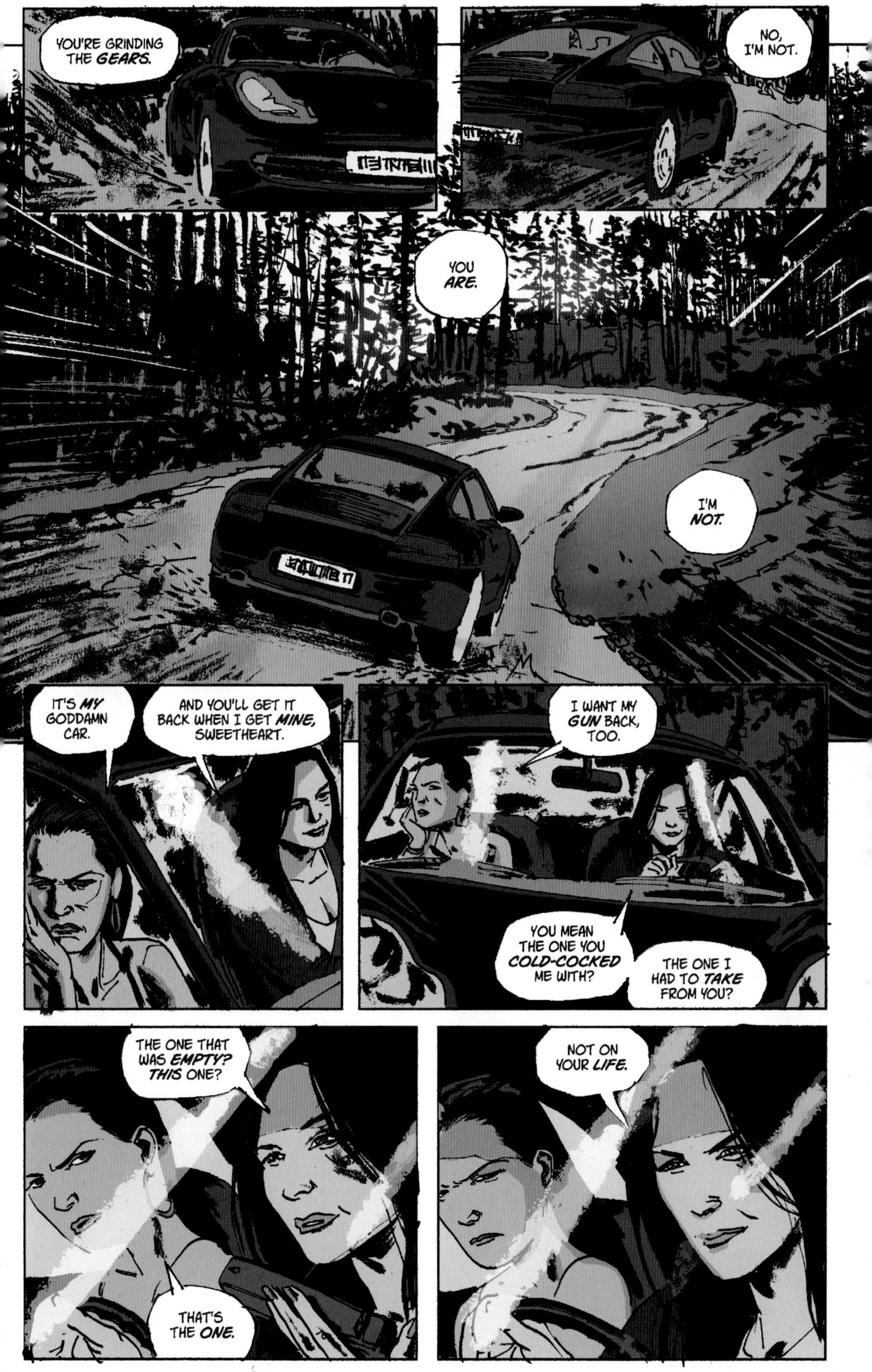

YOU'RE GRINDING THE GEARS.
NO, I'M NOT.
YOU ARE.
I'M NOT.
IT'S MY GODDAMN CAR.
AND YOU'LL GET IT BACK WHEN I GET MINE, SWEETHEART.
I WANT MY GUN BACK, TOO.
YOU MEAN THE ONE YOU COLD-COCKED ME WITH?
THE ONE I HAD TO TAKE FROM YOU?
THE ONE THAT WAS EMPTY? THIS ONE?
THAT'S THE ONE.
NOT ON YOUR LIFE.

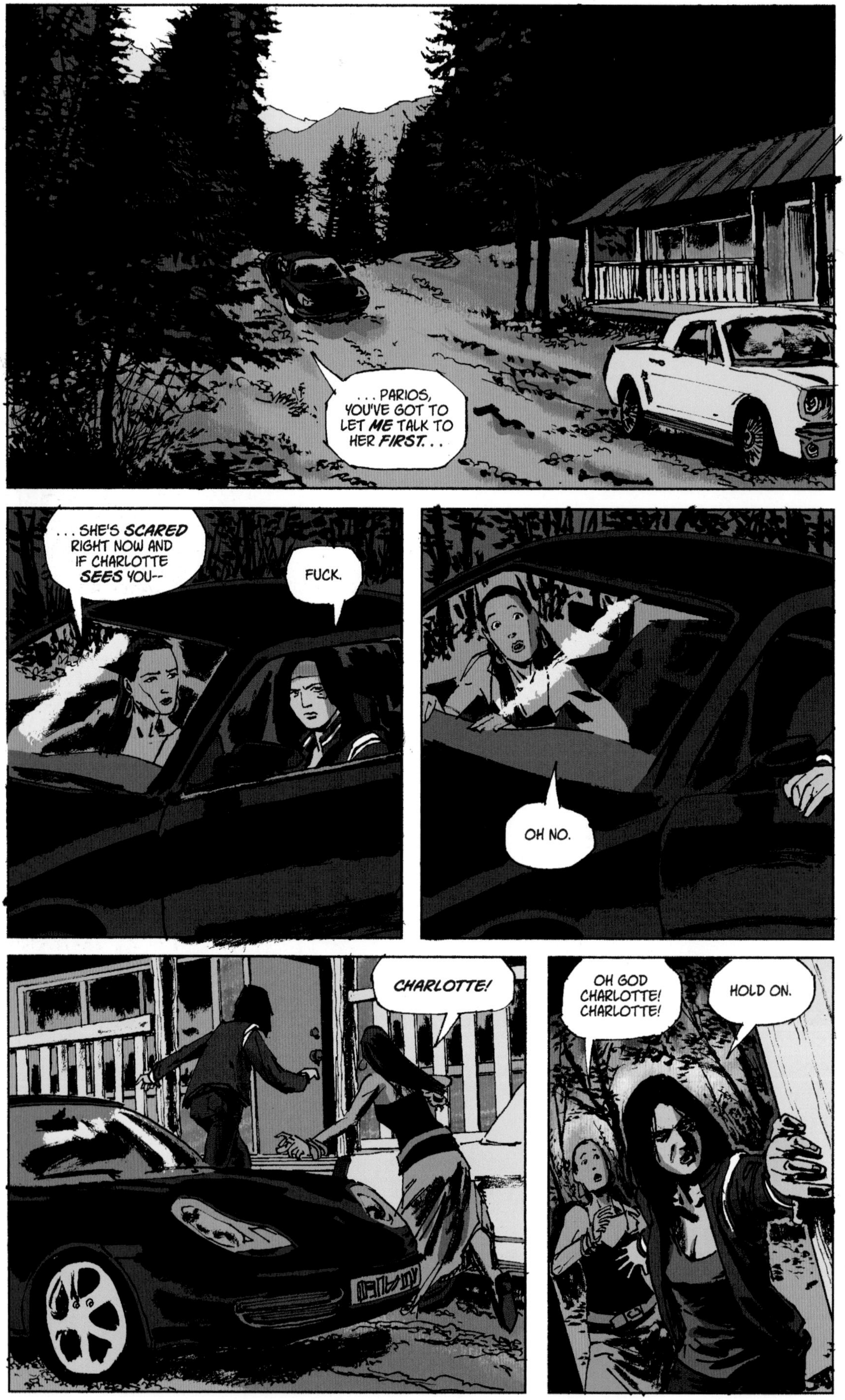
. . . PARIOS, YOU'VE GOT TO LET ME TALK TO HER FIRST. . .
. . . SHE'S SCARED RIGHT NOW AND IF CHARLOTTE SEES YOU--
FUCK.
OH NO.
CHARLOTTE!
OH GOD CHARLOTTE! CHARLOTTE!
HOLD ON.

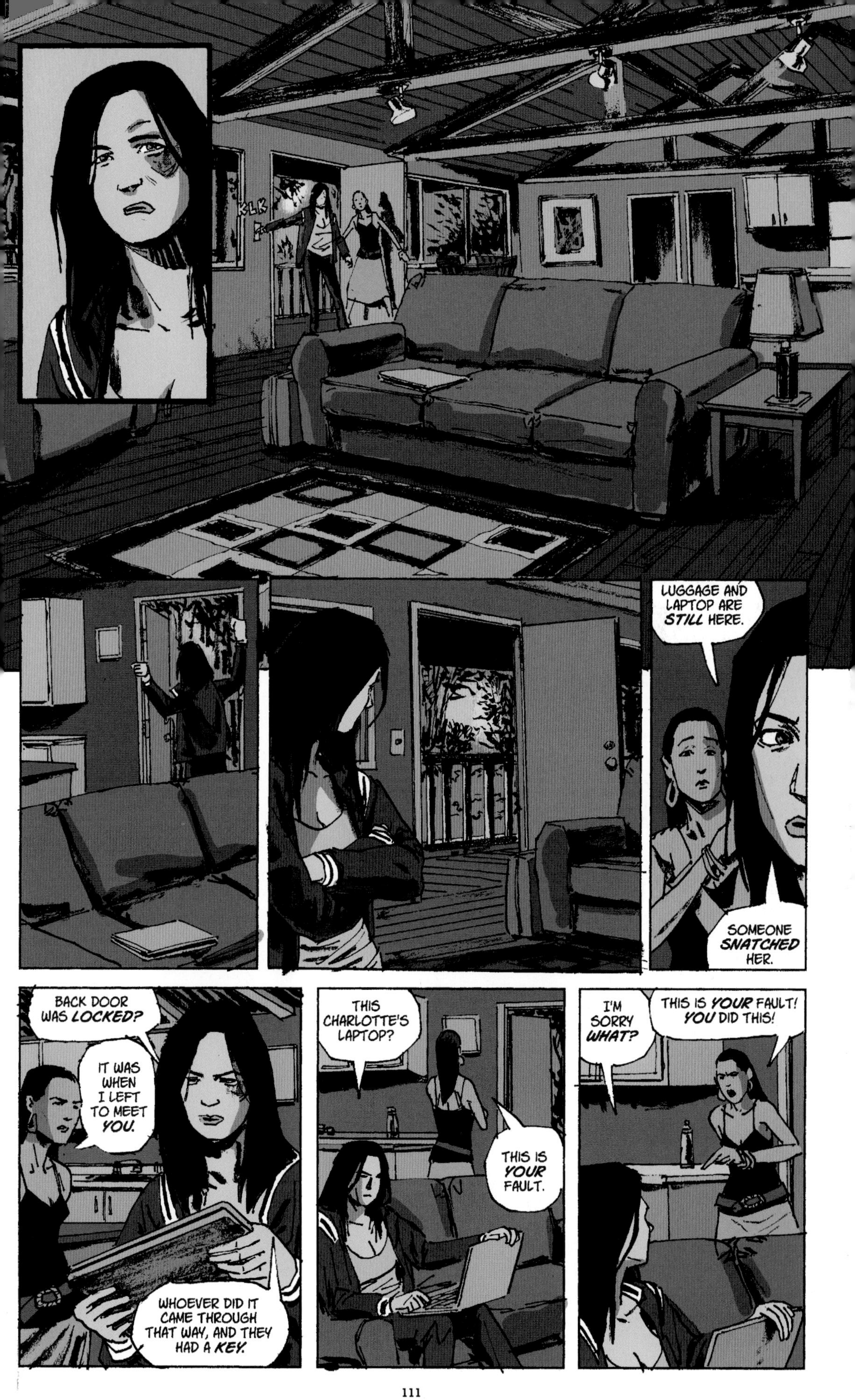
KLK
LUGGAGE AND LAPTOP ARE *STILL* HERE.
SOMEONE *SNATCHED* HER.
BACK DOOR WAS *LOCKED?*
IT WAS WHEN I LEFT TO MEET *YOU.*
WHOEVER DID IT CAME THROUGH THAT WAY, AND THEY HAD A *KEY.*
THIS CHARLOTTE'S LAPTOP?
THIS IS *YOUR* FAULT.
I'M SORRY *WHAT?*
THIS IS *YOUR* FAULT! *YOU* DID THIS!

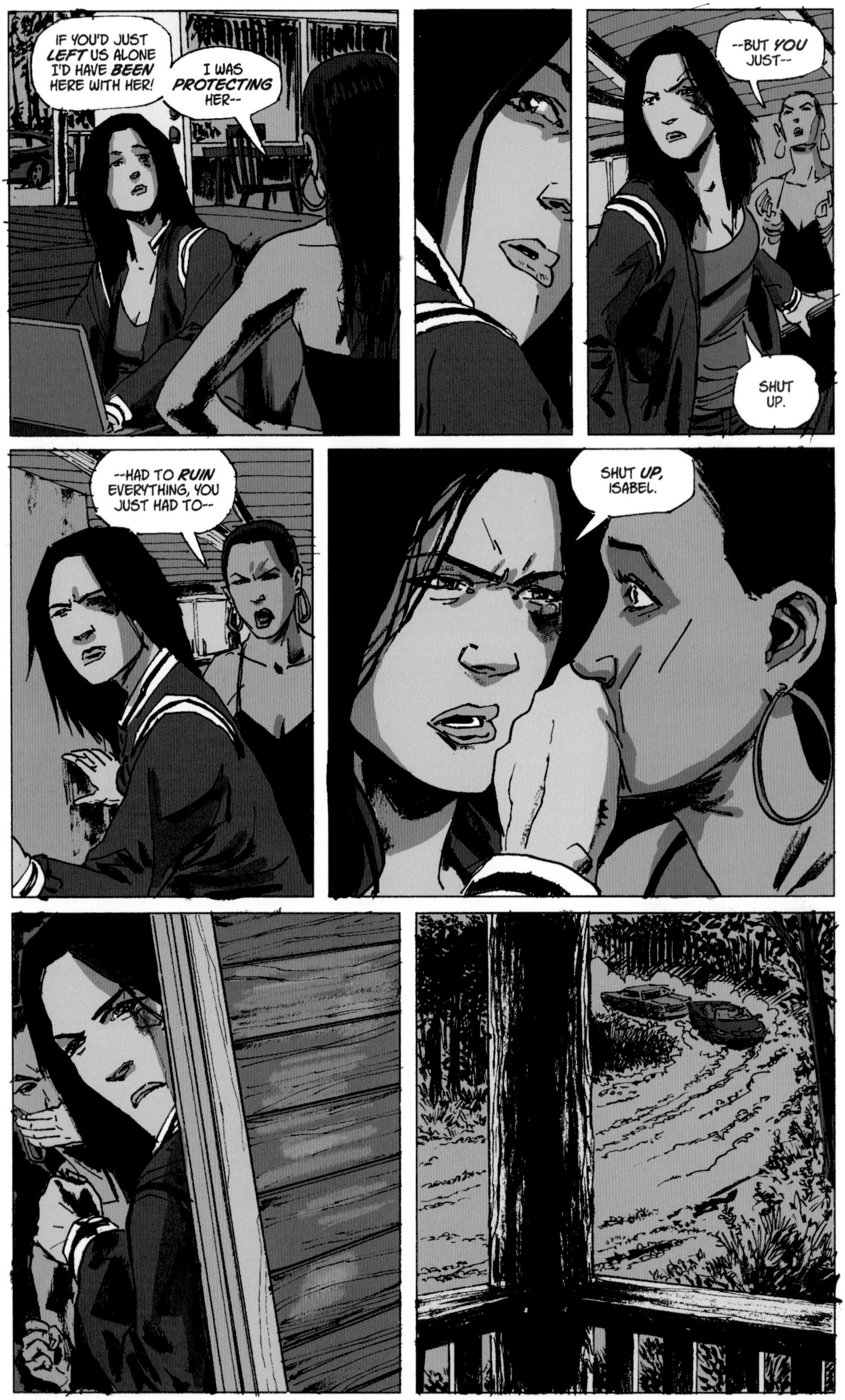
IF YOU'D JUST LEFT US ALONE I'D HAVE BEEN HERE WITH HER!
I WAS PROTECTING HER--
--BUT YOU JUST--
SHUT UP.
--HAD TO RUIN EVERYTHING, YOU JUST HAD TO--
SHUT UP, ISABEL.

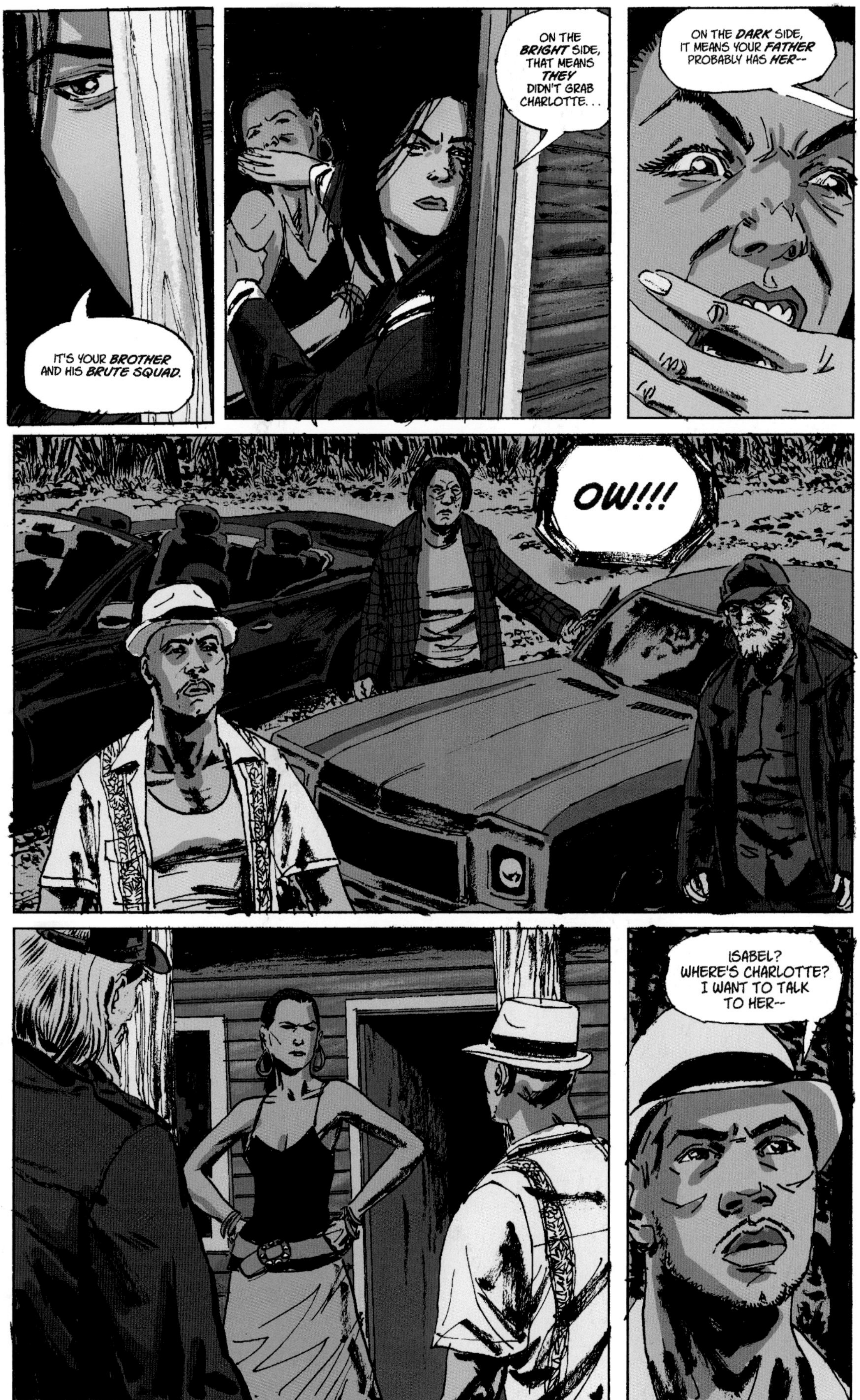
IT'S YOUR BROTHER AND HIS BRUTE SQUAD.
ON THE BRIGHT SIDE, THAT MEANS THEY DIDN'T GRAB CHARLOTTE...
ON THE DARK SIDE, IT MEANS YOUR FATHER PROBABLY HAS HER--
OW!!!
ISABEL? WHERE'S CHARLOTTE? I WANT TO TALK TO HER--

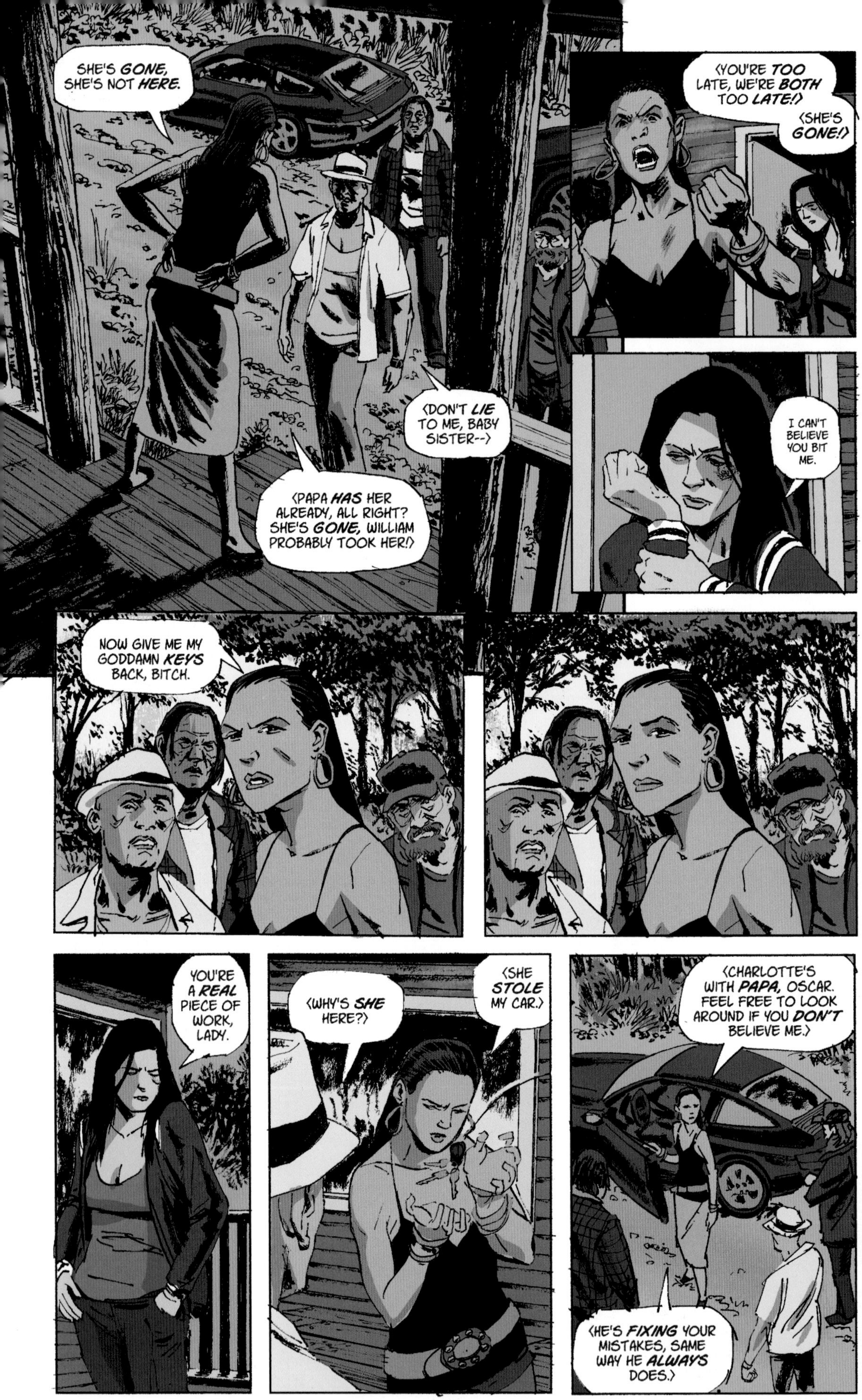

SHE'S GONE, SHE'S NOT HERE.
<YOU'RE TOO LATE, WE'RE BOTH TOO LATE!>
<SHE'S GONE!>
<DON'T LIE TO ME, BABY SISTER-->
<PAPA HAS HER ALREADY, ALL RIGHT? SHE'S GONE, WILLIAM PROBABLY TOOK HER!>
I CAN'T BELIEVE YOU BIT ME.
NOW GIVE ME MY GODDAMN KEYS BACK, BITCH.
YOU'RE A REAL PIECE OF WORK, LADY.
<WHY'S SHE HERE?>
<SHE STOLE MY CAR.>
<CHARLOTTE'S WITH PAPA, OSCAR. FEEL FREE TO LOOK AROUND IF YOU DON'T BELIEVE ME.>
<HE'S FIXING YOUR MISTAKES, SAME WAY HE ALWAYS DOES.>

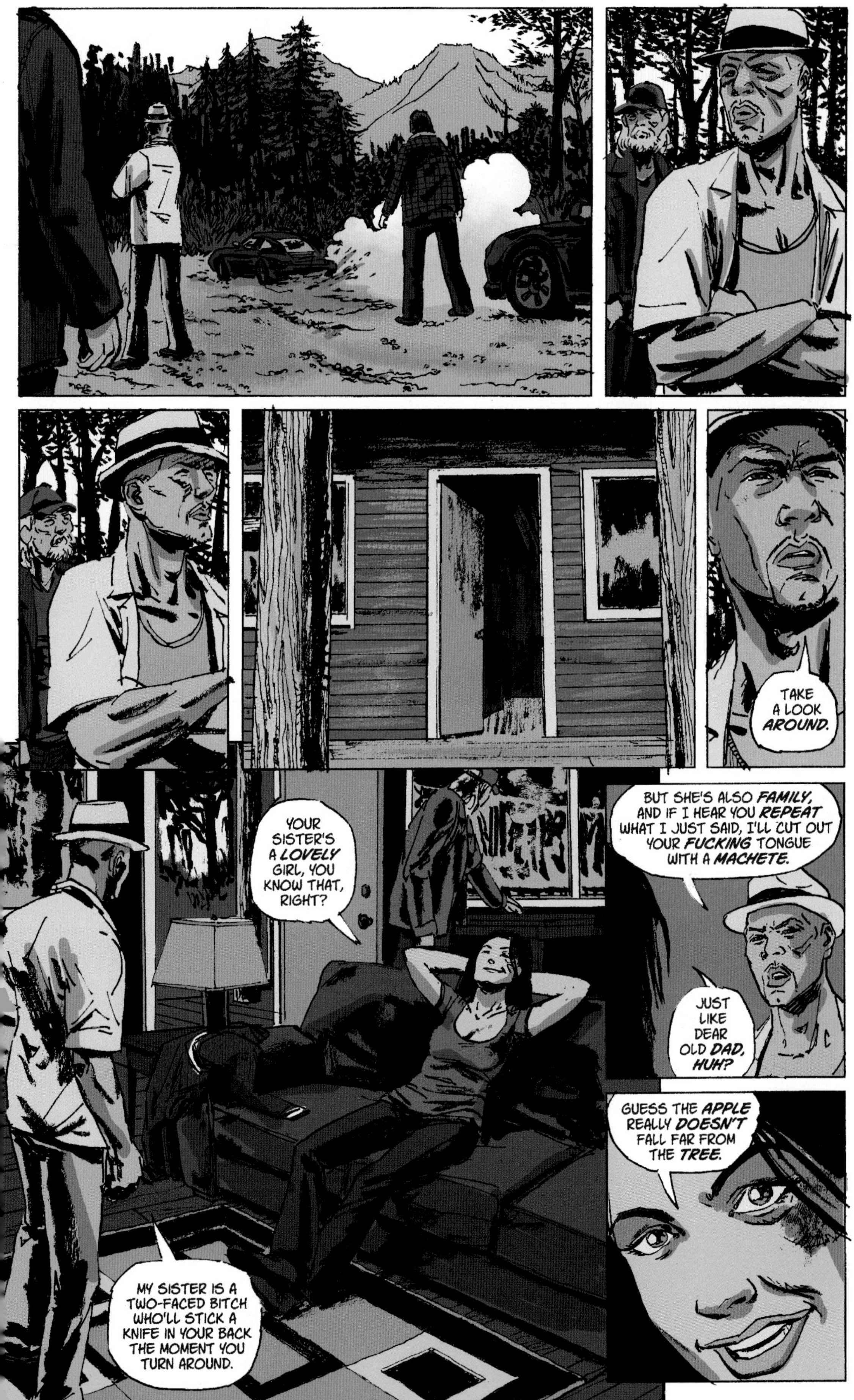
TAKE A LOOK AROUND.
YOUR SISTER'S A LOVELY GIRL, YOU KNOW THAT, RIGHT?
MY SISTER IS A TWO-FACED BITCH WHO'LL STICK A KNIFE IN YOUR BACK THE MOMENT YOU TURN AROUND.
BUT SHE'S ALSO FAMILY, AND IF I HEAR YOU REPEAT WHAT I JUST SAID, I'LL CUT OUT YOUR FUCKING TONGUE WITH A MACHETE.
JUST LIKE DEAR OLD DAD, HUH?
GUESS THE APPLE REALLY DOESN'T FALL FAR FROM THE TREE.

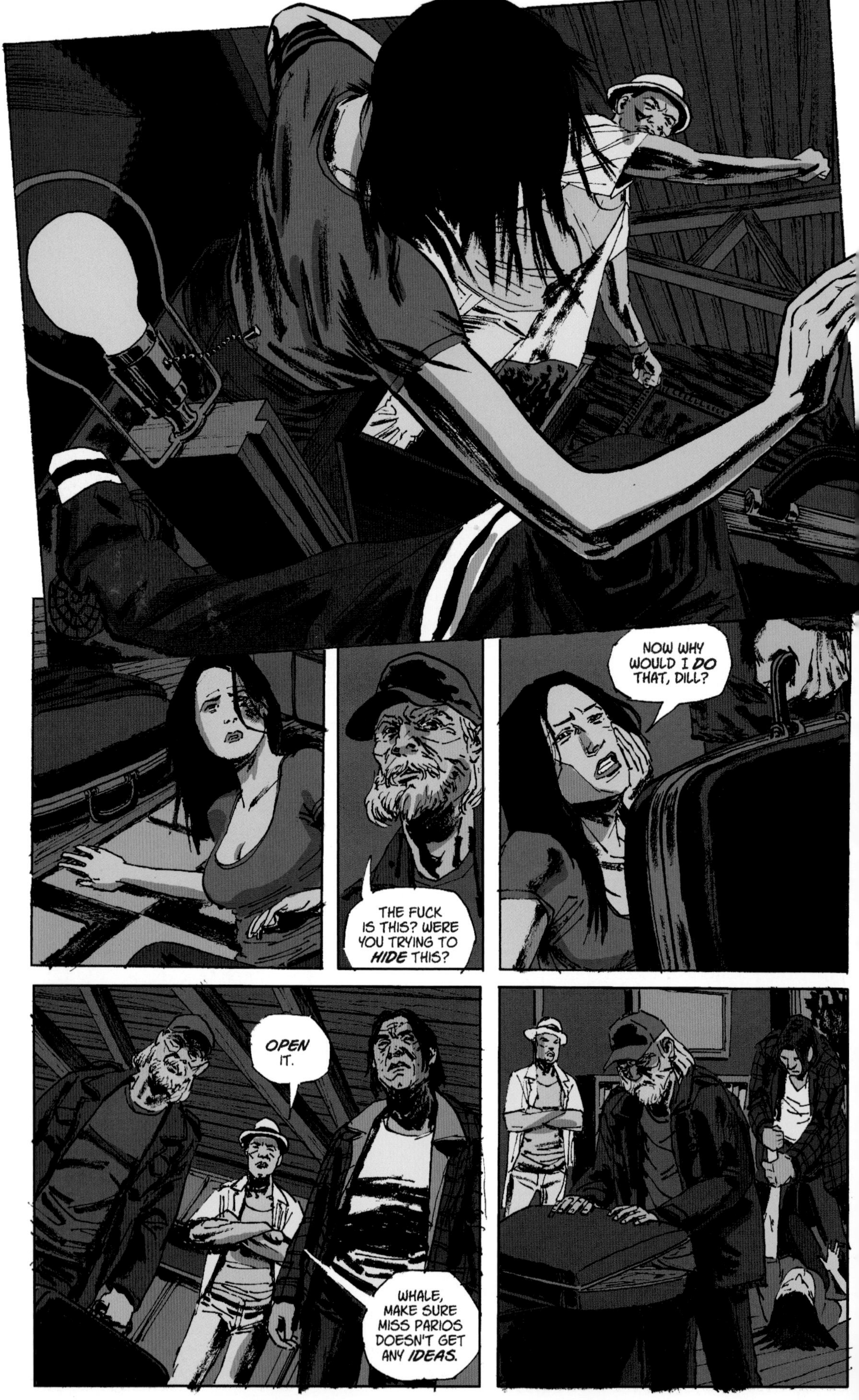
THE FUCK IS THIS? WERE YOU TRYING TO HIDE THIS?
NOW WHY WOULD I DO THAT, DILL?
OPEN IT.
WHALE, MAKE SURE MISS PARIOS DOESN'T GET ANY IDEAS.

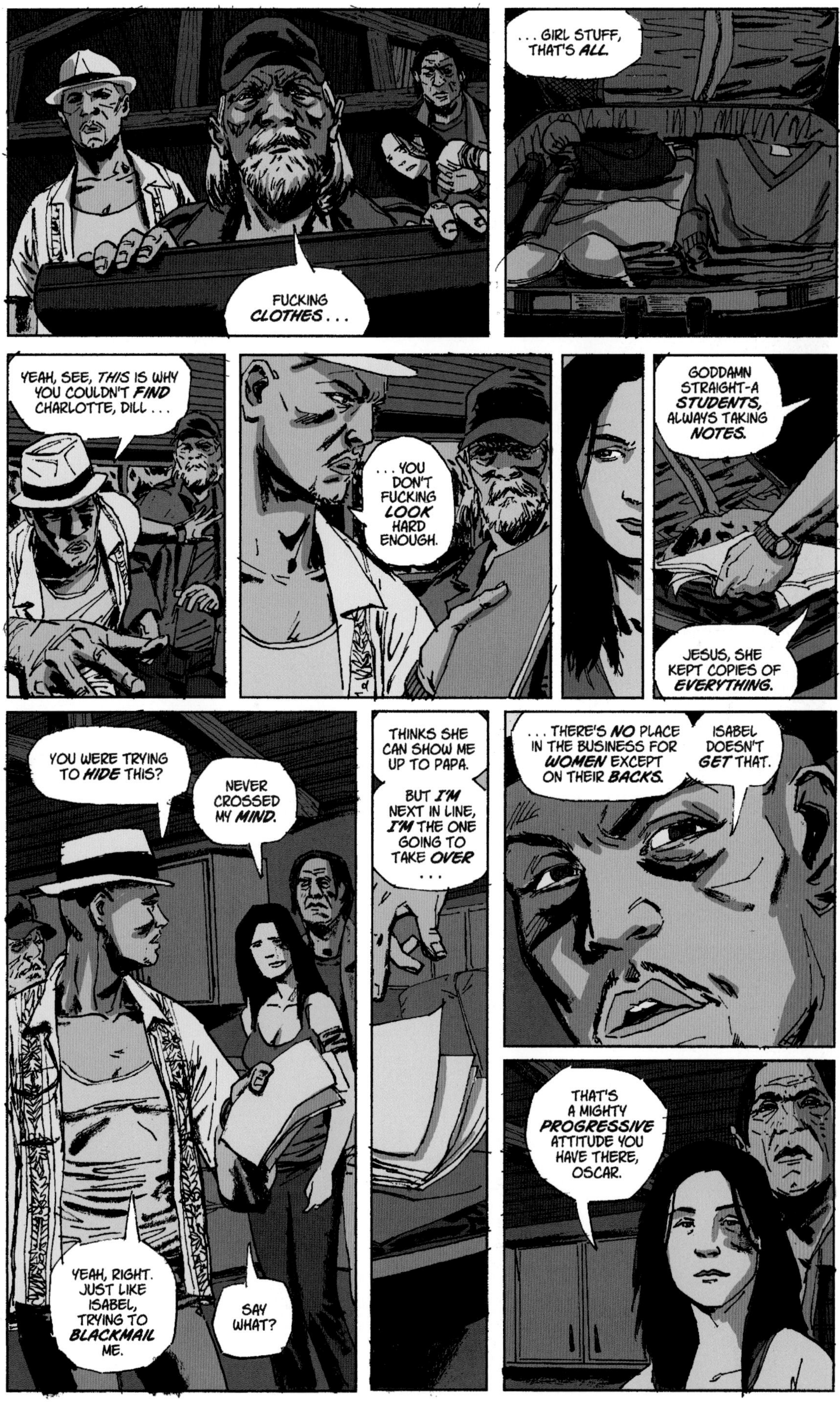

FUCKING CLOTHES . . .
. . . GIRL STUFF, THAT'S ALL.
YEAH, SEE, THIS IS WHY YOU COULDN'T FIND CHARLOTTE, DILL . . .
. . . YOU DON'T FUCKING LOOK HARD ENOUGH.
GODDAMN STRAIGHT-A STUDENTS, ALWAYS TAKING NOTES.
JESUS, SHE KEPT COPIES OF EVERYTHING.
YOU WERE TRYING TO HIDE THIS?
NEVER CROSSED MY MIND.
YEAH, RIGHT. JUST LIKE ISABEL, TRYING TO BLACKMAIL ME.
SAY WHAT?
THINKS SHE CAN SHOW ME UP TO PAPA.
BUT I'M NEXT IN LINE, I'M THE ONE GOING TO TAKE OVER . . .
. . . THERE'S NO PLACE IN THE BUSINESS FOR WOMEN EXCEPT ON THEIR BACKS.
ISABEL DOESN'T GET THAT.
THAT'S A MIGHTY PROGRESSIVE ATTITUDE YOU HAVE THERE, OSCAR.

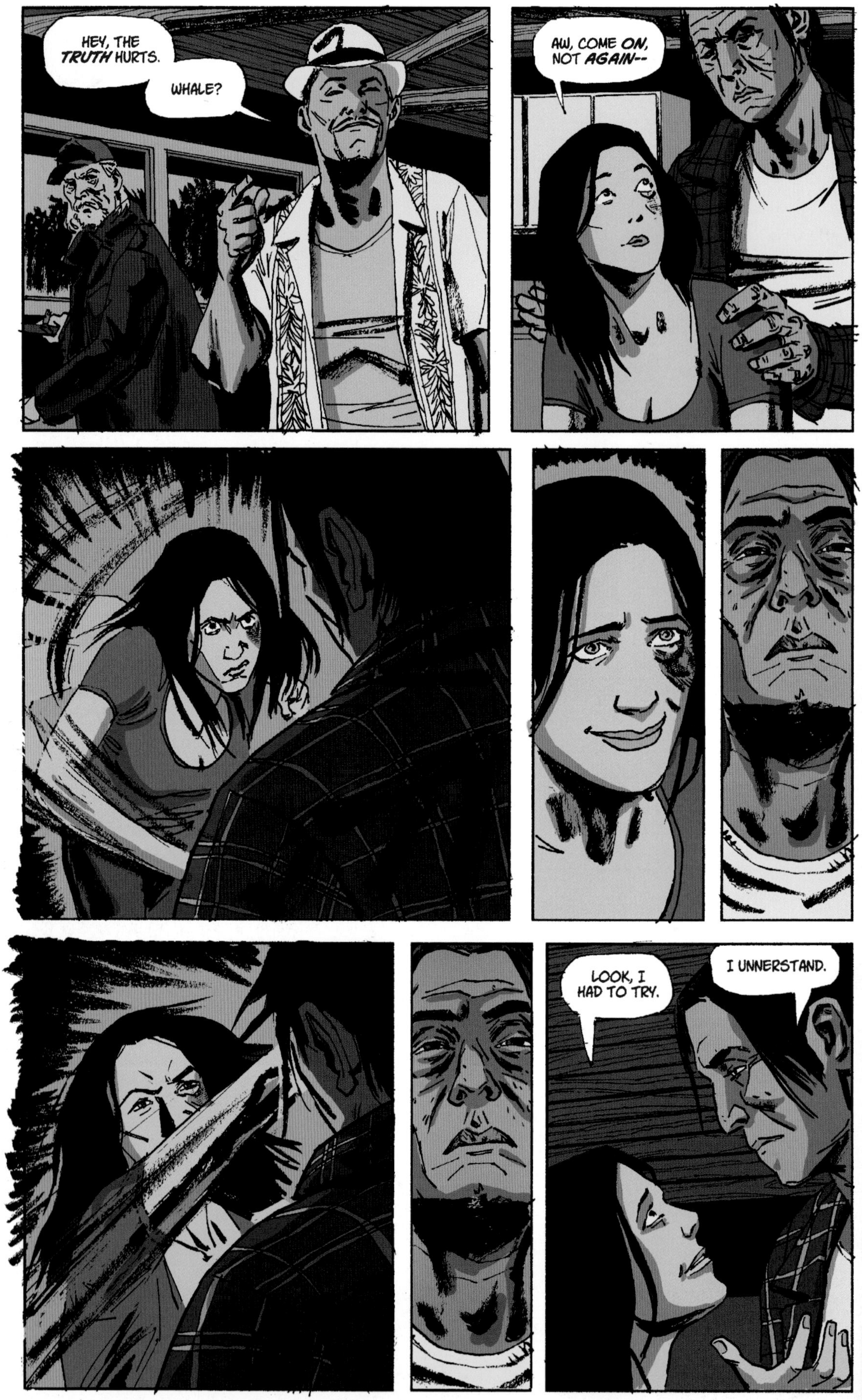
HEY, THE TRUTH HURTS.
WHALE?
AW, COME ON, NOT AGAIN--
LOOK, I HAD TO TRY.
I UNNERSTAND.

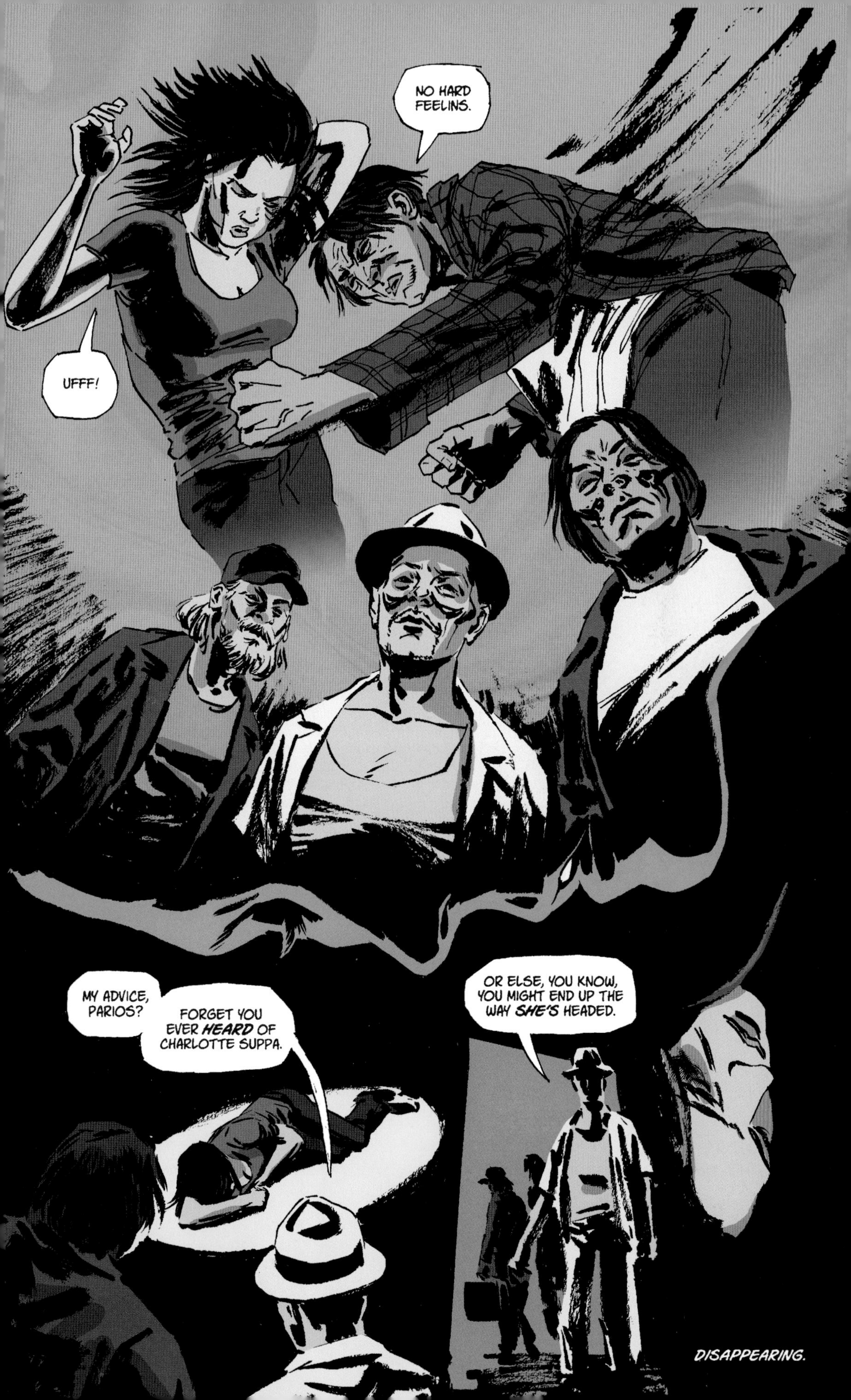
NO HARD FEELINS.
UFFF!
MY ADVICE, PARIOS?
FORGET YOU EVER HEARD OF CHARLOTTE SUPPA.
OR ELSE, YOU KNOW, YOU MIGHT END UP THE WAY SHE'S HEADED.
DISAPPEARING.

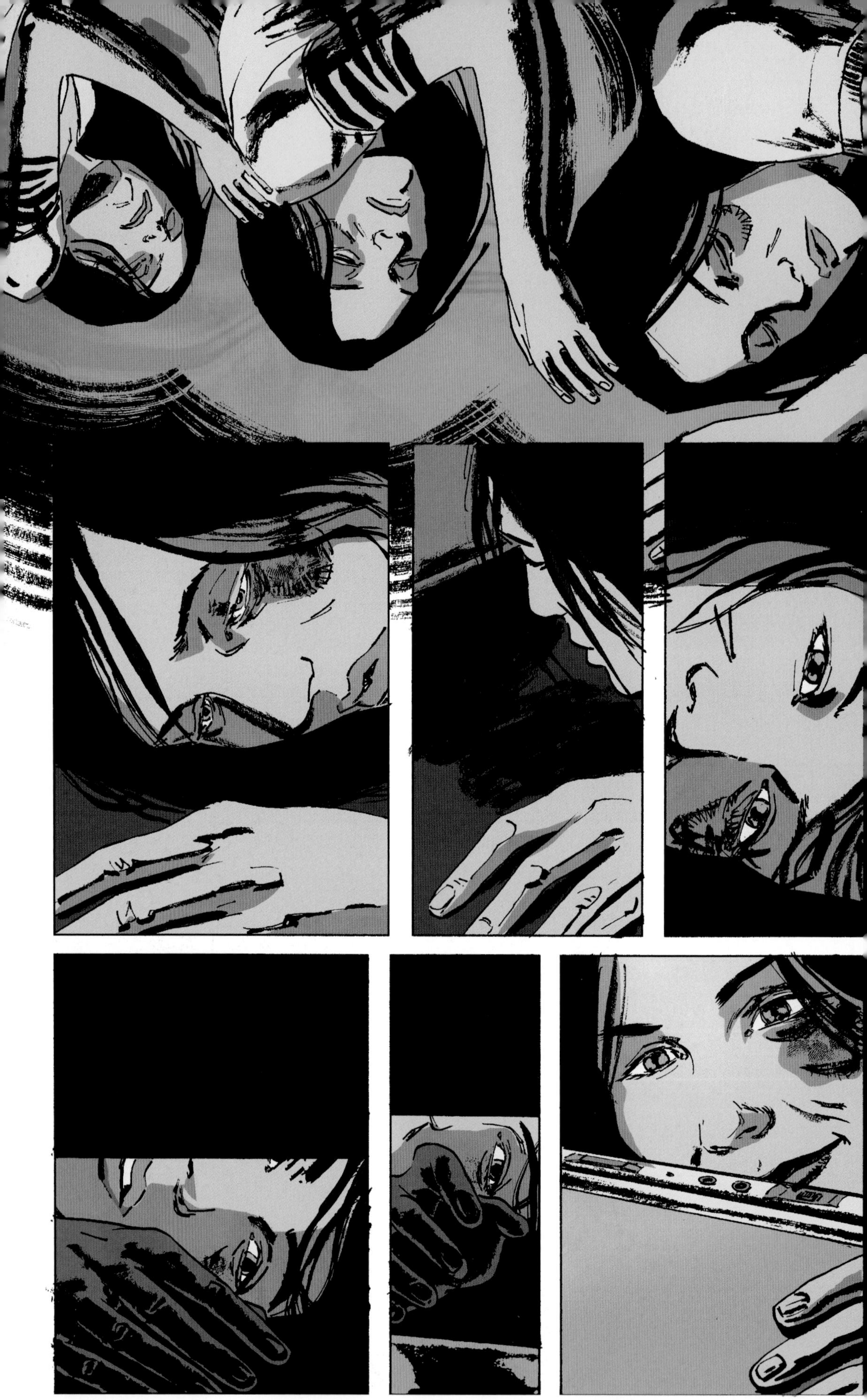

⟨WHERE'S MY DAD?⟩

⟨HE'S IN HIS OFFICE, MR. MARENCO--⟩

⟨--YOUR *SISTER* IS WITH HIM.⟩

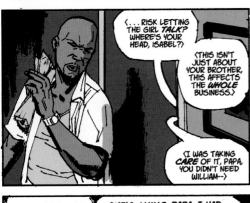

⟨. . . RISK LETTING THE GIRL *TALK?* WHERE'S YOUR HEAD, ISABEL?⟩

⟨THIS ISN'T JUST ABOUT YOUR BROTHER, THIS AFFECTS THE *WHOLE* BUSINESS.⟩

⟨I WAS TAKING *CARE* OF IT, PAPA, YOU DIDN'T NEED WILLIAM--⟩

⟨*YOU* WERE TAKING CARE OF IT? HOW? BY HIDING IN HOTEL ROOMS WITH THIS GIRL?⟩

⟨I HAD A *PLAN,* WHICH IS MORE THAN *OSCAR* EVER HAS! FIRST IT WAS *ELECTRONICS,* THEN *METH,* NOW *THIS,* PAPA!⟩

⟨*EACH* TIME, YOU HAVE WILLIAM *FIX* HIS *MISTAKES!*⟩

--YOU *FUCKING BITCH!*

SHE'S *LYING,* PAPA, I HAD THIS ALL *UNDER CONTROL*--

--SHE'S *ALWAYS* TRYING TO--

--MAKE ME LOOK *BAD* IN FRONT OF YOU--

I DON'T HAVE TO DO *ANYTHING,* YOU DO IT *YOURSELF*--

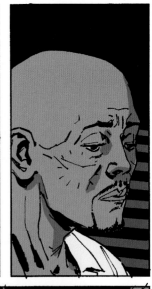

〈YOU *NEVER* SPEAK THAT WAY *TO* OR *ABOUT* YOUR *SISTER*.〉

〈YES, PAPA.〉

〈UNDERSTAND?〉

〈IS THIS *EVERYTHING?* NO *OTHER* EVIDENCE, ONLY THE GIRL'S *WORD*?〉

〈YES, PAPA.〉

〈YOU'RE *CERTAIN*?〉

〈YES, PAPA.〉

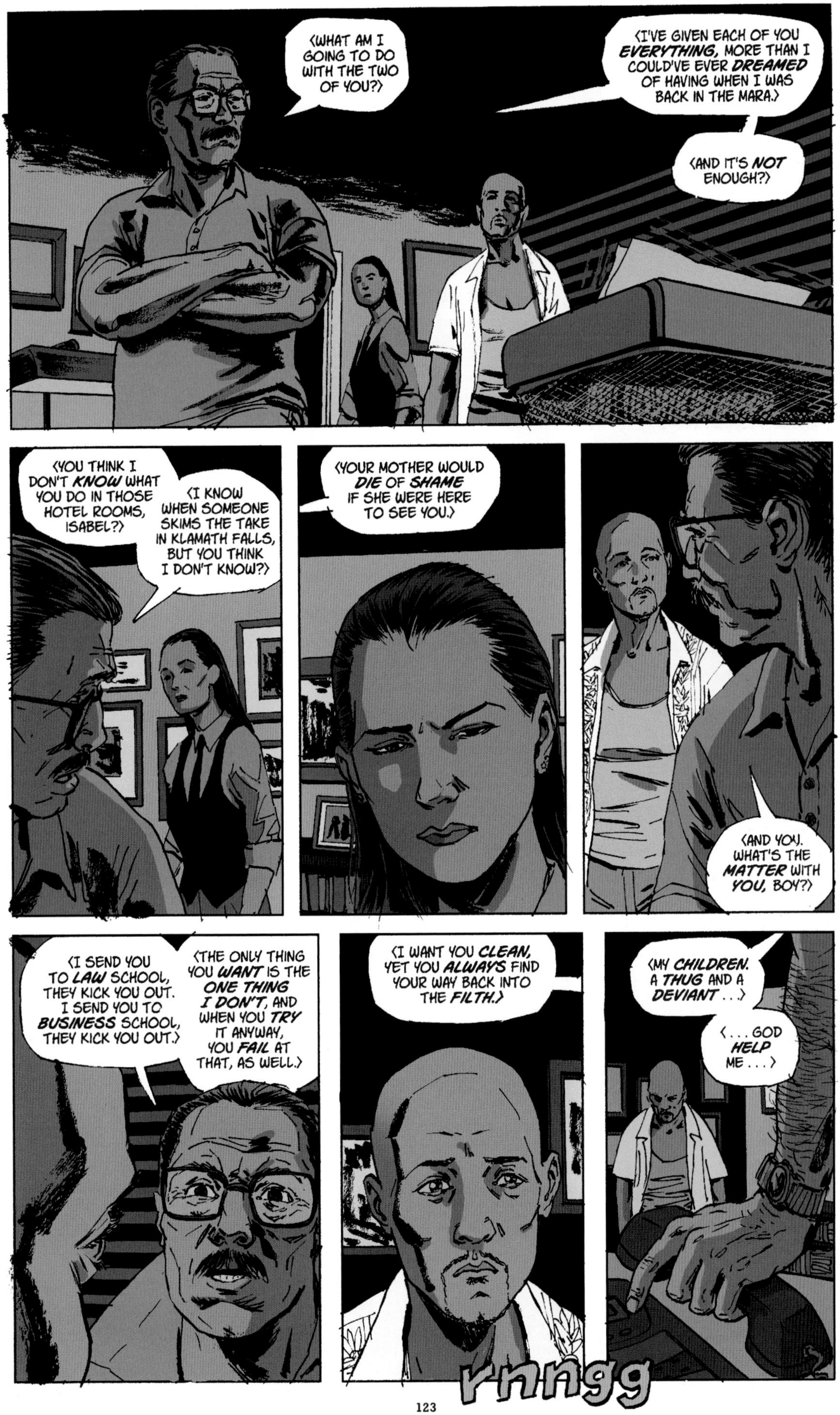
⟨WHAT AM I GOING TO DO WITH THE TWO OF YOU?⟩
⟨I'VE GIVEN EACH OF YOU EVERYTHING, MORE THAN I COULD'VE EVER DREAMED OF HAVING WHEN I WAS BACK IN THE MARA.⟩
⟨AND IT'S NOT ENOUGH?⟩
⟨YOU THINK I DON'T KNOW WHAT YOU DO IN THOSE HOTEL ROOMS, ISABEL?⟩
⟨I KNOW WHEN SOMEONE SKIMS THE TAKE IN KLAMATH FALLS, BUT YOU THINK I DON'T KNOW?⟩
⟨YOUR MOTHER WOULD DIE OF SHAME IF SHE WERE HERE TO SEE YOU.⟩
⟨AND YOU. WHAT'S THE MATTER WITH YOU, BOY?⟩
⟨I SEND YOU TO LAW SCHOOL, THEY KICK YOU OUT. I SEND YOU TO BUSINESS SCHOOL, THEY KICK YOU OUT.⟩
⟨THE ONLY THING YOU WANT IS THE ONE THING I DON'T, AND WHEN YOU TRY IT ANYWAY, YOU FAIL AT THAT, AS WELL.⟩
⟨I WANT YOU CLEAN, YET YOU ALWAYS FIND YOUR WAY BACK INTO THE FILTH.⟩
⟨MY CHILDREN. A THUG AND A DEVIANT . . .⟩
⟨. . . GOD HELP ME . . .⟩
rnngg

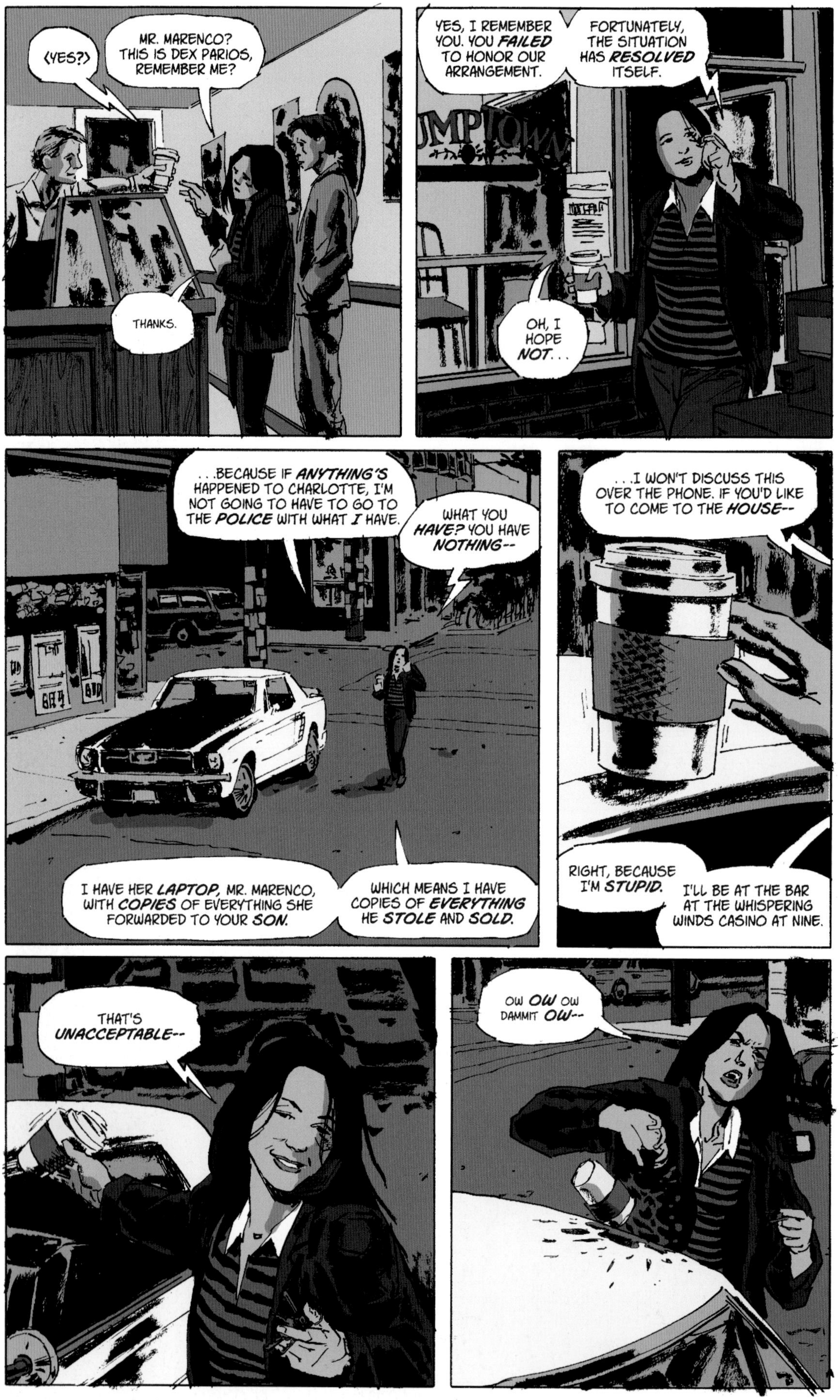

MR. MARENCO? THIS IS DEX PARIOS, REMEMBER ME?
‹YES?›
THANKS.
YES, I REMEMBER YOU. YOU FAILED TO HONOR OUR ARRANGEMENT.
FORTUNATELY, THE SITUATION HAS RESOLVED ITSELF.
UMPTOWN
OH, I HOPE NOT. . .
. . .BECAUSE IF ANYTHING'S HAPPENED TO CHARLOTTE, I'M NOT GOING TO HAVE TO GO TO THE POLICE WITH WHAT I HAVE.
WHAT YOU HAVE? YOU HAVE NOTHING--
I HAVE HER LAPTOP, MR. MARENCO, WITH COPIES OF EVERYTHING SHE FORWARDED TO YOUR SON.
WHICH MEANS I HAVE COPIES OF EVERYTHING HE STOLE AND SOLD.
. . .I WON'T DISCUSS THIS OVER THE PHONE. IF YOU'D LIKE TO COME TO THE HOUSE--
RIGHT, BECAUSE I'M STUPID.
I'LL BE AT THE BAR AT THE WHISPERING WINDS CASINO AT NINE.
THAT'S UNACCEPTABLE--
OW OW OW DAMMIT OW--

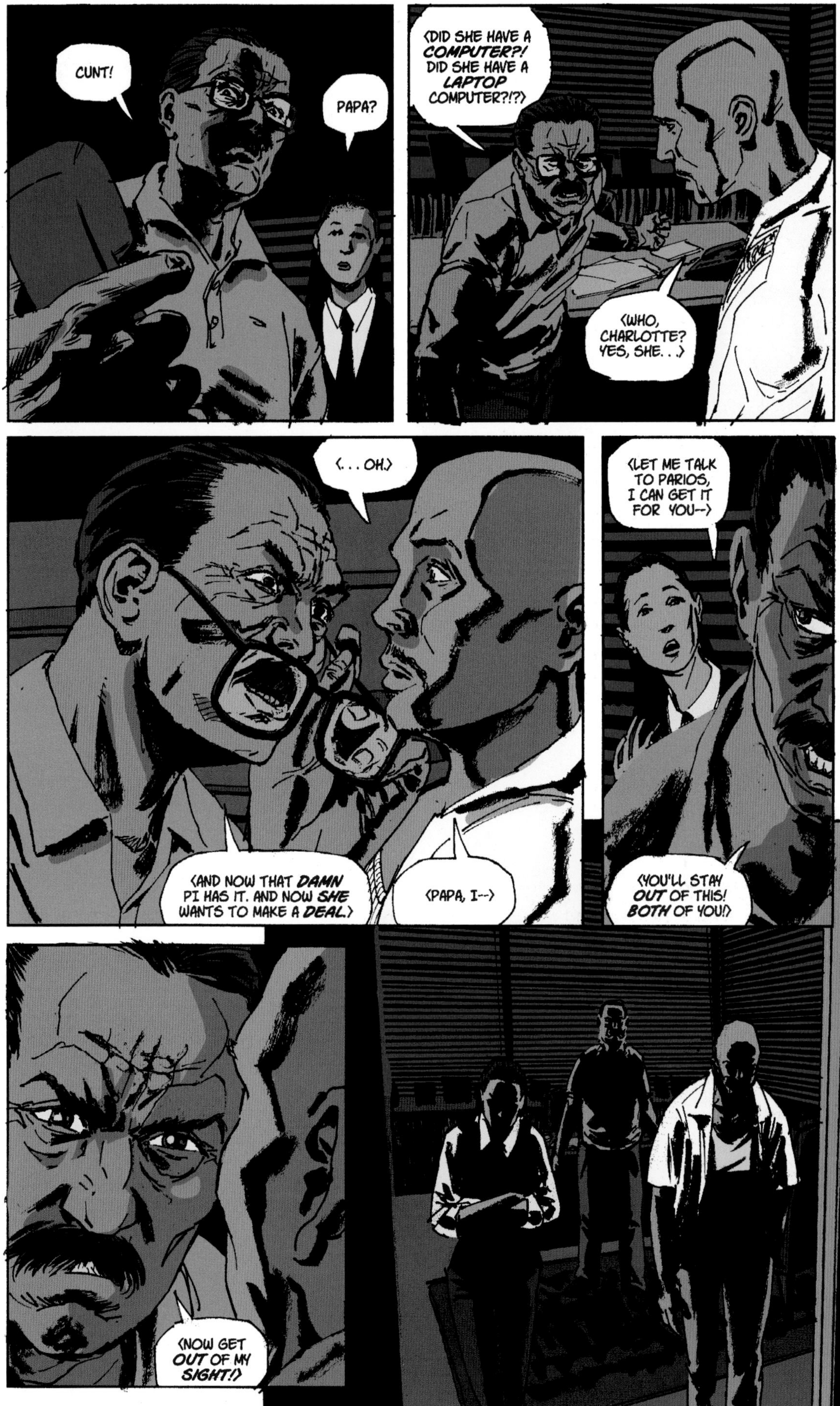
CUNT!
PAPA?
<DID SHE HAVE A COMPUTER?! DID SHE HAVE A LAPTOP COMPUTER?!?>
<WHO, CHARLOTTE? YES, SHE. . .>
<. . . OH.>
<AND NOW THAT DAMN PI HAS IT. AND NOW SHE WANTS TO MAKE A DEAL.>
<PAPA, I-->
<LET ME TALK TO PARIOS, I CAN GET IT FOR YOU-->
<YOU'LL STAY OUT OF THIS! BOTH OF YOU!>
<NOW GET OUT OF MY SIGHT!>

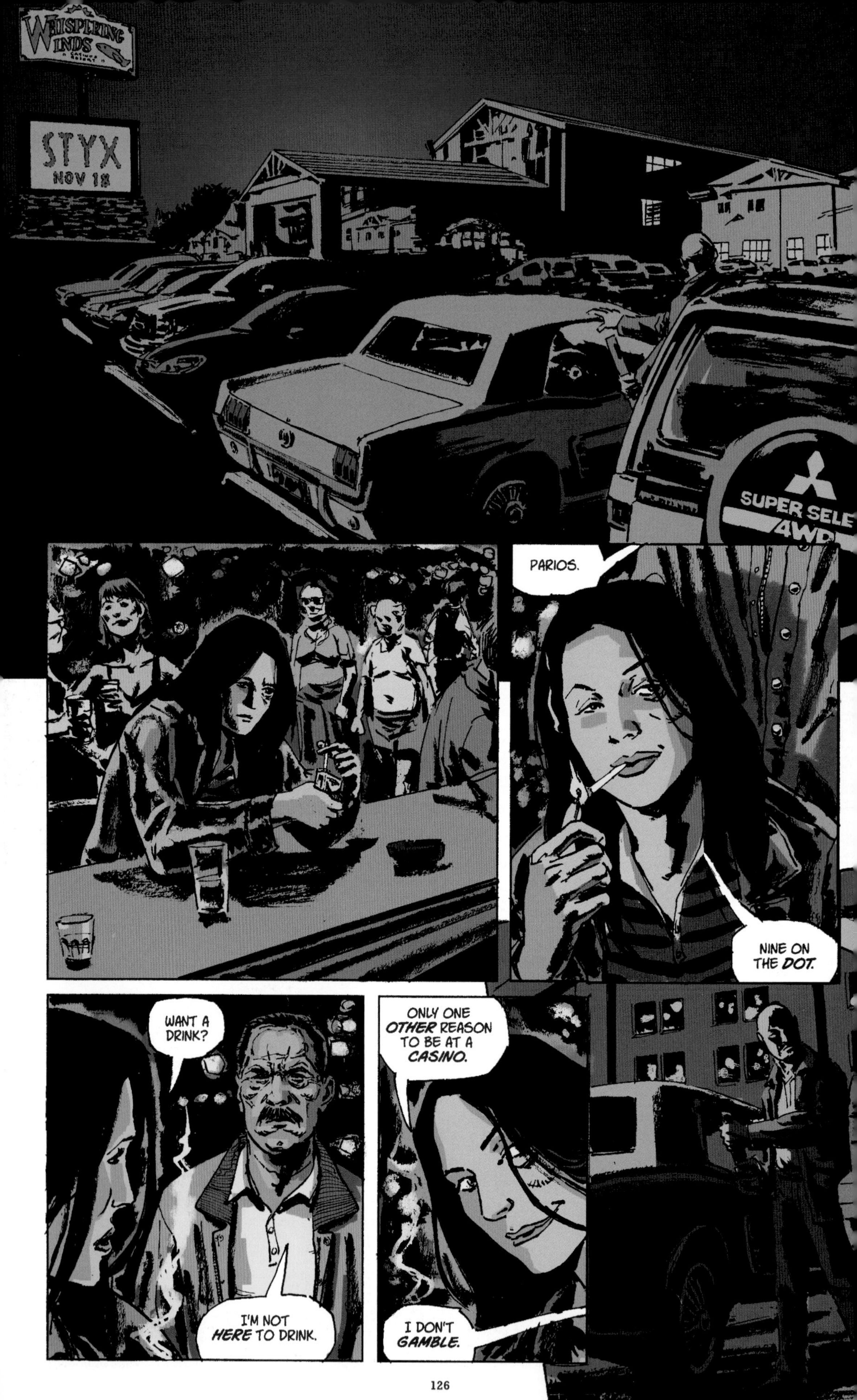
WHISPERING WINDS
STYX
NOV 18
SUPER SELE
4WD
PARIOS.
NINE ON THE DOT.
WANT A DRINK?
I'M NOT HERE TO DRINK.
ONLY ONE OTHER REASON TO BE AT A CASINO.
I DON'T GAMBLE.

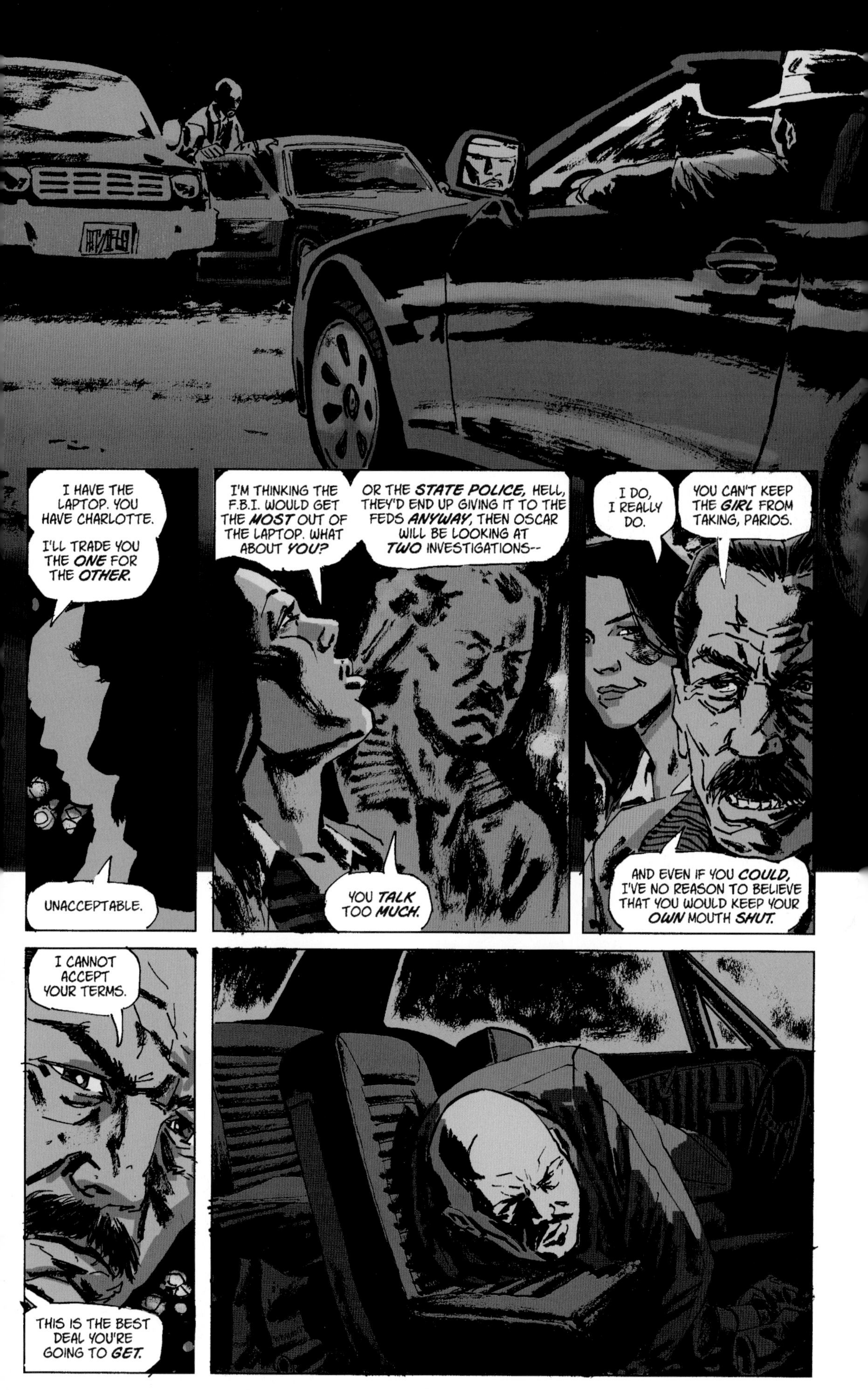
I HAVE THE LAPTOP. YOU HAVE CHARLOTTE.
I'LL TRADE YOU THE ONE FOR THE OTHER.
UNACCEPTABLE.
I'M THINKING THE F.B.I. WOULD GET THE MOST OUT OF THE LAPTOP. WHAT ABOUT YOU?
OR THE STATE POLICE, HELL, THEY'D END UP GIVING IT TO THE FEDS ANYWAY, THEN OSCAR WILL BE LOOKING AT TWO INVESTIGATIONS--
YOU TALK TOO MUCH.
I DO, I REALLY DO.
YOU CAN'T KEEP THE GIRL FROM TAKING, PARIOS.
AND EVEN IF YOU COULD, I'VE NO REASON TO BELIEVE THAT YOU WOULD KEEP YOUR OWN MOUTH SHUT.
I CANNOT ACCEPT YOUR TERMS.
THIS IS THE BEST DEAL YOU'RE GOING TO GET.

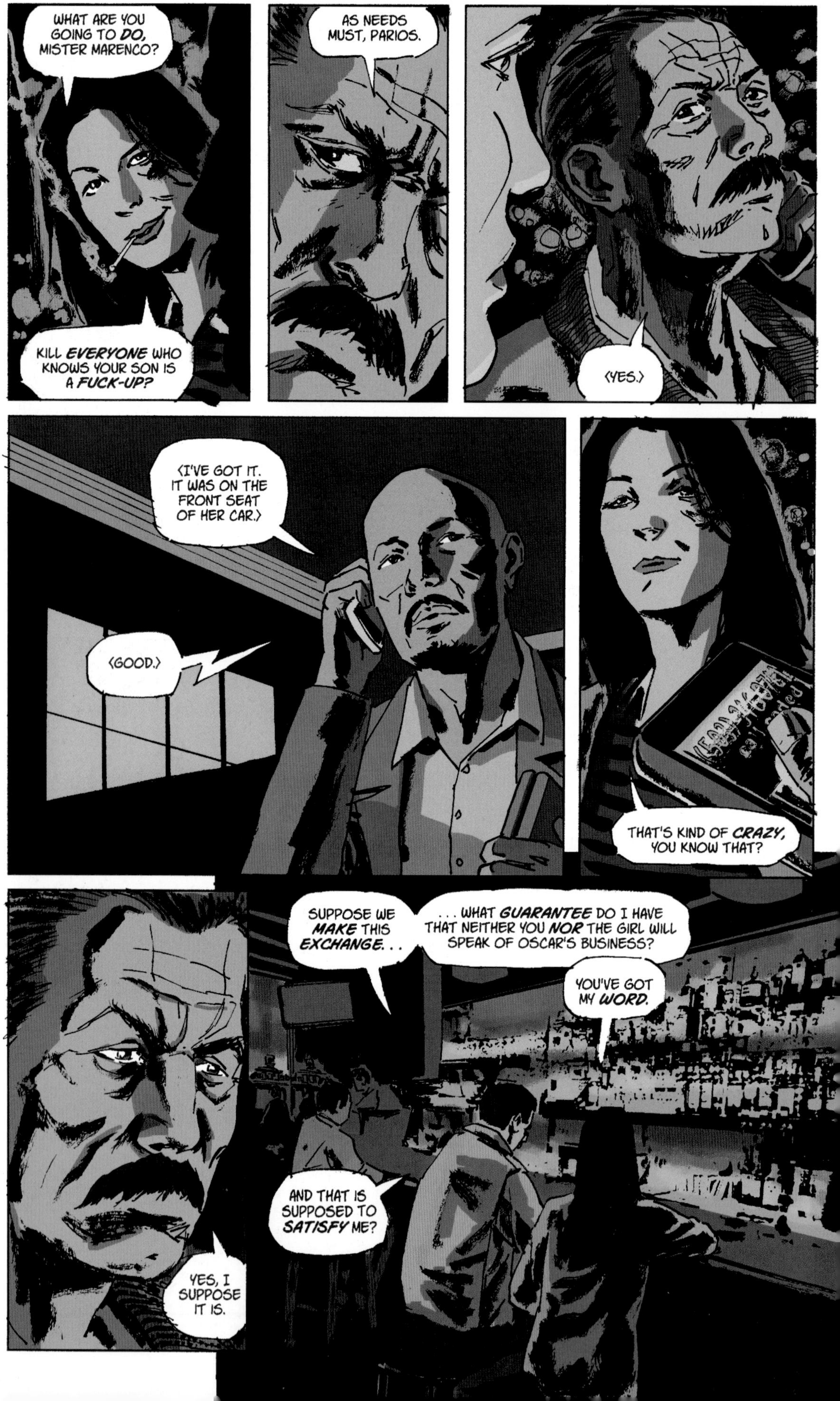
WHAT ARE YOU GOING TO *DO,* MISTER MARENCO?
AS NEEDS MUST, PARIOS.
KILL *EVERYONE* WHO KNOWS YOUR SON IS A *FUCK-UP?*
<YES.>
<I'VE GOT IT. IT WAS ON THE FRONT SEAT OF HER CAR.>
<GOOD.>
THAT'S KIND OF *CRAZY,* YOU KNOW THAT?
SUPPOSE WE *MAKE* THIS *EXCHANGE*...
...WHAT *GUARANTEE* DO I HAVE THAT NEITHER YOU *NOR* THE GIRL WILL SPEAK OF OSCAR'S BUSINESS?
YOU'VE GOT MY *WORD.*
AND THAT IS SUPPOSED TO *SATISFY* ME?
YES, I SUPPOSE IT IS.

MISTER MARENCO, I GAMBLE, I DRINK, I SMOKE, AND I'VE GOT A CAR THAT RUNS *HALF* THE TIME.

I JUST TOOK OUT MY *SECOND* MORTGAGE, HALF MY BILLS ARE PAST DUE, AND MY MENTALLY RETARDED BROTHER PULLS A STEADIER INCOME THAN ME.

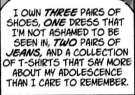

I OWN *THREE* PAIRS OF SHOES, *ONE* DRESS THAT I'M NOT ASHAMED TO BE SEEN IN, *TWO* PAIRS OF *JEANS*, AND A COLLECTION OF T-SHIRTS THAT SAY MORE ABOUT MY ADOLESCENCE THAN I CARE TO REMEMBER.

I'M THIRTY-TWO, SINGLE, UNATTACHED, AND THE LAST TIME I WENT ON A DATE THE PRESIDENT WAS *WHITE* AND IN HIS *FIRST TERM*.

MY *WORD* IS *ALL* I HAVE.

WILLIAM JUST REMOVED THE LAPTOP FROM YOUR CAR. HE IS VERIFYING THE CONTENTS.

IF EVERYTHING IS AS YOU CLAIM, I WILL CALL YOU IN THIRTY MINUTES WITH A LOCATION WHERE WE CAN MEET.

I WILL HAND OVER THE GIRL AT THAT TIME.

AND WHAT'S TO STOP YOU FROM PUTTING A BULLET IN *EACH* OF US THEN AND THERE?

NOTHING BUT MY *WORD*.

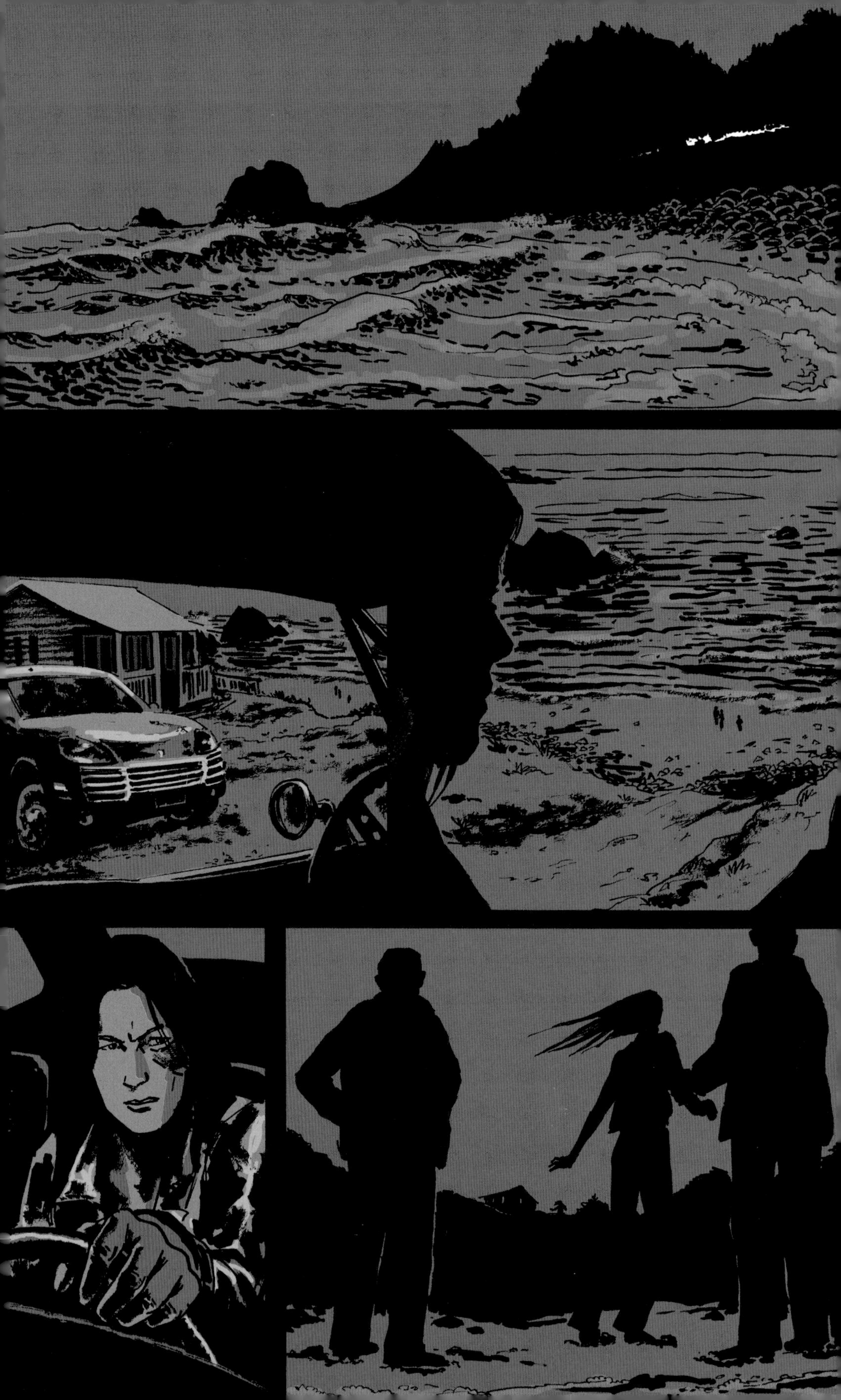

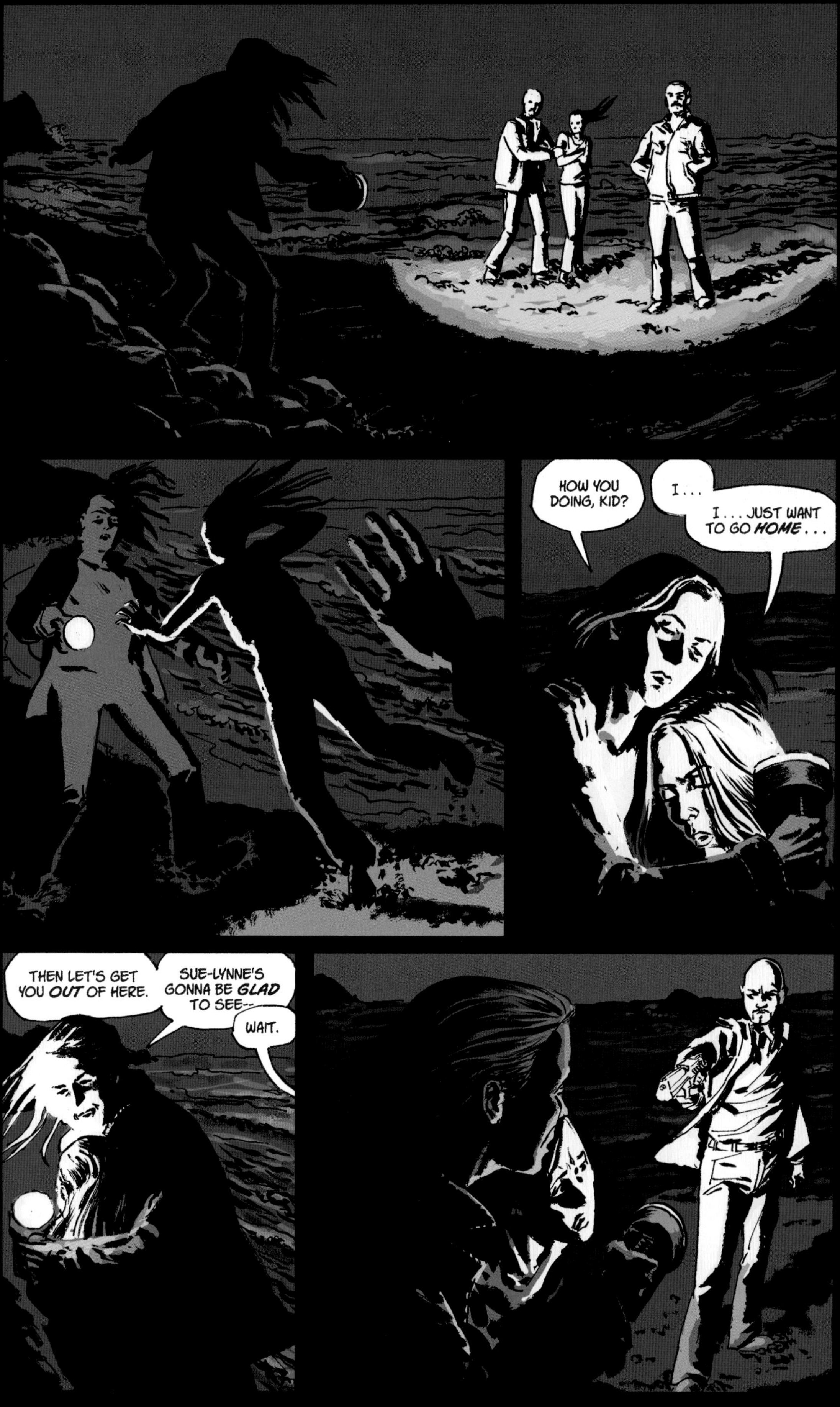
HOW YOU DOING, KID?
I...
I... JUST WANT TO GO HOME...
THEN LET'S GET YOU OUT OF HERE.
SUE-LYNNE'S GONNA BE GLAD TO SEE--
WAIT.

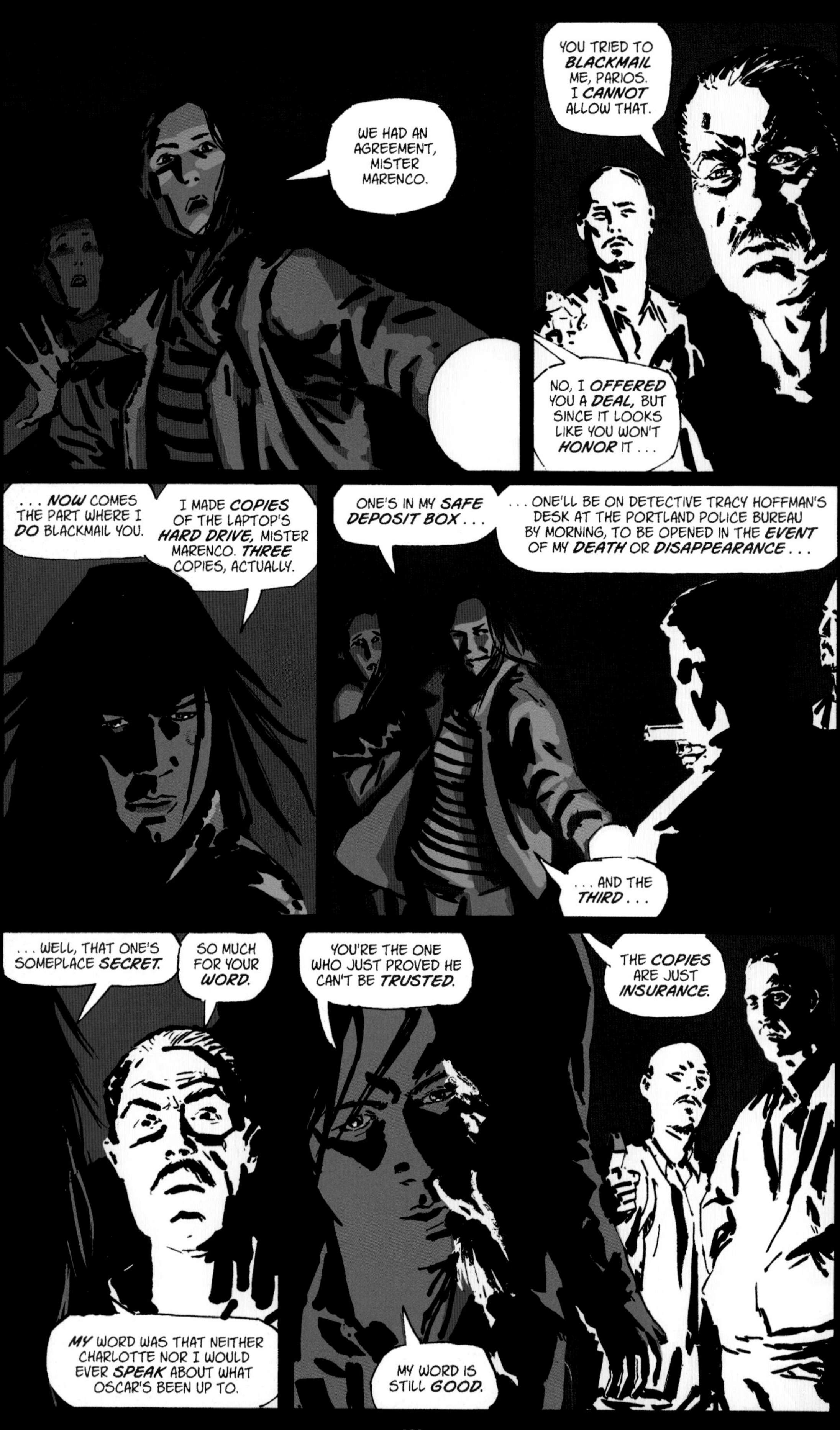

WE HAD AN AGREEMENT, MISTER MARENCO.
YOU TRIED TO BLACKMAIL ME, PARIOS. I CANNOT ALLOW THAT.
NO, I OFFERED YOU A DEAL, BUT SINCE IT LOOKS LIKE YOU WON'T HONOR IT . . .
. . . NOW COMES THE PART WHERE I DO BLACKMAIL YOU.
I MADE COPIES OF THE LAPTOP'S HARD DRIVE, MISTER MARENCO. THREE COPIES, ACTUALLY.
ONE'S IN MY SAFE DEPOSIT BOX . . .
. . . ONE'LL BE ON DETECTIVE TRACY HOFFMAN'S DESK AT THE PORTLAND POLICE BUREAU BY MORNING, TO BE OPENED IN THE EVENT OF MY DEATH OR DISAPPEARANCE . . .
. . . AND THE THIRD . . .
. . . WELL, THAT ONE'S SOMEPLACE SECRET.
SO MUCH FOR YOUR WORD.
MY WORD WAS THAT NEITHER CHARLOTTE NOR I WOULD EVER SPEAK ABOUT WHAT OSCAR'S BEEN UP TO.
YOU'RE THE ONE WHO JUST PROVED HE CAN'T BE TRUSTED.
MY WORD IS STILL GOOD.
THE COPIES ARE JUST INSURANCE.

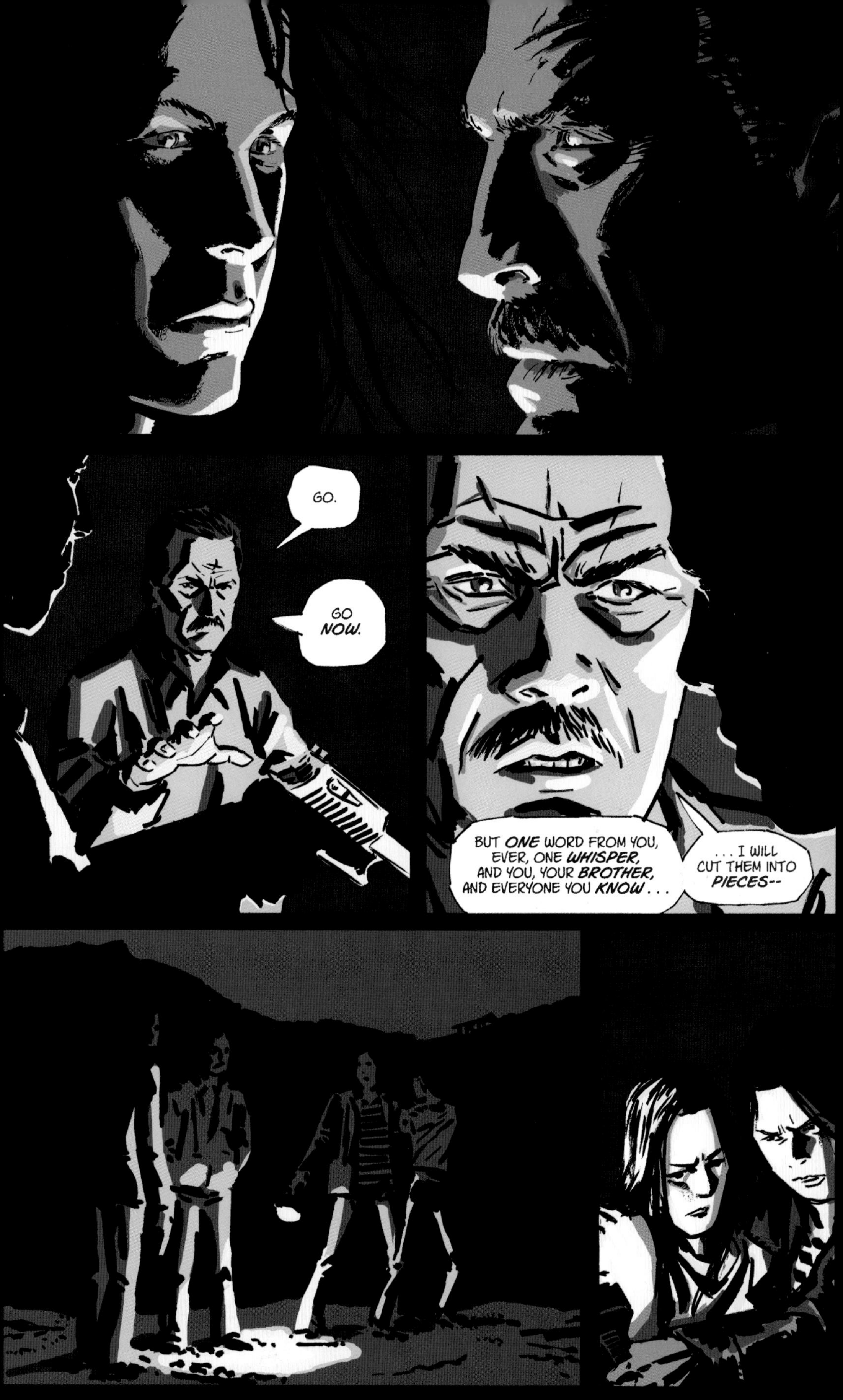
GO.
GO NOW.
BUT ONE WORD FROM YOU, EVER, ONE WHISPER, AND YOU, YOUR BROTHER, AND EVERYONE YOU KNOW . . .
. . . I WILL CUT THEM INTO PIECES--

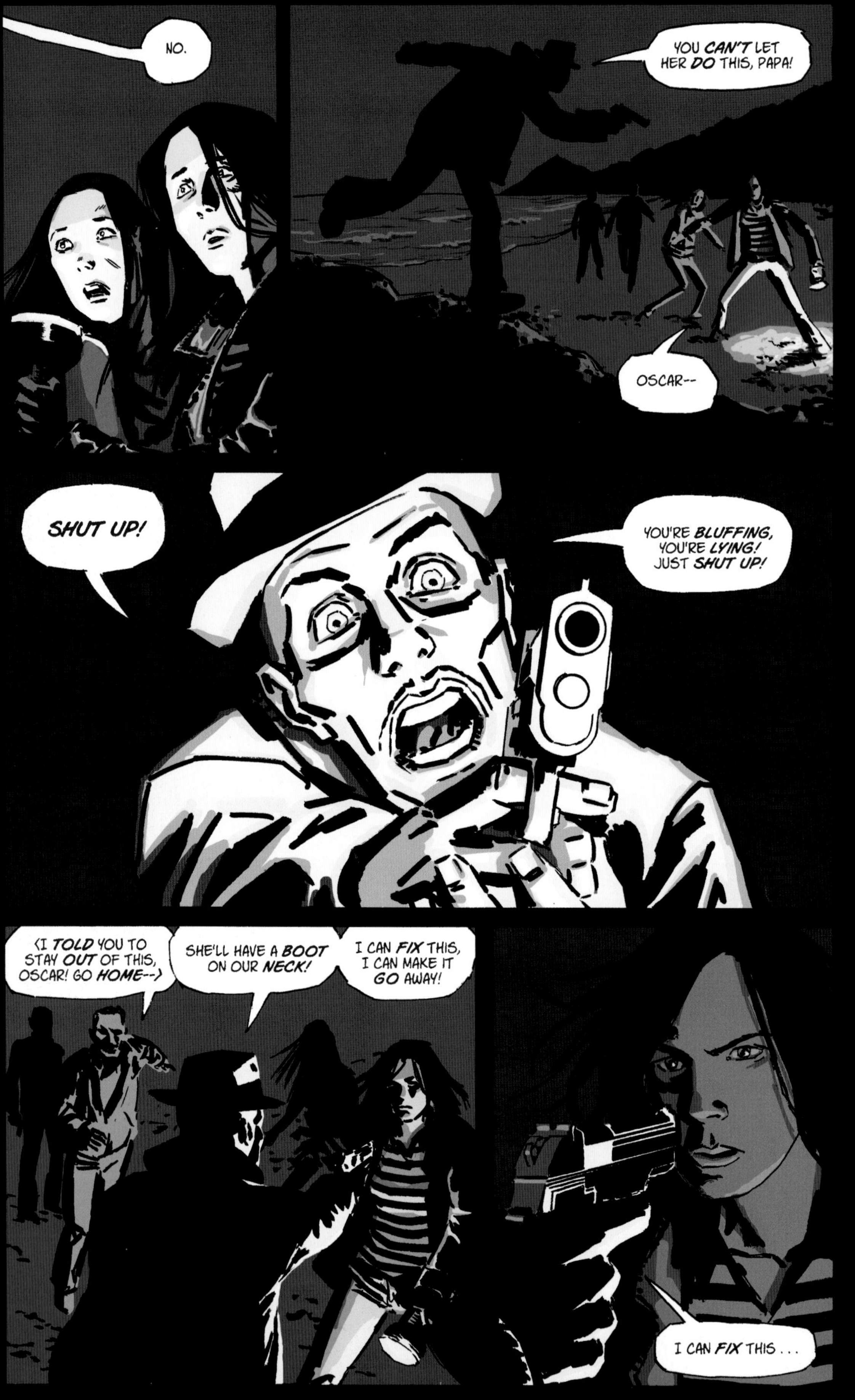
NO.
YOU CAN'T LET HER DO THIS, PAPA!
OSCAR--
SHUT UP!
YOU'RE BLUFFING, YOU'RE LYING! JUST SHUT UP!
<I TOLD YOU TO STAY OUT OF THIS, OSCAR! GO HOME-->
SHE'LL HAVE A BOOT ON OUR NECK!
I CAN FIX THIS, I CAN MAKE IT GO AWAY!
I CAN FIX THIS . . .

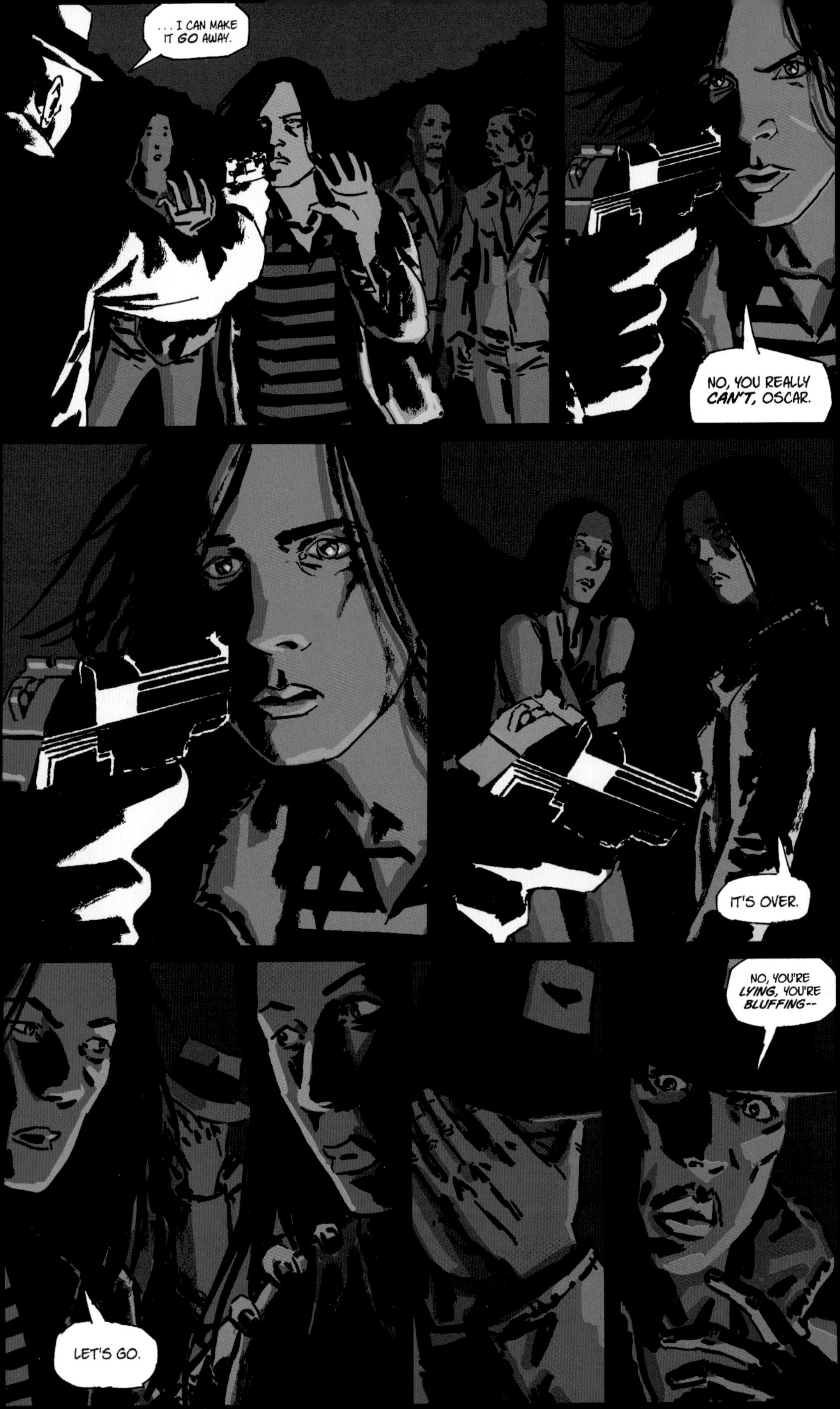
. . . I CAN MAKE IT GO AWAY.
NO, YOU REALLY CAN'T, OSCAR.
IT'S OVER.
NO, YOU'RE LYING, YOU'RE BLUFFING--
LET'S GO.

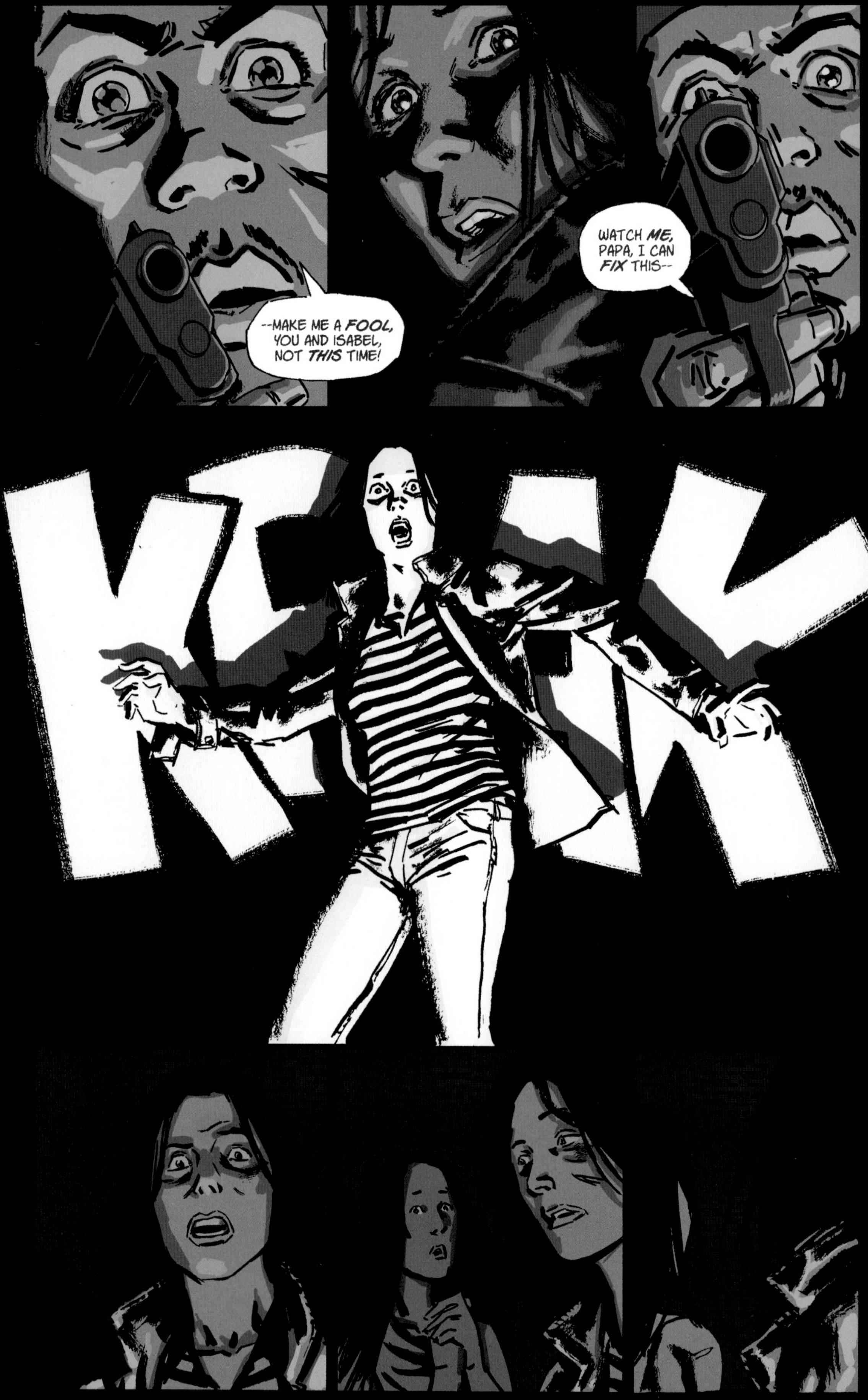
--MAKE ME A *FOOL,* YOU AND ISABEL, NOT *THIS* TIME!
WATCH *ME,* PAPA, I CAN *FIX* THIS--

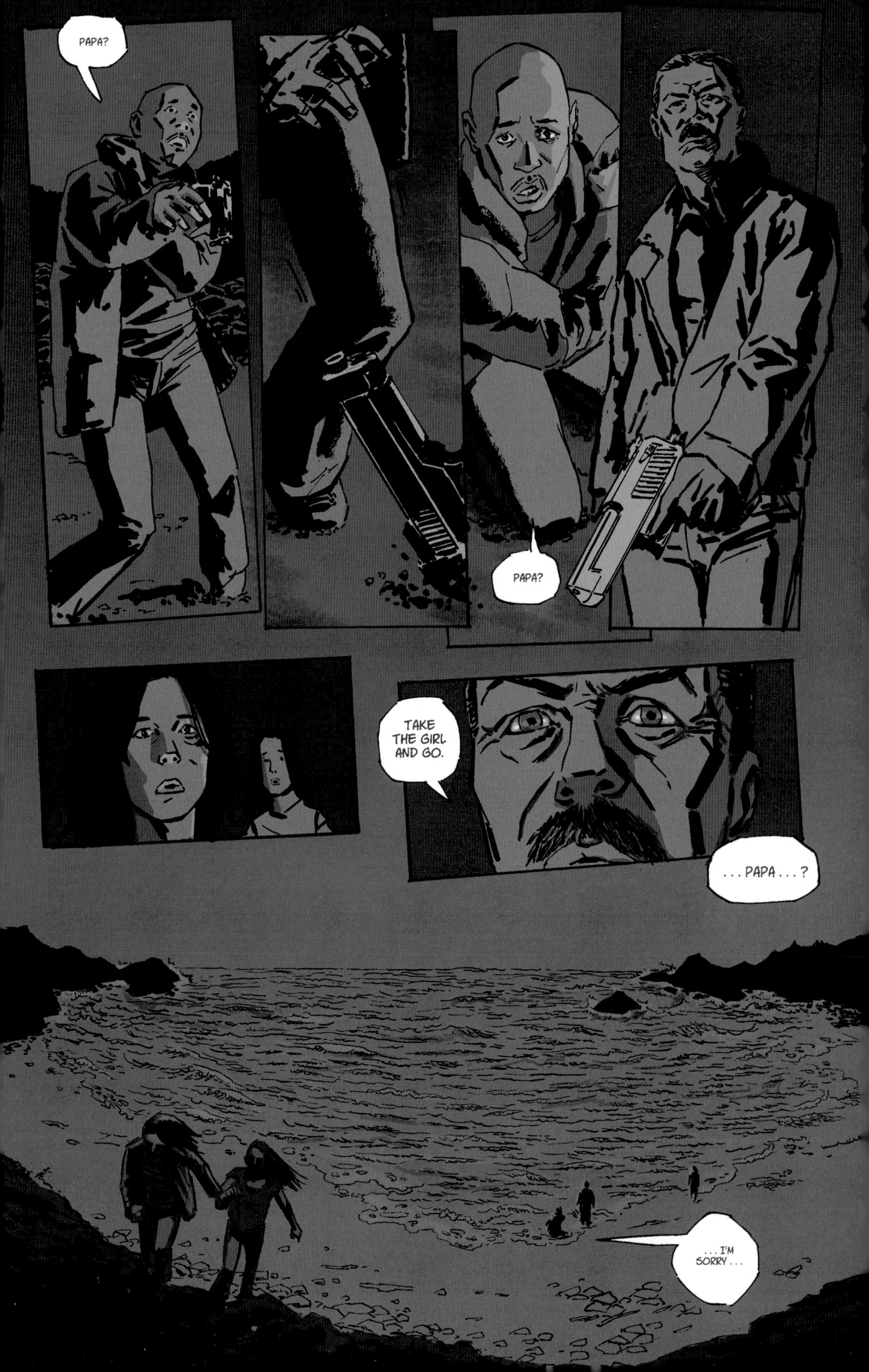
PAPA?
PAPA?
TAKE THE GIRL AND GO.
. . . PAPA . . . ?
. . . I'M SORRY . . .

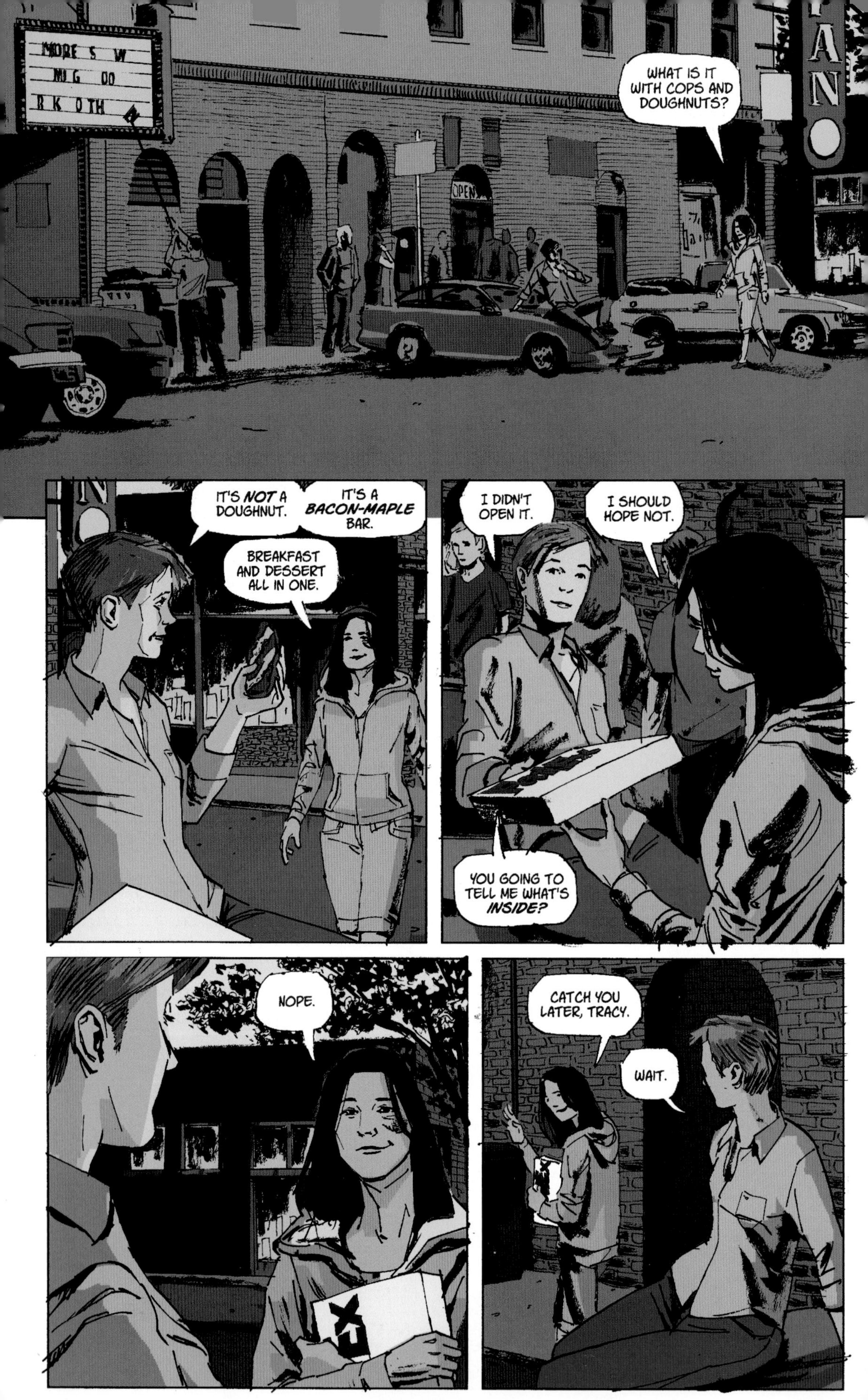
MORE S W
MIG OO
R K OTH
OPEN
WHAT IS IT WITH COPS AND DOUGHNUTS?
IT'S *NOT* A DOUGHNUT.
IT'S A *BACON-MAPLE* BAR.
BREAKFAST AND DESSERT ALL IN ONE.
I DIDN'T OPEN IT.
I SHOULD HOPE NOT.
YOU GOING TO TELL ME WHAT'S *INSIDE?*
NOPE.
CATCH YOU LATER, TRACY.
WAIT.

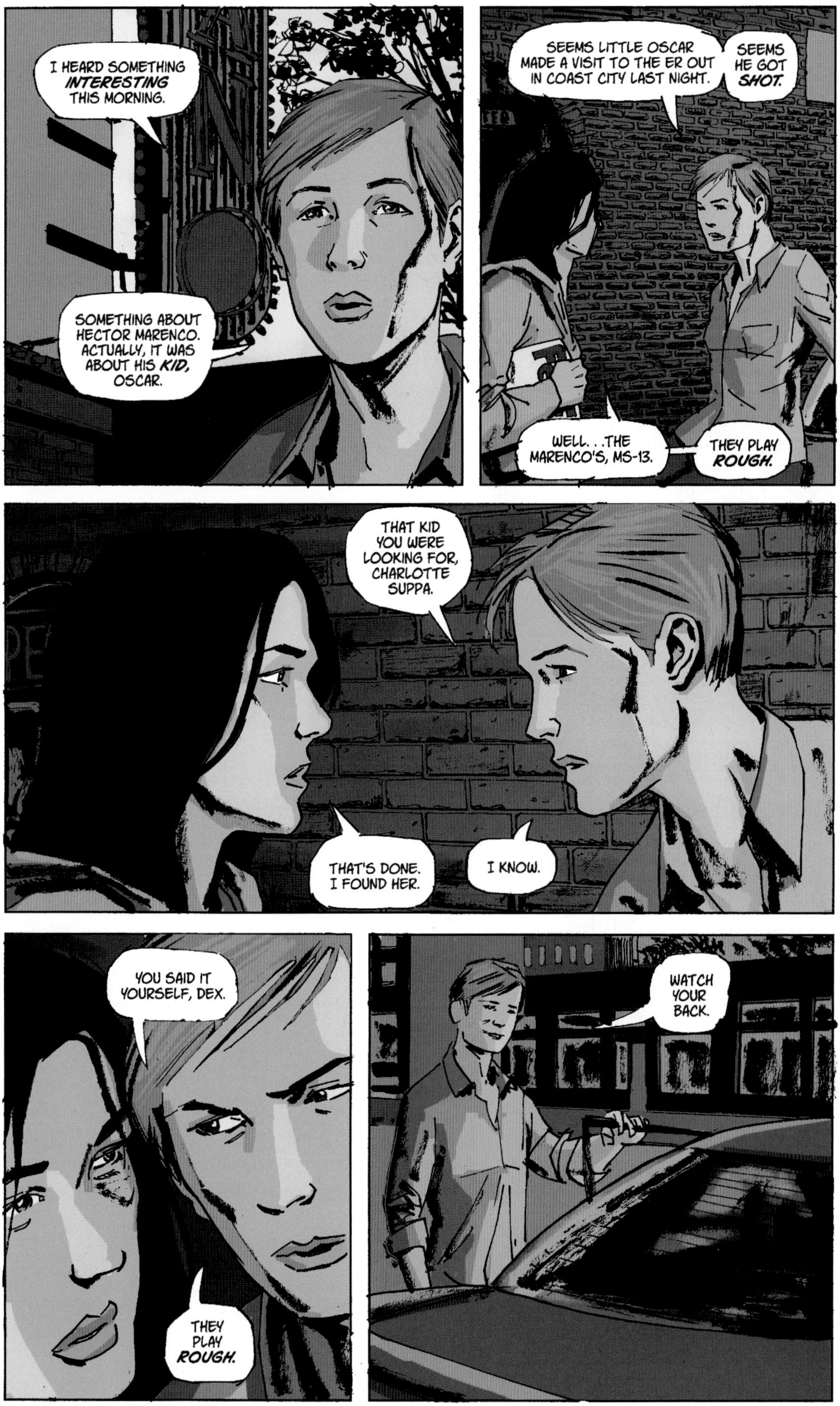
I HEARD SOMETHING INTERESTING THIS MORNING.
SOMETHING ABOUT HECTOR MARENCO. ACTUALLY, IT WAS ABOUT HIS KID, OSCAR.
SEEMS LITTLE OSCAR MADE A VISIT TO THE ER OUT IN COAST CITY LAST NIGHT.
SEEMS HE GOT SHOT.
WELL. . .THE MARENCO'S, MS-13.
THEY PLAY ROUGH.
THAT KID YOU WERE LOOKING FOR, CHARLOTTE SUPPA.
THAT'S DONE. I FOUND HER.
I KNOW.
YOU SAID IT YOURSELF, DEX.
THEY PLAY ROUGH.
WATCH YOUR BACK.

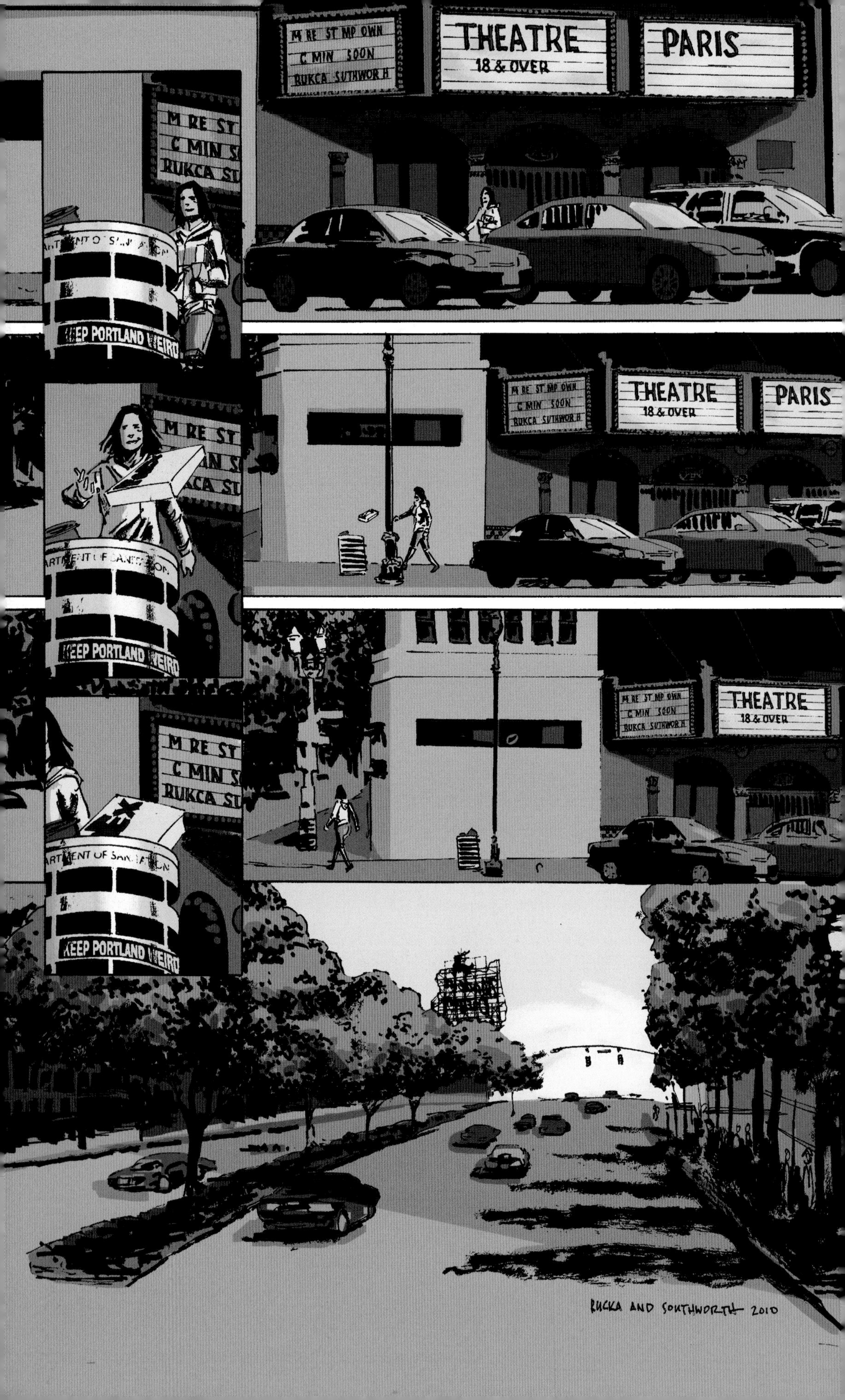
M RE ST
C MIN S
RUKCA SU
ARTMENT OF SANITATION
KEEP PORTLAND WEIRD
M RE ST MP OWN
C MIN SOON
RUKCA SUTHWORH
THEATRE
18 & OVER
PARIS
M RE ST
C MIN S
RUKCA SU
ARTMENT OF SANITATION
KEEP PORTLAND WEIRD
M RE ST MP OWN
C MIN SOON
RUKCA SUTHWOR H
THEATRE
18 & OVER
PARIS
M RE ST
C MIN S
RUKCA SU
ARTMENT OF SANITATION
KEEP PORTLAND WEIRD
M RE ST MP OWN
C MIN SOON
RUKCA SUTHWOR H
THEATRE
18 & OVER
RUCKA AND SOUTHWORTH 2010

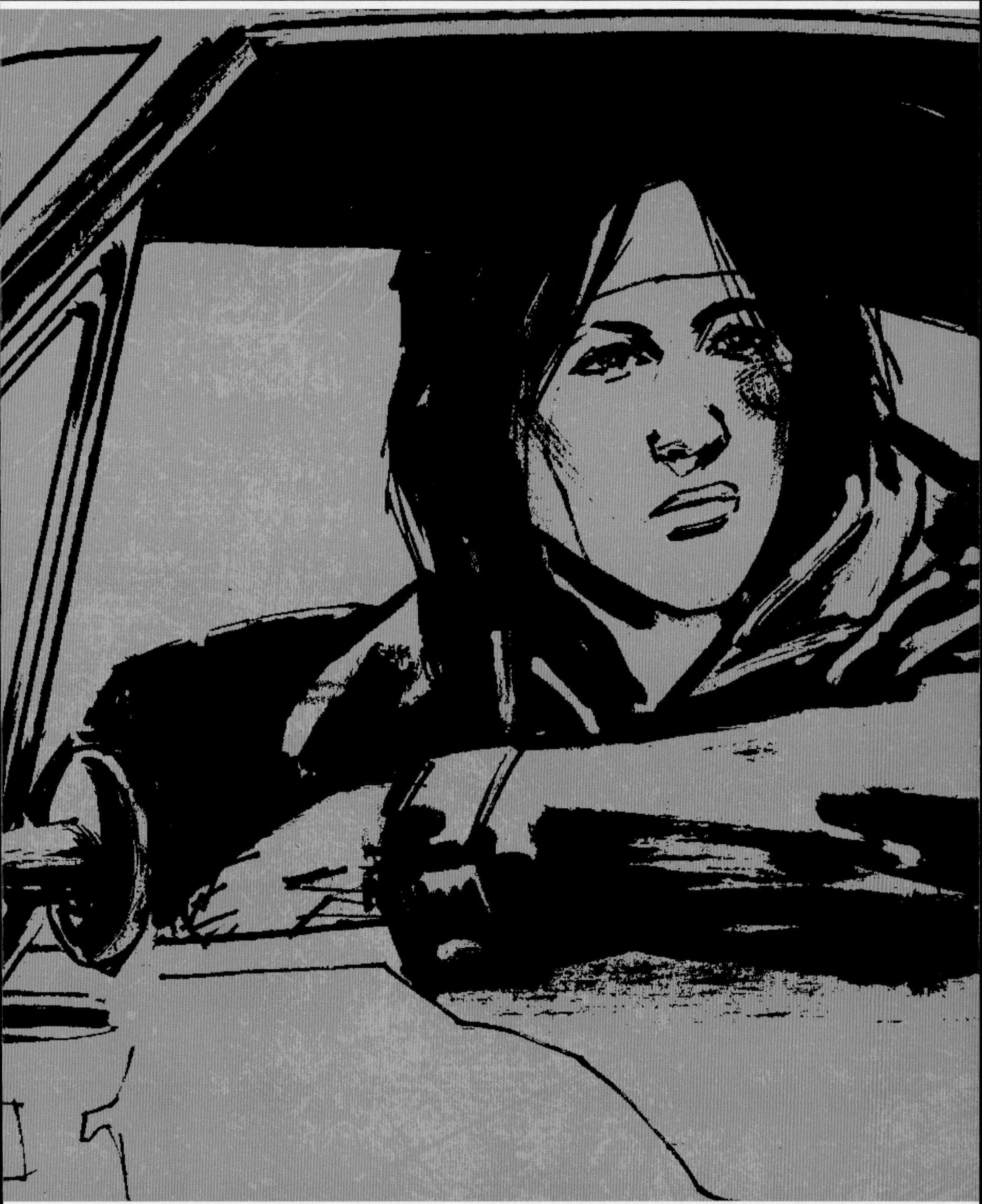

Artist Bios

GREG RUCKA was born in San Francisco and raised on the Central Coast of California, in what is commonly referred to as "Steinbeck Country." He began his writing career in earnest at the age of 10 by winning a county-wide short-story contest, and hasn't let up since. He graduated from Vassar College with an A.B. in English, and from the University of Southern California's Master of Professional Writing program with an M.F.A.

He is the author of nearly a dozen novels, six featuring bodyguard Atticus Kodiak, and three featuring Tara Chace, the protagonist of his *Queen & Country* series. Additionally, he has penned several short-stories, countless comics, and the occasional non-fiction essay. In comics, he has had the opportunity to write stories featuring some of the world's best-known characters—Superman, Batman, and Wonder Woman—as well as penning several creator-owned properties himself, such as *Whiteout* and *Queen & Country*, both published by Oni Press. His work has been optioned several times over, and his services are in high-demand in a variety of creative fields as a story-doctor and creative consultant.

Greg resides in Portland, Oregon, with his wife, author Jennifer Van Meter, and his two children. He thinks the biggest problem with the world is that people aren't paying enough attention.

MATTHEW SOUTHWORTH is a musician, playwright, filmmaker, and cartoonist who has lived in Nashville, Los Angeles, Louisville, Pittsburgh, and now Seattle.

He used to lead a band called the Capillaries, and they never broke up. He directed an independent feature film that he very nearly finished. He came this close to getting his Masters in playwriting and directing from Carnegie Mellon University.

He has undiagnosed (but undeniable) attention deficit disorder and has trouble sitting still long enough to get his work done. Nonetheless, in addition to *Stumptown*, he has drawn comics for Marvel, DC, and Image.

READ MORE FROM ONI PRESS!

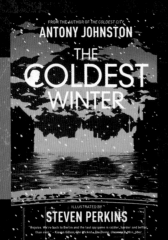